Best Dives

of the

Bahamas & Bermuda

Florida Keys, Turks & Caicos

Joyce & Jon Huber

HUNTER

Acknowledgments

The authors thank all Best Dives' contributors, correspondents, photographers and researchers for their enormous effort in preparing material for this edition.

A special thanks to Lissa Dailey and Michael Hunter of Hunter Publishing. For work on GRAND TURK: Cecil Ingham and Connie Rus. BAHAMAS: Michelle Landa, BSMG Marketing, Larry Speaker, Stuart Cove's Dive South Ocean, John Stewart, UNEXSO, Lynn Dixon, Nekton Cruises; Anita, Amanda, Neil and Ken Liggett, Rick and Lisa Ocklemann. BERMUDA: Olivia Serafin, Porter Novelli. FLORIDA KEYS: Tom McKelvey, Jim and Nadia Spencer, Andy Dear, Andy Newman, Stuart Newman Associates. GENERAL: Dennis and Karen Sabo, Barbara Swab, Frank Holler, Holler Swab & Partners, Bob DiChiara, Dr. Susan Cropper.

Contents

Introduction 1
Resources & Travel Tips. 3
Diver Safety 9
Nitrox. 10
BAHAMAS 11
New Providence Island 15
   Best Dive and Snorkeling Sites 16
   Accommodations 20
Grand Bahama Island 22
   Best Dive and Snorkeling Sites 24
   Accommodations 27
THE OUT ISLANDS 29
The Abaco Islands 29
   Best Dive and Snorkeling Sites 30
   Accommodations 32
Andros Island 35
   Best Dive and Snorkeling Sites 36
   Accommodations 38
The Berry Islands 39
   Best Dive and Snorkeling Sites 39
   Accommodations 40
Bimini. 40
   Best Dive and Snorkeling Sites 42
   Accommodations 43
Cat Island 43
   Best Dive and Snorkeling Sites 44
   Accommodations 44
Crooked Island 45
   Best Dive and Snorkeling Sites 46
   Accommodations 45
Eleuthera 46
   Best Dive and Snorkeling Sites 46
   Accommodations 48
The Exumas. 49
   Best Dive and Snorkeling Sites 50
   Accommodations 51
Long Island 51
   Best Dive and Snorkeling Sites 52
   Accommodations 55

San Salvador 56
   Best Dive and Snorkeling Sites 56
   Accommodations 56
Bahamas Live-Aboards 60
Cruise Ship Island Retreats 62

TURKS & CAICOS 67
Grand Turk 68
   Best Dive and Snorkeling Sites 68
   Accommodations 71
Salt Cay 73
   Best Dive and Snorkeling Sites 73
   Accommodations 74
Providenciales Island & North Caicos 74
   Best Dive and Snorkeling Sites 74
   Accommodations 77
South Caicos 79
   Best Dive and Snorkeling Sites 79
   Accommodations 79

BERMUDA 83
   Best Dive and Snorkeling Sites 86
   Accommodations 99

THE FLORIDA KEYS 105
Key Largo and the Upper Keys 108
   Best Dive and Snorkeling Sites 108
   Accommodations 118
Islamorada 122
   Accommodations 122
Marathon and the Middle Keys 125
   Best Dive and Snorkeling Sites 125
   Accommodations 127
The Lower Keys and Key West 129
   Best Dive and Snorkeling Sites 129
   Accommodations 131
The Florida Keys Shipwreck Trail 140
Eco Tips 151
First Aid for Coral Cuts and Sea Stings 155
What About Sharks? 159
Index 161

Introduction

Best Dives of the Bahamas and Bermuda takes divers and snorkelers through the grandest places to explore in the Bahamas, Bermuda, Florida Keys and Turks & Caicos.

Romanticized by Ernest Hemingway's *Islands in the Stream*, these islands share the marine richness carried by the Gulf Stream, a broad current that sweeps the entire area with powerful flows of warm water, nutrients and fish. Collectively, the area attracts more than 2,000,000 divers each year.

The Gulf Stream shapes the climates too. Tropical temperatures predominate in the southernmost islands year-round. Bermuda, the northernmost island chain, cools off during winter, but retains sufficient warmth to sustain lush vegetation and hard corals.

Text, maps and photos in *Best Dives of the Bahamas and Bermuda* describe and illustrate the incredible variety of treasures to found both above and beneath the sea throughout this unique area. In addition to starfish-rated dive and snorkeling sites for every skill level, the guide describes accommodations for every budget, suggests fast-food and gourmet restaurants and lists helpful travel information Rated dive sites include shallow reefs, wall dives, exhilarating drift dives, submerged movie sets, underwater sculptures, train, plane and shipwrecks.

Travel tips, listed at the end of each chapter, cover airlines, documents, transportation, currency, climate, language, gear, electricity, clothing and where to find more information.

Mystery abounds too, with stories of Bermuda's historic shipwrecks, the Bahamas' Stones of Atlantis – the lost continent, the Sand Mound Sculptures of Bimini – so vast they can only be recognized from the air, The Florida Keys National Marine Sanctuary Shipwreck Trail and the former salt plantations of the Turks and Caicos.

We hope you find *Best Dives of the Bahamas and Bermuda* a useful tool for vacation planning. Have a great trip, and when you get home let us know the highs and lows of your vacation. We'll pick some to run in our next edition. Write to us care of the publisher's address listed on the copyright page or e-mail us at jonhuber@worldnet.att.net or bestdives@att.net.

Using This Guide

Quick-reference symbols are used throughout this guide to identify diving and snorkeling areas. Each has been given a rating from one to five starfish by prominent divemasters in the area.

☆☆☆☆☆   **Five Starfish**. Best of the best diving; best visibility, best marine life, best reef or kelp dive.

☆☆☆☆   **Four Starfish**. Fantastic dive. Outstanding marine life or visual interest.

☆☆☆   **Three Starfish**. Superb dive. Excellent visibility and marine life or wreck.

☆☆   **Two Starfish**. Good dive. Interesting fish and plant life. Good visibility.

☆   **One Starfish**. Pleasant dive. Better than average.

Map Symbols

Dive site 🐟   Shipwreck ⛵

Snorkeling area ∫   Airport ✈

Resources & Travel Tips

Scuba Certifying Organizations

Locations for scuba instruction near your home may be obtained from one of the following organizations.

IDEA, International Diving Educators Association, PO Box 8427, Jacksonville, FL 32239-8427. ☎ 904-744-5554.

NASDS, National Association of Scuba Diving Schools, 1012 S. Yates, Memphis, TN 38119. ☎ 800-735-3483; 901-767-7265. Website: www.divesafe. com.

NAUI, National Association of Underwater Instructors, PO Box 14650, Montclair, CA 91763. ☎ 800-553-6284; 909-621-5801. Lost cards 909-621-6210; fax 901-621-6405. Website: www.naui.org.

PADI INTERNATIONAL, Professional Association of Diving Instructors, 1251 E. Dyer Rd., Suite 100, Santa Ana, CA 92705-5605. ☎ 800-729-7234; 714-540-7234. Website: www.padi.com.

PDIC INTERNATIONAL, Professional Diving Instructors Corporation 1554 Gardener Ave, Scranton, PA 18509. ☎ 717-342-9434; fax 717-342-1480. E-mail: info@PDIC-INTL.com. Website: www.pdic-intl.com.

SSI, Scuba Schools International, 2619 Canton Court, Fort Collins, CO 80525. ☎ 800-892-2702; 303-482-0883. E-mail: admin@ssiusa.com or ssilen@aol.com.

YMCA, National YMCA Scuba Program, Oakbrook Square, 6083-A Oakbrook Parkway, Norcross/Atlanta, GA 30093. ☎ 770-662-5172; fax 770-242-9059. E-mail: scubaymca@aol.com. Website: www.webcom. com/cscripts/-ymca/ymca.html.

Cruises & Package Tours

Package vacations may save you hundreds of dollars, but be sure to read the fine print carefully when you are comparing tours. Consider transfers, sightseeing tours, meals, auto rentals, acceptable accommodations, and taxes. Tanks and weights may or may not be included. Also ask whether extra airline weight allowances are included for dive gear.

Oceanic Society Expeditions, a non-profit environmental group, offers research-oriented snorkel trips and dolphin swims to a variety of destinations. ☎ 415-441-1106 or 800- 326-7491 or write to the Oceanic Society, Fort Mason Center, Bldg. E, San Francisco CA 94123. Website: www.oceanic-society.org.

Landfall Dive and Adventure Travel offers hassle-free, money-saving tours for groups and individual divers to the Bahamas, Caribbean, Turks and Caicos and the Pacific. ☎ 916-563-0164, fax 916-924-1059. E-mail: landfall@pattravel.com. Website: landfallproductions.com.

CEDAM (Conservation, Ecology, Diving, Archaeology, Museums) offers programs as varied as an underwater archaeological dig on an ancient shipwreck or a mapping tour of the Turks & Caicos. Write them at 1 Fox Rd., Croton NY 10520. ☎ 914-271-5365; fax 914-271-4723. E-mail: cedamint@ aol.com. Website: www.cedam.org.

Tropical Adventures offers more than 27 destinations and live-aboards worldwide. ☎ 800-247-3483. Website: www.divetropical.com.

Handicapped Divers

Handicapped divers will find help and information by contacting the **Handicapped Scuba Association** (HSA). The association has provided scuba instruction to people with physical disabilities since 1975. Over 600 instructors in 24 countries are HSA-trained. HSA has developed the "Resort Evaluation Program" to help handicapped divers select a vacation destination. They check out facilities and work with the staff and management to ensure accessibility. Once a resort is totally accessible, it is certified by HSA.

For a list of HSA-certified resorts, group-travel opportunities and more information on HSA's programs, instruction and activities, ☎ 949-498-6128. E-mail: hsahdq@compuserve.com.

Money

Most large resorts, restaurants and dive operators will accept major credit cards, although you risk being charged at a higher rate if the local currency fluctuates. Traveler's checks are accepted almost everywhere and often you'll get a better exchange rate for them than cash. It's always a good idea to have some local currency on hand for cabs, tips and small purchases.

Insurance

Many types of travel insurance are available, covering everything from lost luggage and trip cancellations to medical expenses. Since emergency medical assistance and air ambulance fees can run into thousands of dollars, it is wise to be prepared. Trips purchased with some major credit cards include life insurance.

Divers Alert Network (DAN) offers divers' health insurance for $35 a year plus an annual membership fee of $25 ($35 for a family). Any treatment required for an accident or emergency that is a direct result of diving, such as decompression sickness (the bends), arterial gas embolism or pulmonary barotrauma is covered up to $125,000. Air ambulance to the closest medical care facility, recompression chamber care and in-patient hospital care are covered. Non-diving travel-related accidents are NOT covered.

Lacking the ability to pay, a diver may be refused transport and/or treatment. For more information write to DAN, PO Box 3823, Duke University Medical Center, Durham, NC 27710. ☎ 919-684-2948. For emergencies worldwide call collect ☎ 800-446-2671 or 919-684-4DAN (4326). E-mail: dan@ dan.ycg.org. Website: www.dan.ycg.org.

International SOS Assistance is a medical assistance service to travelers who are more than 100 miles from home. For just $55 per person for seven to 14 days, or $96 per couple, SOS covers air evacuation and travel-related assistance. Evacuation is to the closest medical care facility, which is determined by SOS staff doctors. Representative Michael Klein states that SOS will send out a private Learjet if necessary to accommodate a patient. Hospitalization is NOT covered. Standard Blue Cross and Blue Shield policies do cover medical costs while traveling. For individual and group information write to International SOS Assistance, Box 11568, Philadelphia, PA 19116. ☎ 800-523-8930 or 215-244-1500. E-mail: jfahy @intsos.com. Website: www.intsos.com.

Lost luggage insurance is available at the ticket counters of many airlines. If you have a homeowner's policy, you may already be covered. Be sure to check first with your insurance agent.

Keep a list of all your dive equipment and other valuables, including the name of the manufacturer, model, date of purchase, new price and serial number, if any, on your person when traveling. Immediately report any theft or loss of baggage to the local police, hotel security people or airline and get a copy of that report. Both the list and the report of loss or theft will be needed to collect from your insurance company. Do not expect airlines to cheerfully compensate you for any loss without a lot of red tape and hassle. Regardless of the value of your gear the airline pays by the weight ($9 per pound) of what is lost. Be sure to tag your luggage with your name and address. Use a business address if possible.

Packing Checklist

___ MASK

___ SNORKEL

___ FINS

___ REGULATOR

___ DEPTH GAUGE

___ BUOYANCY COMPENSATOR (stab jacket)

___ WET SUIT, SHORTIE OR LYCRA WET SKIN

___ WET SUIT BOOTS

___ MESH CATCH BAG

___ U/W DIVE LIGHTS

___ DRAMAMINE or other seasickness preventative

___ GEAR MARKER

___ DIVER CERTIFICATION CARD (C-card)

___ DIVER LOG BOOK

___ SUNGLASSES

___ SPARE MASK STRAP

___ SPARE SNORKEL RETAINER RING

___ SPARE STRAPS

___ SUBMERSIBLE PRESSURE GAUGE

___ WATCH/BOTTOM TIMER

___ WEIGHT BELT (no lead)

___ DE-FOG SOLUTION

___ REEF GLOVES (not for use in marine parks)

___ CYALUME STICKS (chemical light sticks)

___ U/W CAMERA AND FILM

___ FISH ID BOOK

___ DIVE TABLES

___ PASSPORT or proof of citizenship as required

___ DIVE TABLES (or computer)

___ SUNTAN LOTION

___ HAT (with visor or brim)

Documents

Carry your personal documents on you at all times. Be sure to keep a separate record of passport numbers, visas, or tourist cards in your luggage.

Security

Tourists flashing wads of cash and expensive jewelry are prime targets for robbers. Avoid off-the-beaten-track areas of cities, especially at night. Do not carry a lot of cash, expensive cameras or jewelry. Keep alert to what's going on around you. Stay with your luggage until it is checked in with the airlines. Jewelry should be kept in the hotel safe.

Rental cars have become a target for robbers in some areas. To avoid problems, try to rent a car without rental company markings. If someone bumps into your car, do not stop. Drive to a police station and report the incident. Do not stop for hitchhikers or to assist strangers.

Drugs

Penalties for possession of illegal drugs are very harsh and the risk you take for holding even a half-ounce of marijuana cannot be stressed enough. Punishment often entails long jail terms. In certain areas, such as Mexico, your embassy and the best lawyer won't be much help. You are guilty until proven innocent. Selling drugs is still cause for public hanging in some areas.

Cameras

Divers traveling with expensive camera gear or electronic equipment should register each item with customs *before* leaving the country.

Sundries

Suntan lotion, aspirin, antihistamines, decongestants, anti-fog solutions, or mosquito repellent should be purchased before your trip. These products are not always available and may cost quite a bit more than you pay for them at home.

First Aid

Every diver should carry a small first aid kit for minor cuts, bruises or ailments. Be sure to include a topical antihistamine ointment, antihistamine tablets, seasickness preventive, decongestant, throat lozenges, band-aids, aspirin and diarrhea treatment.

Sunburn Protection

Avoid prolonged exposure to the sun, especially during peak hours, 10 am to 3 pm. Since most dive trips occur during peak hours, whenever possible opt for trips on dive boats with sun canopies, use sunblock lotions or a sunscreen with a protection factor of at least 15, select hats with a wide brim and wear protective clothing of fabrics made to block the sun's ultraviolet rays.

Diver Identification

Most dive operations require that you hold a certification card and a logbook. A check-out dive may be required if you cannot produce a log of recent dives.

New Divers

Every dive shop in the US offers a "resort course" or introductory class. If you have not yet learned to dive and want to find out more, stop in at your local dive shop. You'll find learning the sport or deciding whether you really want to before you travel much easier than trying to do it all at a resort destination. Once you commit, it's a good idea to get certified before you go. Stretching out the certification course over a few weeks gives you more time to absorb what you're learning. Plus, you'll have ample opportunity to solve problems and ask questions in a pool rather than the ocean. You can take the open-water portion of the certification at any of the destinations in this book. You'll notice we list "referrals" under many of the resort area dive shops. That means they can complete your certification.

Additional Reading

Undercurrent, a monthly newsletter, is a must for avid divers. Each issue packs in fascinating stories on a variety of dive subjects ranging from the Bermuda Triangle to using mosquito nuts as malaria prophylaxis, diving, dive resorts, live-aboards, and treasure hunting. New subscribers pay $39. ☎ 800-326-1896 or 415-5906. Website: www.undercurrent.org. Send checks to Undercurrent, PO Box 1658, Sausalito CA 94966.

Splashadventures.com, a new website, promises continuous updates on dive travel resorts.

Diver Safety

Support "C-CARDS ON BOARD for DIVERS DOWN"

The idea of surfacing to discover that the dive boat left without you can be frightening. It rarely happens, and certainly never by intent, but it does happen. In most cases the missing diver is noticed and the boat returns to the rescue.

The key words here are "most" and "rarely." If you're the diver floating 10 miles offshore as the tour boat disappears over the horizon, the fact that this rarely happens or the boat returns most of the time doesn't offer much comfort.

To eliminate this possibility we ask you to support the "C-Cards on Board for Divers Down" concept. Talk it up and whenever you go out on a dive boat or live-aboard yacht insist that the crew keep a container – a bowl, sack or box – for divers to deposit their c-cards when entering the water. Or find out which crew member is responsible for the head count and ask him/her to hold your card while you're in the water. Upon return from each dive, individual divers must take responsible for picking up their own cards. When the cards are all picked up, with the box empty, the crew knows everyone has made it back.

The container should be safe from wind and wave effects. Buddies or mates should not pick up each other's cards.

Snorkelers who want cards or divers who don't want to leave their c-cards can order a plastic "Wait for Me" ID card from PhotoGraphics. Send a self-addressed, stamped envelope and check or money order for $3 to PhotoGraphics, 629 Edgewater Avenue, Ridgefield, NJ 07657. Allow two to three weeks for delivery.

Nitrox

Nitrox, a mixture of nitrogen and oxygen, replaces compressed air in your scuba cylinder and can extend your bottom time and reduce your nitrogen load. Some people feel less tired and warmer, both during and after a dive. The time or depth advantage of Nitrox is significant.

Equivalent Nitrox Depths		
Air Depth (Feet)	With a mix of 32% oxygen, 68% nitrogen	With a mix of 40% oxygen, 60% nitrogen
40	51	63
50	63	76
70	75	89
80	86	99 (Max)
90	109	
100	121	
110	132 (Max)	

Nitrox diving can be simple or complex. Basic Nitrox dive training will have you in the water with your standard scuba gear. This is the easiest, least expensive and probably the safest way for a sport diver to reap the benefits of Nitrox.

The maximum benefits of Nitrox can only be achieved with rebreather equipment. A rebreather is a self-contained breathing device which reuses at least part of each breath. Regular scuba equipment expels the entire breath into the surrounding water when the diver exhales. Although rebreathers have some significant advantages in technical diving applications, their use and training are outside the scope of this book.

Contact your local dive shop or certifying agency about training (listed on page 3).

Bahamas

The Bahamas stretch between southern Florida and southeastern Cuba, encompassing 700 islands and more than 2,500 cays – an area with more diving and snorkeling variety than imaginable, from dramatic walls and dropoffs, shipwrecks and sharks to shallow reefs and dolphin encounters.

The islands vary in size too, with Andros being the largest. The most visited tourist areas include Nassau, the capital on New Providence Island; the Abacos chain, including Great Abaco, Little Abaco, Elbow Cay, Treasure Cay and others; Eleuthera/Harbour Island; the Exumas; Bimini; the Berry Islands; Cat Island; Long Island; Crooked Island; San Salvador; Grand Bahama Island; and Andros.

Geographically, all are similar, with low, thick pine forests sloping to mangrove swamps, lagoons and lakes. Many coastlines are rimmed with shimmering pink or white sandy beaches. The highest point in the country is Mount Alvernia, which rises 206 feet above sea level.

Dive adventures can begin almost anywhere, when you consider that the islands cap two barrier reefs (the Little and Great Bahama banks) that wander through 500 miles of tropical ocean and cover 100,000 square miles. This dense coral reef system winds through hundreds of historic wrecks, mysterious blue holes and vacated movie sets.

A magnificent trench known as The Tongue of the Ocean (TOTO) starts off of New Providence Island's south end and runs along the eastern side of Andros. TOTO offers shark encounters at the Deer Island Buoy (aka Shark Buoy), which was tethered 12 miles offshore in 6,000 ft of water by the US Navy as part of the Sound Surveillance System (SOSUS) for tracking submarines, whales and underwater seismic events.

Old-world charm and new world glamour combine in Nassau, the capital of the Bahamas on New Providence Island, and in its world-class resort areas, Cable Beach and Paradise Island. Grand Bahama Island has modern resorts in Freeport/Lucaya and the rustic charm of old settlements such as West End. The Out Islands offer pampered seclusion in Robinson Crusoe-style hideaways. Together, the Bahamas provide every style of dive and snorkeling vacation, from sophisticated to simple. And it's easy to get there, via frequent flights by major airlines or on the national flag carrier, Bahamasair. If you can't decide on one area, inter-island air services enable you to combine a visit to Nassau or Freeport with a trip to the Out Islands.

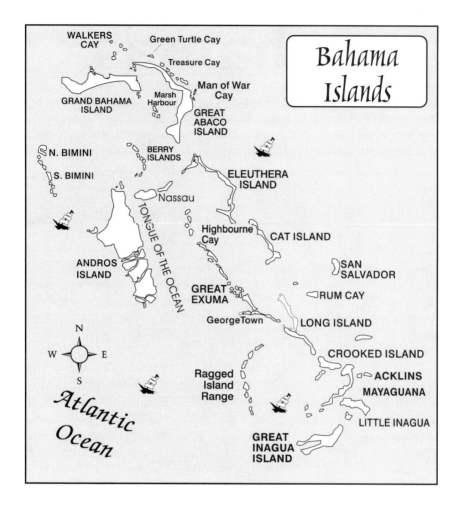

History

The Commonwealth of the Bahamas was originally settled by Lucayan Indians who paddled their way north from the Caribbean, though credit for "discovering" the islands is given to Christopher Columbus, who landed on Guanahani, now San Salvador, in 1492. Conquistadors soon followed in pursuit of gold, killing off the Lucayans with disease, enslavement and hardship. English settlers arrived in1647 seeking religious freedom. They named the island where they landed Eleuthera – the Greek word for freedom. After years of unstable rule, the islands became a Crown Colony. Captain Woodes Rogers was the first Royal Governor. During the American Revolution, the islands fell to Spain and were not restored to Great Britain until 1783. British

Loyalists soon emigrated to the islands of the Bahamas, many bringing black slaves with them. A slave-free society was declared in 1834 by the British Emancipation Act.

Many island inhabitants are descendants of British Loyalists, slaves or pirates who shipwrecked on the islands.

After nearly 250 years of British colonial rule, on July 10, 1973 the Commonwealth of the Bahamas declared its independence. The Bahamas now has a parliamentary democracy, with a Governor-General as head of state.

When to Go

The high season runs from mid-December through mid-April, though some divers and snorkelers prefer the warmer, and sometimes calmer, waters of late April, May and June. Hurricane season occurs from late July through mid-November, with most activity in September. Seawater temperature ranges from 73°F in February to 82°F in August.

The climate of the Bahamas is idyllic, with the mean air temperature in January about 77°F and in August, 89°. The difference between the warmest and coolest months is only about 12°.

Sightseeing

In Nassau, Cable Beach, and Paradise Island you can enjoy topside scenery by taxi, bicycle or horse-drawn surrey complete with fringed top.

To get a personal view, ask for a driver who is a Bahamahost. They are certified by the Bahamas Ministry of Tourism and extremely knowledgeable about native history, folklore, flora, sports and just about everything else.

People-to-People Program

One fun way to meet Bahamians is through the People-to-People Program. Organized by the Ministry of Tourism 20 years ago, it matches visitors with Bahamians of similar age and interests for a day or evening of activities that might include boating, fishing, shopping, a back-street tour or a home-cooked meal of peas'n rice, fried fish, and guava duff.

The program also has a list of volunteers who are ready to assist visitors with their weddings. To sign up, ☎ 242-36-0435.

Junkanoo

This exciting parade in celebration of winter goes so far back that its origin is obscure. Some say it can be traced to a festival held on the Gold Coast of Africa and is named after an early 18th-century African prince, John Connu, who promoted revelry as a release from the oppression of slavery. Others say the name comes from the French "gens inconnus" or "unknown people," describing those who paraded in masks. In any case, the fun begins on January 1 with a raucous parade of costumed revelers dancing in the streets to the music of goatskin drums, horns, whistles, and bugles. Crowds dance and sing. Costumes are outsized extravaganzas constructed on wood and cardboard frames and covered with brightly colored designs. Junkanoo is celebrated in Nassau, Grand Bahama, Exuma, Eleuthera, Harbour Island and Freeport.

Dining

Bahamian cuisine also shares an African accent. Some dishes are simple, with ingredients such as cornmeal flour. Others are more elaborate, using tropical spices and fruits, such as soursop, tamarind, coconut or banana.

A staple of the Bahamian diet is "johnnycake," a rich pan-cooked bread much like cornbread. The recipe arrived with early settlers, who may have called it "journey cake" because it fed them during their journey.

Conch (pronounced "konk"), a mollusk whose pink-lipped shells are often heaped along Bahamian beaches, is as integral to the Bahamian diet as the hamburger is to America. Culinary variations on conch include conch fritters, cracked conch, conch burgers, conch chowder, conch salad, and scorched conch. Served with all Bahamian meals is "peas 'n rice," a satisfying combination of pigeon peas and spicy white rice. Naturally, seafood is a specialty throughout the islands. Almost every restaurant offers fresh fish: groupers, yellowtail, crab, lobster, scallops, snappers and tile fish. Several Bahamas restaurants offer haute cuisine.

Although you can enjoy the most refined Continental cuisine prepared by some of the world's finest chefs, for a genuinely Bahamian experience try the authentic local cooking. Its rich tradition and exotic ingredients make for memorable meals.

Shopping

Shopping has long been an exciting side-venture for divers visiting the Bahamas. The Bahamian dollar is equal in value to and interchangeable with the US dollar and you'll find a great selection of top quality items from all over the globe to choose from. Shoppers are sometimes surprised to find that they can buy luxury items at 20 to 40% below what they cost in the United States. Cameras, cashmere cardigans, watches and emerald jewelry head the list of items bought by tourists and "professional" shoppers alike.

In Nassau, stroll along bustling **Bay Street**, where you'll find one of the largest selections of china and crystal outside centers like Paris and New York. For less expensive gifts like handmade straw hats, handbags, dolls and straw bags, visit the **Straw Market** in the Market Plaza on Bay Street, which is open seven days a week. Here you can test your skills at bartering for many hand-made creations.

In Freeport, the **International Bazaar** is an irresistible lure. There are more than 65 shops on this 10-acre site, with architectural styles reflecting the country whose merchandise is featured. Here you can go "around the world" in a matter of hours or minutes! Since it was designed by movie special effects artist Charles Drew, it not only offers a wide selection of high-quality items from five continents, but the dramatic settings are straight from Hollywood.

In the bazaar, you will find yourself treading the streets of Japan, buying embroidered silk robes, beaded bags and incense. Around the corner, in the Middle East, you may select from a stunning collection of carved ivories, shining brass work or lifelike wooden animals. The International Bazaar is a special place for the shopper who likes to explore.

Also on Grand Bahama is **Port Lucaya**'s multi-million-dollar shopping and entertainment complex, offering a vibrant cultural mix of fine shopping, Bahamian-style restaurants and entertainment, all complemented by the natural brilliance of the turquoise waterfront. The shops are housed in 12 buildings, each with its own individual design.

Other Activities

Besides the dive operations on 18 islands offering scuba and snorkeling, there are more than 200 tennis courts, including almost 100 in the Nassau/Paradise Island/Cable Beach area. There are championship golf courses, casinos, more than 30 major annual fishing tournaments, marinas for motor boating and sailing and airports for private aviators. Squash, polo, parasailing, board sailing, horseback riding, water skiing, and bicycling are some of the other things you can do. There's also shelling, softball, cricket, motor biking, volleyball, ping-pong, skeet shooting, shuffleboard, surfing, jet skiing and paddle boating. Non-diving family members looking for a unique experience can swim cheek-to-cheek with six specially trained, bottle-nosed dolphins at Port Lucaya and Blue Lagoon Island, off Paradise Island.

New Providence Island

New Providence Island, the site of Nassau, the capital of the Bahamas and two famous resort areas (Cable Beach and Paradise Island), offers casino gambling and a wealth of on-shore activities in addition to virgin reef diving and snorkeling. Divers know New Providence best as the sub-sea movie setting for Disney's *20,000 Leagues Under the Sea, Splash, Jaws IV*, and *Cocoon*, not to mention the James Bond thrillers *Thunderball, Never Say Never,* and *For Your Eyes Only*. Diving around New Providence offers steep walls, drop-offs, caves, shallow reefs, ocean holes, and wrecks.

Best Dives of New Providence

Interesting dives exist all around New Providence and adjacent Paradise Island. The north side of Paradise Island shelters a number of shipwrecks and the Lost Ocean Hole.

The southwest area, which skirts the eastern rim of the Tongue of the Ocean, is where you'll find the old movie sets and the best wall dives. Most diehard Bahama divers head for this area while new divers and snorkelers enjoy the special attention offered by the Cable Beach and Paradise Island operators.

☆☆☆☆☆ **Northwest Shipwrecks** off Paradise Island include ***The Mahoney***, a steamship that went down in a hurricane near the turn of the century. She rests in 30 to 40 ft on one end and 100 ft at the other. There is also the ***Ana Lise***, a 150-ft freighter at 90 ft, the adjacent ***Bahama Shell***, a 90-ft tanker, and the ***Helena C***, a 90-ft freighter. Nearby the ***De La Salle*** sits upright at 70 ft.

☆☆☆☆ Southwest of New Providence, **Thunderball Reef**, named for the James Bond film, offers good visibility and a very photogenic setting for shallow water dives and snorkeling. Although small in size, this spot shelters gorgonians, staghorn, and elkhorn corals. The reef supports a dense population of tropicals, queen angels, lobsters and other small critters. Sea conditions are calm with little or no current. Depths are 10 to 30 ft. Boat access.

Courtesy Stuart Cove's Dive South Ocean

Shark Arena.

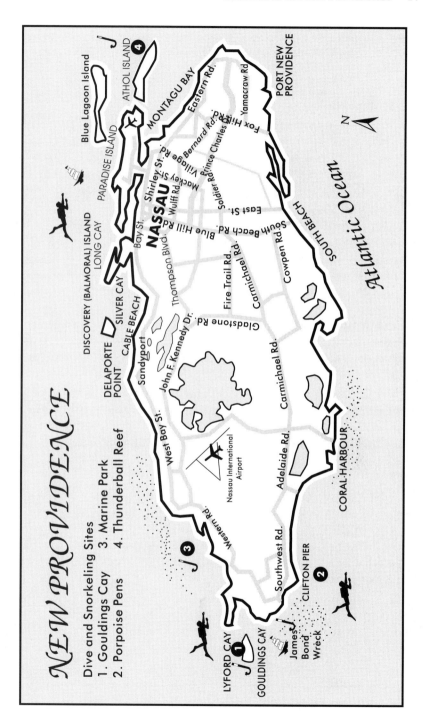

NEW PROVIDENCE

Dive and Snorkeling Sites
1. Gouldings Cay   3. Marine Park
2. Porpoise Pens   4. Thunderball Reef

Courtesy Stuart Cove's Dive South Ocean

Dive Boat, Nassau.

☆☆☆ **New Providence Wrecks** off the southwest coast include the *Bahama Mama*, intentionally sunk in 1995 at 40 ft, the *Willaurie*, a 130-ft freighter at 50 ft, the *Sea Viking*, a 60-ft fishing boat and the *David Tucker II* at 50 ft.

☆☆☆☆ **Gouldings Cay**, a tiny island located off the west end of New Providence, borders a very pretty coral reef that was used as a setting for the films *Cocoon, Never Say Never, 20,000 Leagues Under the Sea* and *Splash*. The area encompasses several acres and offers both shallow snorkeling sites and deeper dives. Eagle rays, turtles, old wreck sections, schools of tropicals, morays, and acres of elkhorn make this spot a favorite.

The *Tears of Allah* wreck from the James Bond movie *Never Say Never* sits in 45 ft of water, as does the nearby *Vulcan Bomber* from *Thunderball*.

☆☆☆☆☆**Lost Blue Hole**, about 10 miles east of Nassau, measures more than 100 ft in diameter. Numerous grunts, Nassau groupers, eels and barracudas inhabit coral heads that surround the top of the hole at 45 ft. Light current. Boat access. Scuba.

☆☆☆ **Shark Wall**, off the southwest side of New Providence Island, is a 50-ft drop-off along the deep-water abyss known as the Tongue of the Ocean. Caribbean reef sharks, lemon and bull sharks cruise the area. The *David Tucker II* sits off the wall. Boat access. Experienced scuba divers.

☆☆☆☆ **Schoolhouse Reef**, on the south side of New Providence Island, is a super snorkeling and shallow scuba spot. Every imaginable fish and sea critter encircle two huge coral mounds. Depths average 15 ft. Boat access.

✮✮✮✮ **Southwest Reef,** a tongue-and-groove formation on the south side of New Providence bottoms at 25 ft. Lots of soft corals. Good for diving and snorkeling. Light current. Boat access.

✮✮✮ **Blue Lagoon Island**, a small watersports and picnic island located approximately one-half mile from Paradise Island, is surrounded by a three-acre marine park. It's home to groupers, moray eels, crawfish, barracudas and a group of affectionate southern stingrays. Dolphin Encounters at Blue Lagoon offers a swim-with-the-dolphins program for snorkelers that allows you to get close up during a half-hour session. ☎ 242-327-5066.

New Providence Dive Operators
(rates subject to change)

Dive Dive Dive Ltd. offers dive/accommodation packages in five deluxe villas on the quiet south side of New Providence Island. Newly renovated villas sleep up to four divers. Each has a kitchen, cable TV and VCR player. Dive boats visit the James Bond Wreck, the Tongue of the Ocean and several reef areas. Two dives cost $70, shark dives $115. Snorkel trips $25 (free gear). Daily pickups from all hotels. Certification and Nitrox courses. Videos, camera and gear rentals. Nitrox and Trimix blends. Friendly staff. Will pick up divers from any hotel on the island. Call for special dive/hotel packages that can save you money. ☎ 800-368-3483, 954-785-3501, fax 954-786-9356. E-mail: info@divedivedive.com. Website: www.divedivedive.com.

Stuart Cove's Dive South Ocean sits on the southwest, lee side of New Providence Island – minutes from sheltered reefs and wrecks. The shop offers shark adventures, reef, wreck and wall dives, snorkeling programs every afternoon and dive-hotel packages with neighboring Clarion South Ocean Dive, Beach and Golf Resort and the Nassau Marriott. Extreme Adventures include Wall Flying via submersible scooter, Shark Adventures and Rebreather Adventures. Pick-up service for divers is provided from any resort. Two-tank, à la carte dives cost $70, full day $115, shark dives $115, snorkel trip, $30. Tanks, weights and belt included for divers; mask, fins, snorkel, and vest for snorkelers. Reduced-rate multiple-dive packages are available. Friendly, helpful service. ☎ 800-879-9832 or 954-524-5755, fax 954-524-5925. E-mail: info@stuartcove.com. Website: www.stuartcove.com.

Nassau Scuba Centre offers shark and shark chainmail suit dives, rebreathers, Nitrox and PADI instruction. Two-tank dives include tanks, weights and belt for $67. Day trips to Andros or Chub Cay cost $115. Lost Blue Hole Dive Trip (minimum 10 divers) costs $85. Hotel packages are offered with Casuarinas of Cable Beach, Orange Hill Beach Inn and the Nassau Beach Hotel. ☎ 888-962-7728, 800-327-8150, 954-462-3400, 242-362-1964 or 242-362-1379. Fax 954-462-4100. Write to: PO Box 21766, Ft.

Bahamas

Lauderdale FL 33335. E-mail: dive@nassau-scubacentre.com. Website: www.nassau-scubacentre.com or www.nealwatson.com.

Bahama Divers serves hotels on Paradise Island with three boats and nine instructors. Packages with all hotels on Paradise Island and Cable Beach. Resort courses. ☎ 800-398-DIVE or 954-351-9533, fax 954-351-9740. Write to PO Box 21584, Ft. Lauderdale, FL 33335. E-mail: bahdiver@ bahamadivers.com.

Divers Haven sells gear, sundries, resort courses, dive trips. Hotel packages with Comfort Suites, Red Carpet Inn, Radisson Cable Beach. ☎ 242-393-0869 or 242-393-3285, fax 242-393-3695. Write to: PO Box N 1658, Nassau, Bahamas.

New Providence Island Accommodations

Clarion South Ocean Golf, Beach & Dive Resort, on the southwest side of New Providence Island, features 250 guest rooms in two categories – standard or deluxe oceanfront, two freshwater pools, a 1,500-ft natural beach, 18-hole golf course, tennis courts, two restaurants, beach bar and golf bars. Babysitting, tour desk, watersports center with snorkeling, board sailing and sailing. Stuart Cove Dive shop on premises. The resort is just four miles from the airport, 10 miles from Nassau. Oceanfront rooms are closest to the dive shop. Standard rooms (lovely) are around the golf course, a seven-minute walk to the dive shop docks. All rooms have phones, A/C, color cable TV. High-season rates for a standard room, double occupancy, are from $695 for five nights, four two-tank dives. Non-divers pay $450. Oceanfront rooms – five nights, three dives – cost $855 for a diver, $610 for non-diver. Summer rates (April 13 to December 23) for the standard room drop to $585 for the diver and $340 for the non-diver. Summer rates for oceanfront, five nights/ three dives, drop to $755 for the diver and $510 for the non-diver. Airport transfers are not included. ☎ 800-879-9832 or 954-524-5755, fax 954-524-5924. Website: www.stuartcove.com.

Dive Dive Dive offers lovely villas on the quiet south side of New Providence. Dive boats are docked outside. Each villa has a kitchen, A/C, TV, VCR, patio with barbecue. Packages with Dive Dive Dive include airport transfers, diving, continental breakfast, trip to shopping center. Each villa accommodates four. Winter rates for a double are from $655 for five nights with four dives. Tanks, weights and belts included. ☎ 800-368-3483, fax 242-362-1994. Website: www.divedivedive.com.

Nassau Marriott Resort and Crystal Palace Casino offers 860 guest rooms and suites with phones, air-conditioning, satellite TV. Amenities include an 800-seat theater with Las Vegas-style shows, a private lagoon bordered by two acres of beach, a swimming pool with water slide and pool bar, fitness center, 18 tennis courts lighted for night play, four racquetball courts, two squash courts, casino gambling, and numerous dining options, including a pizzeria, New York-style deli open 24 hours, a seaside buffet, a snack shop, Chinese and seafood restaurants, plus a dinner theater.

If you want the glitz, glamour and gambling opportunities of Nassau and Cable Beach, this is the place, but expect a 25-minute ride to the dive shop docks. Room rates in winter start at $310 per night. Package rates vary depending on whether day of arrival and departure fall on a weekend or weekday. Rates with Stuart Cove for five nights and four dives in winter start at $1,248 per diver, $1,023 per non-diver. Summer rates are from $800 for five nights/four dives and $575 for a non-diver. Complimentary transfers to the dive shop are included. ☎ 800-879-9832 or 954-524-5755, fax 954-524-5925. Hotel direct, 800-331-6358 or 800-222-7466.

Casuarinas of Cable Beach, also a 25-minute ride to dive-shop docks, is a family-owned 78-room hotel. All rooms have TV, air-conditioning, phone and private bath. The resort features a small beach, two restaurants, two pools. Some oceanfront rooms. Packages with Nassau Scuba Centre during winter start at $538 for five nights. Package includes two boat dives daily, tanks, weights and belts, complimentary transportation to the dive shop. Non-divers deduct $65 per dive day. Summer rates drop to $483 for five nights/three dives. ☎ 888-962-7728, or 954-462-3400, fax 954-462-4100.

Orange Hill Beach Inn is a quiet 320-room inn four miles from the Cable Beach hotels and casinos, 100 yards from the beach. Rooms have TV, A/C, kitchen facilities, private bath. Pool. Packages with Nassau Scuba Centre start at $543 for five nights, two boat dives daily – three days of diving, tanks, weights and belts, transportation to dive shop. Low season rates for five nights are from $490. Travel time to dive shop about 15 minutes. Local bus service to downtown and the Straw Market. ☎ 888-962-7728 or 954-462-3400. Hotel direct 800-805-5485 or 242-327-7157.

Nassau Beach Hotel offers all-inclusive or SuperSaver packages. The 411-room resort sits on Cable Beach, five minutes from the center of town, 20 minutes from south side dive boat docks. Rooms have safes, a balcony, A/C, hair dryers, phone, cable TV. Free non-motorized watersports. Six restaurants, four bars, pool. Golf course and casino next door. All-inclusive packages through Nassau Scuba Centre during the high season range from $1,095 for five nights. Includes meals, daily transportation to the Nassau Scuba Centre, all taxes and gratuities, wine or soft drink with lunch and dinner, upgraded room. The SuperSaver Package booked through Nassau Scuba Centre does not include meals. For five nights with three two-tank dives, rates are from $669. ☎ 888-962-7728 or 954-462-3400, fax 954-4100. Hotel direct: 242-327-7711, fax 242-327-8829.

Bahamas

Atlantis, Paradise Island is a wonderful resort for travelers headed to nearby Blue Lagoon Island. This gigantic 1,147-room property includes a 14-acre waterscape, four lagoons with waterfalls, an underwater grill and bar, the largest open-air aquarium in the world, two freeform pools, and 12 restaurants – one with an underwater view. The dive shop on premises offers visits to wrecks around Paradise Island. Winter rates start at $350 per room, per day, summer from $290. ☎ 800-321-3000 or 242-363-3000, fax 242-363-3524.

Sandals Royal Bahamian Resort & Spa on Cable Beach features eight gourmet restaurants, seven pools, 406 guest rooms, 240 suites, a private offshore island, a water sports complex, and The Spa, featuring facials, hydrotherapy, mud baths and massages. Diving and snorkeling are included in their all-inclusive rates, which vary greatly depending on the accommodations. Winter rates for six nights in a premium room run from $1,840 per person. Summer rates drop to $1,710. Spa services are extra. Call or visit their Website for a complete list of rates for suites and rooms. ☎ 800-SANDALS or 242-327-6400, fax 242-327-6961. Write to: PO Box 39-CB-13005, Cable Beach, Nassau, Bahamas. Website: www.sandals.com.

Grand Bahama Island

Grand Bahama Island, the fourth largest in the Bahamas chain, lies about 60 miles east of Florida, a 30-minute flight from Fort Lauderdale or Miami. Whether diving for the first time, or the hundredth, you'll find Grand Bahama Island an easy spot to enjoy coral reefs, ancient caves, mysterious shipwrecks and every type of marine life from dolphins to angelfish. It is also home to UNEXSO, the Underwater Explorers Society.

Tourist activity centers around **Freeport/Lucaya**, the capital of Grand Bahama and the second largest city in the Bahamas. It is the site of many tourist beaches and activities as well as the International Bazaar and Port Lucaya Marketplace.

West End, a picturesque fishing village on the western tip of the island, is the oldest city and a popular sightseeing spot. It is known for its history as a liquor smuggling town during Prohibition. Driving the coast road from West End to town brings you past Deadman's Reef and Paradise Cove, where you can swim out to some terrific snorkeling reefs.

The Blue Holes

The Islands of the Bahamas were once joined together as a huge underwater mountain range. However, during the Ice Age giant glaciers built up. Water levels dropped and the land began to protrude above the water's surface. As the glaciers melted, the "sponge-like" surface caused holes to form, along

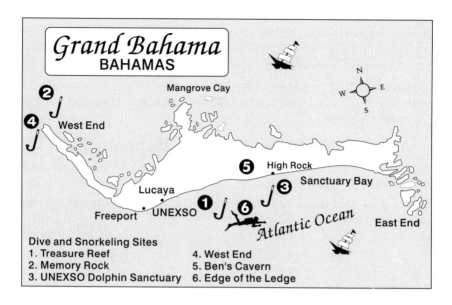

Grand Bahama
BAHAMAS

Mangrove Cay

West End

High Rock

Sanctuary Bay

Lucaya

Freeport UNEXSO

Atlantic Ocean

East End

Dive and Snorkeling Sites

1. Treasure Reef
2. Memory Rock
3. UNEXSO Dolphin Sanctuary

4. West End
5. Ben's Cavern
6. Edge of the Ledge

Bahamas

with an intricate labyrinth of underground caverns. **Gold Rock Blue Hole**, Grand Bahama Island, has fascinated geologists and researchers for years. **Ben's Cavern** (see *Best Dives of Grand Bahama*) offers divers a look at an inland sinkhole. Others may be seen offshore.

Diving

More than 60 identified and buoyed dive sites exist along the South shore of Grand Bahama Island, including two huge wrecks sunk as artificial reefs. Shallow reefs, such as **Rainbow Reef** and the **Fish Farm**, range from four to 15 ft deep and feature forests of elkhorn and staghorn coral interspersed with hard coral, gorgonians and seafans. Thousands of reef fish inhabit this area, including large schools of grunt, snappers, goatfish and sergeant majors.

Depths on the medium reef average about 40 ft. This area is typified by large mushroom-shaped coral heads scattered across a soft sandy bottom. The heads rise about 10 ft from the sea bottom. **Angel's Camp** and **Eden Banks** are two nice areas. Larger pelagic fish are often seen here.

The reef averages 75 ft in depth and is riddled with undersea canyons and caves. Divers are flanked by massive coral buttresses as they swim down perpendicular surge channels. Larger groupers and turtles inhabit the depths.

Less than a mile out from the Lucaya beach, the continental shelf abruptly drops off from a depth of 80 ft to more than 2,000. The face of this wall is deeply pocketed with coral overhangs and is covered with fuzzy sea whips and blood-red sponges. There is an aura of beauty and mystery as one hangs suspended over the indigo blue abyss.

Overall, the reefs are healthy, with good displays of soft corals, sponges and tropicals, but the big attractions here are the dolphin and shark dives. Alternate dive attractions include caverns and blue holes.

The Gulf Stream passes through many of the best dive sites around the island, providing visibility that can exceed 200 ft. Dive sites are close (most less than 15 minutes from shore).

Best Dives of Grand Bahama

Most sites are within a 15-minute boat ride. Sea conditions are usually calm, but can kick up with storms or high winds.

☆☆☆☆☆ **Dolphin Dives**, created by UNEXSO (Underwater Explorers Society), allows divers to swim alongside trained dolphins in the open ocean. Non-diving partners can meet the dolphins at a holding facility in Sanctuary Bay, a 20-minute ferry ride from UNEXSO's dock. Participants first sit on a dock with their feet in the water while dolphins swim around. They later move into waist-deep water and interact with the dolphins.

A **Dolphin Assistant Trainer Program** allows snorkeling, feeding and training sessions. Assistant trainers must be at least 16 years old and speak English.

☆☆☆☆☆ **Shark Dives** offered by UNEXSO and Xanadu Undersea Adventures enable you to observe a number of sharks at close range. Exciting, but not for the timid.

☆☆☆☆☆ **Theo's Wreck** is the favorite dive on Grand Bahama. This 230-ft steel freighter sits in 100 ft of water and is dramatically perched on a ledge that drops off to 2,000 ft.

☆☆ *The José*, a 60-ft tugboat, was intentionally sunk to serve as an artificial reef and dive attraction. She rests at 45 ft and shelters a number of small fish. Boat access.

☆☆ *Poppa Doc*, a 50-ft cargo boat sunk during a storm, offers divers a fun site at 60 ft. Boat access.

☆☆☆ **The *Ethridge* Wreck**, nearby at 60 ft, is another favorite.

☆☆☆☆☆ **Edge of the Ledge** sits less than a mile out from the Lucaya beach. Here the continental shelf abruptly drops off from a depth of 80 ft to more than 2,000 ft. The face of this wall is deeply pocketed with coral overhangs and covered with fuzzy sea whips and blood-red sponges. Good for novice and experienced divers. Seas vary with wind conditions. Often calm. Boat access.

☆☆☆☆ **Ben's Cavern** offers an opportunity to go cave diving without going into a cave. Located within a 40-acre national park, this inland cavern developed centuries ago when the level of the sea was much lower than it is now. Giant stalactites grew down from the ceilings and stalagmites grew up from the floors. Eons later, the level of the ocean rose, flooding the cavern. Eventually the ceiling of Ben's Cavern collapsed, resulting in a crystal clear inland pool. Divers entering this 50-ft-deep pool are able to explore the cave without losing quick access to the cavern opening above.

At approximately 35 ft (sea level), divers swim through a halocline (a transition zone of cool fresh water to warmer saltwater) where vision is blurred for a few feet.

Certified guides take divers thorugh the "breakdown pile" (a large pile of stones from the collapsed ceiling), drapery-like "flowstones" (which look like moving water frozen into positions), a number of types of fossils (shells, corals, conchs, sand dollars, and chrinoids), "Table Rock" (a large column broken from the ceiling), stalagmites, stalactites, and smaller "soda straws."

Ben's Cavern lies about 20 miles east of UNEXSO. There parking close to the cavern opening, and a spiral staircase leads down to a dock-like entry point at the side of the pool. Guided dive shop trips must be arranged on a custom basis with UNEXSO, who supervise a limited number of diver permits for the Bahamas National Trust. Reservations should be made well in advance.

Snorkeling Grand Bahama

☆☆☆ **Treasure Reef** is the site where more than $2.4 million in Spanish Treasure was discovered in the 1960s. Thousands of reef fish inhabit this area, including large schools of grunt, snappers, goatfish, and sergeant majors. Depths range from four to 15 feet. Elkhorn and staghorn corals, gorgonians, and colorful seafans decorate the bottom. Boat access.

☆☆☆ **Memory Rock** offers a look at spectacular brain, pillar and star coral formations. Friendly fish and usually calm seas make this a favorite snorkeling and photo spot. Boat access.

☆☆ **Paradise Cove** is the best spot to snorkel over a reef from the shore. To reach this spot from Freeport/Lucaya, drive the main highway west toward West End. Turn off at Deadman's Reef where you'll find Paradise Cove. Usually calm.

Grand Bahama Dive Operators

UNEXSO, short for the **Underwater Explorers Society**, is world renowned for expert diver training and unusual underwater activities like the Dolphin Experience and Marine Identification Workshops, during which the resident naturalist will put you on a "first name basis" with dozens of marine creatures. Their dive sites are close-in, yet so varied they can accommodate both novice and experienced divers as well as snorkelers. UNEXSO's dive fa-

Bahamas

UNEXSO diver wearing chain mail suit hand-feeds shark, Grand Bahama.

Photo © UNEXSO

cility is world class, with two pools, a well-stocked dive shop and boutique, a fully equipped photo/video center, the largest professional scuba training staff in the Bahamas, and a lively après-dive restaurant and pub. Their unique chain mail suit shark-feeding course costs $2,500 at press time. Reliable dive gear rentals are available, as are reef tours, video and still camera rentals, E-6 processing, and multiple dive packages. ☎ 800-992-DIVE for further information or write UNEXSO, Box F-2433, Freeport, Bahamas.

Xanadu Undersea Adventures, located at the Xanadu Beach Resort, offers resort, certification, rescue, first aid, deep dive, wreck dive, Dive Master and Scuba Instructor courses, open-water and rusty diver checkouts. A two-tank dive costs $55. Packages up to 20 tanks for $394 are available. Add $15 for a night dive, $30 for a shark dive. Non-diving companions pay $15 to ride on the boat, snorkelers pay $20, which includes use of a mask, fins, and snorkel. The shop boats leave at 8 am, 10:30 am and 1 pm. The early dive is 60 to 100 ft, the mid-morning dive usually shallow and the afternoon dive from 40

*Snorkeling
Bahamas Out Islands.*

Photo by Michael Lawrence
©Jean-Michel Cousteau's Out
Islands Snorkeling Adventures

to 60 ft. All dives have guided tours and divemaster assistance. Dives include the use of weights, weight belt, tank and air fills. Hotel packages with Xanadu Beach resort, Royal Islander Hotel, Royal Palm Resort and Running Mon Resort. ☎ 800-327-8150 or 954-462-3400, fax 954-4100. E-mail: xanadu@ nealwatson.com. Website: nealwatson.com/xanadu.htm. Write to PO Box 21766, Fort Lauderdale FL 33335-1766.

Grand Bahama Accommodations

Room rates are subject to a $12 per person, per night tax unless stated otherwise. All rates subject to change. Websites: www.grand-bahama.com/hotels.html or www.grandbahamavacations.com.

Grand Bahama Beach Hotel is on the beach across from the Port Lucaya Marketplace within walking distance of UNEXSO. The recently renovated resort features 250 rooms, a huge pool, lounge and snack bar. Near a variety of restaurants. Shuttle to the Arawak Restaurant. ☎ 800-622-6770 or 305-592-5757, fax 242-373-8662. Room rates are from $129 per day. Packages with UNEXSO for five nights/six dives in winter (December 21-April 18) range upward from $450 (low season from $400). ☎ 800-992 DIVE or 954-351-9889.

Xanadu Beach Resort & Marina, once the home of Howard Hughes, offers two restaurants, lounge, three tennis courts (one lighted), on-site dive center, 77-slip marina, tour desk, babysitting, gift shop, beauty salon, bike and scooter rental, and private beach with its own straw market. Each of the 186 guest rooms and suites have a balcony or patio. Room rates start at $140.

Packages with Xanadu Undersea Adventures start from $498 for five nights/ four dives, $464 during the low season (4/16 -12/14). Includes room taxes, service charges, tanks, weights and belts. ☎ 800-327-8150 or 954-462-3400, fax 954-462-4100. E-mail: xanadu@nealwatson.com. Write to: PO Box 21766, Ft Lauderdale FL 33335. Hotel direct: ☎ 242-352-6782, fax 242-352-5799.

Port Lucaya Resort & Yacht Club, adjacent to the Port Lucaya Market-place, offers 160 rooms, an Olympic pool, Jacuzzi, restaurant, two bars and 50-slip marina. This resort juts out into the bay like a peninsula, with hotel buildings positioned in a circle around the pool and grounds. Built in 1993. Walking distance to UNEXSO. Room rates are from $135 for a single, each person add $25, children under 12 free. ☎ 800-582-2921 or 800-LUCAYA-1, fax 242-373-6652. Dive packages with UNEXSO for five nights, six dives run from $450. Snorkelers from $370. ☎ 800-992-DIVE or 954-351-9889.

Club Fortuna Beach, a 204-room low-rise resort sits on 1,200 ft of white sandy beach away from the hustle and bustle. Amenities include a large pool, restaurant, lounge, tennis, exercise room and shopping arcade. A short drive from UNEXSO and Port Lucaya. All-inclusive rates with three meals per day range from $300 per person, per day in winter, from $240 in summer. ☎ 800-847-4502 or 242-373-4000, fax 242-373-5555. E-mail: maxcar@ batelnet.bs. Packages with UNEXSO for five nights/six dives run from $785 for a diver, $705 for a snorkeler. ☎ 800-992-DIVE.

Royal Islander Hotel features 100 air-conditioned rooms with cable TV, phone and a choice of two doubles or a king-size bed. Non-smoking rooms available. No beach. Pool, restaurant open for three meals a day, children's playground, gift shop, complimentary shuttle to Xanadu Beach. Short drive or walk to Princess Casino and the International Bazaar. Room rates for a double start at $104. Hotel direct: ☎ 242-351-6000, fax 242-351-3546. Packages with Xanadu Undersea Adventures for five nights and four dives start at $498 in winter, $464 in summer. ☎ 800-327-8150. Includes transport to dive shop, taxes, tanks, weights and belts.

Bahamas Princess Resort & Casino, the island's largest resort with 965 rooms, sits on 100 lush acres next to the International Bazaar and Princess Ca-sino. The resort offers nine restaurants and bars, two pools and a beach club. Near UNEXSO. Rooms per day are from $135, from $200 for a suite. ☎ 800-545-1300, fax 954-359-9585. Website: www. grandbahamavacations.com. Packages with UNEXSO for five nights, six dives are from $460 in winter, $395 summer. ☎ 800-992-DIVE or 954-351-9889.

Royal Palm Resort is located five minutes from the airport and a half-mile from downtown. The property consists of 48 rooms with TV, freshwater pool, restaurant and bar. Rates are from $120 per day. ☎ 242-352-3462, fax 242-

352-5759. E-mail: royal@batelnet.bs. Packages with Xanadu Undersea Adventures for four nights/three dives are from $328 in winter, $312 in summer. Includes free transport to the beach and International Bazaar, room taxes, service charges, tanks, weights and belts.

Running Mon Resort, on Freeport's south shore, features air-conditioned rooms with TV and phones. Pool, waterfront restaurant and lounge. No beach. Room rates are from $110 per day for a double. ☎ 242-352-6833, fax 242-352-6835. Packages with Xanadu for five nights, four dives are from $404 in winter, $378 in summer. They include diving, tanks, weights, belts, daily transportation to the dive shop, complimentary transportation to the beach and International Bazaar, room, service charges. ☎ 800-327-8150.

Pelican Bay, on the waterfront adjacent to the shops and restaurants of Port Lucaya Marketplace, features 48 large rooms, pool, Jacuzzi, pool bar next to the Underwater Explorer's Society. Packages with UNEXSO for five nights, six divers are from $460 in winter. ☎ 800-992-DIVE.

The Out Islands

Bahama Out Islands offer pristine reefs for diving and snorkeling. Twenty-six out-island resorts offer a special program just for snorkelers. The Bahama Out Islands Snorkeling Adventures, created by Jean-Michel Cousteau, offer guided reef excursions by professionally trained instructors. Participating resorts are noted under each island description.

The Abaco Islands

The Abaco Islands are the northernmost group in the Bahamas stretching roughly 130 miles from Walker's Cay to Great Abaco. Most of the diving activity takes place around Marsh Harbour, Walker's Cay, and Treasure Cay.

The history of this special island group explains its New England-style villages. Many Abaco residents descend from British Loyalists who left New England and the Carolinas following the Revolutionary War. Some became fishermen, some became wreckers and others learned boat building.

The **Albert Lowe Museum**, a 150-year-old former residence on Green Turtle Cay, is devoted to showcasing the history of the Abacos and its shipbuilding traditions. It was created by Alton Lowe in honor of his father, who was a noted carver of ship models.

Bahamas

Getting to the Abacos

Bahamasair from Nassau to Marsh Harbour. Charter to Walker's Cay from Ft. Lauderdale (see *Walker's Cay* below).

Best Dives of the Abacos

☆☆☆☆☆**Pelican Cay National Park**, a 2,000-acre national underwater preserve offers endless mazes of coral tunnels, walls, pinnacles and remains of modern and ancient wrecks.

The park is shallow and ranges in depth from breaking the surface to about 30 ft. The marine life is spectacular, with eagle rays, jacks, angels, critters, huge groupers, and colorful sponges to be seen. Pelican Park offers the underwater photographer and video enthusiast an abundance of beautiful subseascapes.

☆☆☆☆☆ **Fowl Cays National Park**, an underwater preserve, features more than 20 sites. Coral sea mounts and pinnacles provide great snorkeling in the shallows and fine scuba sites with large groupers, nurse shark and tropical fish. Currents are very light. Depths are from the surface at low tide to 60 ft. Underwater terrain is rocky with many caverns. During summer numerous copper sweepers and silversides crowd the shadows.

☆☆☆☆ **Shark Rodeo**, off Walker's Cay, whirls with adventure as more than 100 sharks circle a frozen barrelful of fishheads affectionately known as the "chumsicle." The sharks take turns feeding in groups of a half-dozen at once while their buddies investigate the surroundings. This attraction is put on by Walker's Cay Undersea Adventures for intrepid divers. The site is a short boat ride from shore.

☆☆☆☆ *USS Adirondack*, a Federal-era battleship resting in 30 ft of water, offers both snorkelers and scuba divers a look at the remains of the superstructure and some interesting antique cannons. A host of colorful reef fish inhabit the area around it. Boat access.

☆☆☆ *Deborah K*, a 165-ft light cargo ship, was used as a mail boat by the Bahamian government until Independence Day, 1998, when she was stripped of hazards to the environment and scuttled off Fowl Cay. She sits upright facing east at 100 ft. Residents include a huge groupers, horse-eyed jacks, angelfish and yellowtails. Top of the mast reaches up to 35 feet. Cargo holds are open. Good visibility. Boat access. Experienced divers only.

☆☆☆☆ **Spiral Cavern**, off Walker's Cay, features walls of fish in caverns and around monster-size coral heads with a maximum depth of 45 ft. Boat access. Experienced divers.

Additional favorite sites, all less than a 10-minute boat ride, are **The Tower**, a 60-ft-tall coral pinnacle, **Grouper Alley**, home to several Nassau groupers,

Shark Alley, a valley of non-aggressive nurse and reef sharks, **Tutts Reef** and **Cathedral**, a bright cavern densely packed with tropical fish and turtles.

Snorkeling the Abacos

The best shore snorkeling sites lie off Guana Cay, where the reef sits less than 50 ft from the beach at the Guana Beach Resort, and Hopetown Harbour Lodge, which has a section of beautiful barrier reef just 30 ft from their lovely two-mile-long beach. Excellent shallow reefs exist less than a mile off Green Turtle Cay and Spanish Cay.

Abaco Dive Operators

Abaco Beach Resort Dive Centre. Located in Marsh Harbour, this upbeat shop offers resort courses and all levels of training, reef trips and equipment rentals. Nitrox. The shop's 36-ft custom dive boat carries a maximum of 20 divers. PADI, YMCA, ANDI, NASDA, CMAS and BSAC training in English, French or Spanish. Rates are $45 for a one-tank dive, $70 for two tanks. Equipment rental. Most dives are about 100 ft. Visits the Tower, Shark Alley, Tutts Reef, Cathedral and the *Deborah K*. Equipment storage at the dive shop. ☎ 800-838-4189 or 242-367-4646. Website: dive@greatabaco.com.

Dive Abaco, at the town marina in Marsh Harbour, offers diving inside the barrier reef at the Tunnels, where trained groupers and snappers pose for photos or the Towers at 60 ft and the Caves at 45 ft, both with awesome corals and marine life. The dive shop owner doubles as boat captain and dive master. Dive Abaco uses a 30-ft custom dive boat with a wide dive platform, open transom and easy-access ladder. Oxygen is on board. This is a nice operation. Hotel/dive packages are available with Abaco Towns by the Sea, the Conch Inn resort, Island Breezes, Lofty Fig Villas and Pelican Beach Villas. Write to: PO Box AB 20555, Marsh Harbour, Abaco, Bahamas. ☎ 800-247-5338 or 242-367-2787, fax 242-367-4779. E-mail: dive.abaco@internetfl.com. Website: www.internetfl.com/abaco.

Brendal's Dive Shop, on Green Turtle Cay at the Green Turtle Club and Marina, caters to novices as well as experienced divers. Tours explore Pelican Park and the Coral Catacombs, both teeming with moray eels, turtles, rays, schools of grunts and porpoises. Resort courses are offered and equipment rentals are available. Dive packages with lodging at the Green Turtle and Bluff House are available. Write to: Brendal Stevens, Green Turtle Cay, Green Turtle Club and Marina, Bahamas. ☎ (US) 800-780-9941 or 242-365-4411.

Divers Down at the Treasure Cay Marina offers two-tank dives to the reefs and wrecks. Snorkelers welcome. Resort and certification courses. Gear rentals. Retail store sells snorkel gear. ☎ 800-327-1584 or 242-365-8465, fax 242-365-8508. E-mail: jic@oii.net.

*Candy-Striped
Lighthouse on
Elbow Cay,
Abaco.*

© Bahamas
Tourist Board

Walker's Cay Undersea Adventures has a staff of six with four instructors, two boats that carry 16 to 25 passengers and a retail shop selling gear and accessories. Rentals. Dive groups can arrange for special tours and cookouts. Packages with Walker's Cay Hotel and Marina on property. ☎ 800-327-8150 or 954-462-3400, fax 954-462-4100. On island, 242-353-1252.

Abaco Islands Accommodations
Rates subject to change

Elbow Cay

The **Abaco Inn** on Elbow Cay features 15 guest rooms and suites, each with a private patio and hammock. On-site Clubhouse Lounge serves beachfront tropical meals. Short walk to Hope Town and the Elbow Cay Lighthouse. Winter rates for a double are from $135. From $195 for a suite. Summer rates from $100. ☎ 800-468-8799 or 242-366-0133, fax 242-366-0113. E-mail: abacoinn@batelnet.bs. Website: www.oii.net/AbacoInn. Participant in the Jean-Michel Cousteau Out Island Snorkeling Adventures program.

Hope Town Harbour Lodge features a nice shallow coral reef 30 feet off the beach. The Lodge offers 20 remodeled rooms. AC and ceiling fans. Overlooks Hope Town Harbour. To reach this resort take a ferry from Marsh Harbour. Rates for a double are from $130. Butterfly House from $1,250 weekly. ☎ 800-316-7844 or 242-366-0095, fax 242-366-0286. E-mail: harbour lodge@batelnet.bs. Participant in the Jean-Michel Cousteau Out Island Snorkeling Adventures program.

Great Abaco

To reach Great Abaco, fly to Marsh Harbour Airport and take a taxi to the resort.

Abaco Beach Resort & Boat Harbour features spacious, air-conditioned rooms, TV, phones, mini-fridges, and patios. Two-bedroom, two-bath villas are also available. Rates are from $145 for a deluxe oceanfront room September 2-December 21. From $185 December 22-September 1. Villas start at $300 during the low season, $400 in the high season. ☎ 800-468-4799 or 242-367-2158, fax 242-367-2819.

Conch Inn Hotel & Marina offers nine recently renovated air-conditioned rooms, each with a single and double bed overlooking Marsh Harbour. Pool, cable TV, mini market. Good restaurant. Full-service marina offers sailboat charters and rentals. The Moorings is on-premises. ☎ 800-688-4752 or 242-367-4000, fax 242-367-4004. Write to PO Box AB-20469. Packages with Dive Abaco.

The Lofty Fig has six nice rooms, each with air-conditioning, a queen-size bed, sofa, small dinette, kitchen and porch. Pool, bicycle, scooter, car and boat rentals. Close to restaurants, bars, and dive shop. Packages with Dive Abaco. ☎ 800-688-4752 or 242-367-2681. Write to PO Box AB 20437, Marsh Harbour, Abaco, Bahamas.

Pelican Beach Villas, at Pelican Shores on Marsh Harbour, features beachfront villas that sleep six, with kitchen, refrigerator, microwave. Near to restaurants and activities. Safe dockage for small boats. Mermaid Reef, a shallow snorkeling area, is nearby. Weekly rates for a double are from $1,045. For a triple, from $1,145. $50 each extra person. ☎ 800-642-4752 or 242-367-3600. Write to Pelican Beach Villas, Marsh Harbour, Abaco, Bahamas.

Great Guana Cay

To reach Guana Cay, fly into Marsh Harbour, taxi to the Conch Inn Marina, where the Guana Cay ferry picks up at 11 am and 3:30 pm. Or take the AIT ferry from Triple J Marina at 12 noon and 4 pm. Boat ride takes 20 minutes.

Guana Beach Resort & Marina offers eight rooms and seven suites with kitchens. Newly renovated bar and restaurant open for breakfast, lunch and dinner. Terrific snorkeling off their seven-mile beach. A 50-ft swim brings you over a lovely reef with healthy seafans and corals. Friendly service. Winter (December 16-May 31) rates are from $140 for a room, from $210 for a two-bedroom suite. ☎ 800-227-3366 or 242-365-5133, fax 242-365-5134. E-mail: guanabeach@guanabeach.com.

Guana Seaside Village, a new romantic beachfront resort, has eight lovely rooms, one suite with kitchenette and a long sandy beach with great snorkeling just 50 ft offshore. Beachside restaurant. Winter (December 15-April 15)

Bahamas

rates are from $145 per day for a double. Suites are $160 for up to four. Summer per-day rates start at $130 for a beachfront room, $145 for the suite. ☎ 800-242-0942 or 242-365-5146. E-mail: guanaseaside@oii.net. Website: www.oii.net/GreatGuana.

Green Turtle Cay

To reach this island, fly into Treasure Cay airport. Taxi to the ferry dock and ferry to Bluff House's or the Green Turtle Inn's docks.

Bluff House Club & Marina is a plush resort with a very attentive staff. Each of the 28 air-conditioned rooms and suites have refrigerators, coffee makers and hair dryers. Restaurant and Beach Club. Room rates in winter are from $110, $135 for a split level, $140 for a studio, $215 for a suite. Villas are from $385 per day. ☎ 800-688-4752 or 242-365-4247, fax 242-365-4248. E-mail: BluffHouse@oii.net. Website: www.oii.net/BluffHouse.

Green Turtle Club & Marina features 34 air-conditioned rooms and cottages on a small island rimmed with white sand beaches. Rooms and villas have a private patio or deck, paddle fans, and refrigerator. Pool, snorkeling, boat rentals, 35-slip marina. Brendal's Dive shop on premises. Fabulous restaurant. Winter rates (January 2-April 14) are $165 per room, $185 for a suite, $269 for a one-bedroom villa, $379 for a two-bedroom villa (one to six persons) ☎ 800-688-4752 or 242-365-4271, fax 242-365-4272. E-mail: greenturtle@batelnet.bs. Website: www.greenturtle club.com.

Spanish Cay

Reach this one-resort island by flying into Spanish Cay. The hotel will pick you up. Or taxi to the government dock at Cooperstown. The Spanish Cay ferry will bring you to Spanish Cay. For private pilots, the island also has a 5,000-ft runway with customs service on Saturday and Sunday. On-island transportation is via bicycle or golf cart. Rates subject to change.

Spanish Cay Resort & Marina has five newer suites, seven one- and two-bedroom apartments and a 70-slip marina. No dive shop or scuba diving services exist, but snorkelers will find a nice reef 50 yards off the beach. Boat rentals available from the marina. This lovely resort appeals to an older crowd. Year-round rates are from $150 for suites, from $225 for apartments. ☎ 888-722-6474 or 242-365-0083, fax 561-655-0172.

Treasure Cay

To reach Treasure Cay, fly into Treasure Cay International Airport, then take a taxi to the resort. The island has an 18-hole golf course, 150-slip marina, restaurants and shops. Rates subject to change.

Banyan Beach Club arranges diving and offshore snorkeling with nearby Divers Down. Snorkelers will find beautiful corals upon entering the water to

the left of the resort property. The resort offers two- and three-bedroom condos. Each unit has an all-electric kitchen, cable TV, air-conditioning, phone.
Golf carts are rented for transportation. Rates for two-bedroom units run
$200 per night, $540 for three nights, $1,050 for seven nights. Beachfront
units are $225, $600, and $1,250. Three-bedroom condos start at $675 for
three nights. ☎ 888-625-3060 or 242-365-8111, fax 561-625-5301.

Treasure Cay Hotel Resort & Marina has a fabulous 3.5-mile beach, a
modern 150-slip marina and an 18-hole golf course. Diver Down Dive Shop
is on premises. Winter rates (December 18-April 27): Standard rooms start at
$130 for a double, suites from $175. Villas from $385 per day. Summer rates
(April 28-December 17): From $95 for a standard room, $155 for deluxe,
$130 for a suite, $315 for villas. Meal plans are $44 per day, per person.
☎ 800-327-1584 or 954-525-7711, fax 954-525-1699. E-mail: abaco@
gate.net. Website: www.treasurecay.com.

Walker's Cay

Walker's Cay Undersea Adventures. Located at the northern end of the
Abacos, this resort and dive center, the only one on the island, offers guests
private air charters to and from Ft. Lauderdale. Walker's Cay Undersea Adventures dive shop is well-equipped and offers a resort course, which includes
a short introductory scuba lesson in a pool, followed by a closely supervised
shallow dive. Open water dives for a PADI certification are available. Access
to most of the dives, which are at the upper end of Barrier Reef, is by boat.
Choose from a scattering of lovely villas and cottages for your stay. ☎ 800-
327-8150 or 954-462-3400. Local 242-353-1252, fax 954-462-4100. E-
mail: nealwatson@aol.com. Website: www.nealwatson.com/walkers.htm.

Andros Island

Andros, the largest of the Bahama islands, yet the least populated, fringes the
second largest barrier reef in the Western Hemisphere. Dive sites sit within 10
minutes from the Small Hope Bay Lodge on the northeastern coast. Superb
visibility and calm seas, ranging from flat during summer months to two to
three feet during the winter, are the norm.

Getting to Andros

Andros has three airports: at centrally located San Andros, at Andros Town,
and at Congo Town in the south. Air service is by Island Express from Fort
Lauderdale, Bahamasair from Nassau and several private charters – Small
Hope Bay Charter, Southern Outbound Air, Miami Air Charter and Air Link.

Folklore buffs might want to pack some flowery bits of fabric for the legendary Chick Charnies of Andros. These are half-bird, half-man creatures that build their nests by bending the tops of two pine trees together. Legend has it the creatures drive away evil spirits and protect the good from the bad. Legend also says visitors to Andros should explore the island carrying flowers and bright bits of fabric to leave for the Chick Charnies, all of which will be returned in riches.

Best Dives of Andros

☆☆☆☆☆ **Brad's Mountain**, a favorite spot for scuba divers of all skill levels, features a huge coral mountain rising from a 50-ft depth to a peak at 20 ft, carved into wonderful arches, caves and crevices loaded with silversides and armies of mini-critters. Festive sea fan, sponge, and coral displays kaleidoscope into a blaze of color. Spade fish, Bermuda chub, parrot fish, grunts and French and Queen angelfish crowd the area. Boat access.

☆☆☆☆☆ **The Blue Hole** is a huge bell-shaped crater, perhaps 300 ft across, which drops off to great depths. It opens at 50 ft in the center of a coral garden. Divers who circle its perimeter at a depth of 100 ft find enormous rock pillars and deep shafts. Huge stingrays glide by amidst super-sized midnight parrot fish, snappers and large crabs. This dive is not recommended for beginners. Do not enter the shafts. Boat access.

☆☆☆☆ **The Barge,** an LC landing craft that sank in 1963, is a delight for a novice diver with a new camera. Sitting in 70 ft of water, the wreck is home to a bevy of friendly morays and groupers. They will greet you at the anchor line, eat from your hand and offer you a tour. Pretty coral formations are found here also. Boat access.

☆☆☆☆ **Giant's Staircase**. Advanced divers will enjoy exploring this wall, which slopes at irregular angles and, as the name implies, looks much like a giant's staircase, with the final step dropping off 6,000 ft into the Tongue of the Ocean. The wall starts at 90 ft. A variety of corals surrounding a huge sand patch adorn the top of the wall, where garden eels peer up from time to time. (They retreat back into the sand when you get too close.) Experienced divers. Boat access.

☆☆☆☆ **Turnbull's Gut**, a fascinating wall dive, starts at 80 ft, then plunges into a wide canyon (the "gut"), which extends laterally 100 ft to a spectacular 6,000-ft drop in the Tongue of the Ocean. The wall shelters lettuce corals, black coral, vibrant sea fans and sponges. The "gut," plentiful with

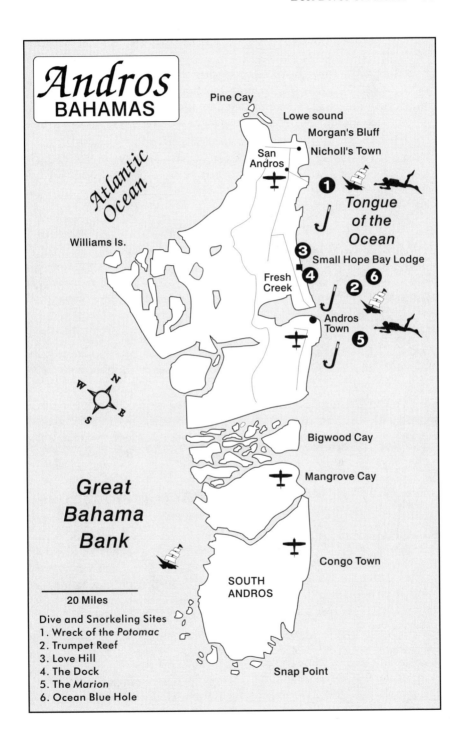

Andros
BAHAMAS

Pine Cay

Lowe sound

Morgan's Bluff

Nicholl's Town

San
Andros

*Atlantic
Ocean*

Williams Is.

*Tongue
of the
Ocean*

Small Hope Bay Lodge

Fresh
Creek

Andros
Town

Bigwood Cay

Mangrove Cay

*Great
Bahama
Bank*

Congo Town

SOUTH
ANDROS

20 Miles

Snap Point

Dive and Snorkeling Sites
1. Wreck of the *Potomac*
2. Trumpet Reef
3. Love Hill
4. The Dock
5. The *Marion*
6. Ocean Blue Hole

fish, often belches large rays. This dive is recommended for those with some experience. Boat access.

☆☆☆ **The *Marion*,** a sunken barge 100 ft long and 40 ft wide, presents a fun dive for all skill levels. With a huge tractor and a crane nearby, the wreckage lies in a large sand patch surrounded by a really pretty coral garden. Residents include spotted groupers, parrot fish, southern sting rays, garden eels, and nurse sharks.

☆☆☆☆ **The Dungeons** are a series of caves weaving in and out of the wall at the Tongue of the Ocean. Some, formed by interconnecting pillars of coral, wind into the wall for 100 ft. Groupers, silversides, rays and sharks are found here. Advanced divers only. Depth range is 70-90 ft. Boat access.

Snorkeling Andros

☆☆☆☆☆ **Trumpet Reef** displays healthy elkhorn, staghorn, brain and soft corals. Trumpet fish are everywhere, joined by beautiful queen and French angels, schools of grunts and yellowtails. Snorkelers and beginning divers get hooked by the bounty and beauty of marine life here. Depths range from two to 15 ft. Boat access.

☆☆☆☆ **Love Hill** rises from a shimmering white sand bottom into huge thickets of elkhorn and staghorn corals. Soft corals and gorgonians hug the hillside. A full range of tropical fish and marine animals inhabit the area. Depths are two to 15 ft. Boat access.

☆☆☆ **The Dock at Small Hope Bay Lodge** is a terrific spot for a night snorkel. Fish are abundant and varied amidst 35 years of stuff that's fallen off the dock, including ruins of the previous dock. Sea life includes snappers, blue tangs, parrot fish, barracuda, angelfish, flounder, puffer fish, eagle rays, and octopus. An occasional dolphin breezes by.

Andros Dive Operators & Accommodations
Rates subject to change.

Small Hope Bay Lodge has been hosting divers since 1960. Guests may choose from 20 one- and two-bedroom cottages at the water's edge and are invited to soothe themselves in a hot tub on the beach or meet with the resident masseuse. Guest cabins feature handmade batik Androsian fabrics and ceiling fans. Excellent meals include Bahamian specialties such as conch chowder, red snapper and lobster.

Besides diving and snorkeling, the resort offers Sunfish sailing, windsurfing and fishing. Small Hope Bay also has Coakley House, a three-bedroom, three-bath oceanfront villa, fully equipped with a dock, beach, patio and bikes. Guests are offered free introductory scuba and snorkeling lessons. Experienced divers are brought to walls and blue holes to dive. Winter rates for a diver are from $220 per day, which includes all meals, help-yourself bar, hors d'oeuvres, airport transfers, and use of snorkel gear, sailboat, kayaks, board surfers and hot tub. For reservations, ☎ 800-223-6961 or 242-368-2014, fax 242-368-2015. Write to PO Box 21667, Fort Lauderdale FL 33335. E-mail: SHBinfo@SmallHope.com. Website: www.SmallHope.com.

Andros Lighthouse Yacht Club & Marina features an 18-slip marina, 20 luxurious air-conditioned rooms with private baths, king size beds or two double beds. Rates for a double in winter range from $150 per day. MAP add $40. Maid service is $2.50 extra per day. Andros Undersea Adventures on premises operates fast custom dive boats, offers package vacations, still and video camera rentals. Diving costs $70 for a two-tank dive (same day). ☎ 800-327-8150 or 954-462-3400, fax 954-462-4100. E-mail: nealwatson@ aol.com. Website: www.neal watson.com. Write to PO Box 21766, Ft. Lauderdale FL 33335.

The Berry Islands

The Berry Islands, a group of small islands and cays, many privately owned, lie just north of New Providence. The best dive and snorkeling areas run along the barrier reef at the northern end of the "Tongue of the Ocean" at Chub Cay.

Best Dives of the Berry Islands

☆☆☆☆ **The Fishbowl**, a wall dive, takes its name from the throngs of fish and marine animals that adorn the area's valleys and ridges. Thriving shallow reefs rich with huge sponges, corals, sea fans and critters welcome snorkelers. Deep dramatic coral cliff drop-offs lure scuba fans. This reef is excellent for underwater photography.

☆☆☆ **Angelfish Reef**, as the name implies, provides shelter to numerous French and queen angels, many of which will pose for a video or still photo. Grunts, rays, turtles, eels, and barracudas are found swimming among the staghorn, elkhorn and brain corals. The average depth is 50 ft and visibility is usually good.

Snorkeling the Berry Islands

☆☆☆ **Moma Rhoda's Reef** delights snorkelers and scuba divers with masses of bright sponges, critters, coral mounds and crevices. Walls of sergeant majors, rays, grunts, hogfish, groupers, jacks, yellowtails and every imaginable critter hang out here. Snorkelers are advised to take care that wave action does not toss them into the shallow areas of the reef. Boat access.

☆☆ **The Reef at Chub Cay** sits off the western coast about 15 ft from the shoreline with depths from three to 60 ft. Undersea Adventures recently installed a concrete pad and steps over the ironshore to allow snorkelers and divers easy entry to the shallow elkhorn gardens. Beach dive.

Berry Islands Dive Operator & Accommodations

The Chub Cay Resort on Chub Cay is a well-planned self-contained dive resort that caters to the special needs of the underwater photographer with a full-service photo lab and custom dive boats. Guests enjoy modern, comfortable, air-conditioned rooms, the Flying Bridge restaurant, pool, and gift shop. Divemaster Bill Whaley has 20 sites within a few minutes of the marina. Rates are from $534 for five days, four nights, with three boat dives daily, tanks, weights, and belts, airport transfers, ☎ 800-327-8150. E-mail: chub@ nealwatson.com. Website: www.chubcaydive.com. Write Undersea Adventures, PO Box 21766, Fort Lauderdale FL 33335.

Getting to the Berry Islands

The Berry islands are reached by private charters. **Island Express** serves Great Harbour Cay from Fort Lauderdale. **Southern Pride Aviation**, ☎ 954-938-8991, provides transportation from Fort Lauderdale Executive Airport to Chub Cay for guests of the Chub Cay Resort and for divers who book a package tour with **Chub Cay Undersea Adventures**. ☎ 800-327-8150. Allow at least 2½ hours between flights if you are arriving at Fort Lauderdale International. You'll need to take a taxi from there to Executive Airport at 1625 W. Commercial Blvd.

Bimini

Bimini divides into two islands, North and South Bimini, separated by a shallow, narrow channel. **Alice Town**, North Bimini, the hub of tourism and commerce, centers around one main road, King's Highway, where you'll find a half-dozen local restaurants and hometown bars. During fishing tournaments the entire town comes to life. Over 50 world records have been set here. Bimini was also the inspiration for Ernest Hemingway's *Islands in the Stream*. South Bimini is very rural and quiet, with just two small hotels and a small airstrip.

Lying 50 miles east of Miami, Bimini edges the warm currents of the Gulf Stream, which nurture and preserve diverse corals, white sand beaches and marine animals.

For the experienced diver, drift dives on the Bimini Wall offer some nice sights; for the novice or snorkeler, Rainbow Reef is the favorite. A playful crowd of fish awaits divers at the shallow freighter wreck *Sapona*.

Overall, Bimini is best known as the one-time stomping ground for Ernest Hemingway and Adam Clayton Powell. What visitors may not know about is Bimini's legend of the **Lost City of Atlantis**. For years, curious scientists have come to Bimini to investigate its mysteries.

According to Greek philosopher Plato, Atlantis was a vast land with an ideal government, advanced agriculture, an elaborate system of canals and bridges and luxurious temples. The kingdom, which was ruled by Poseidon and his 10 sons, threatened to overpower Europe. However, the people became corrupt and the culture was destroyed by volcanoes.

Plato's Mediterranean depiction of Atlantis has since been revived to include the Islands of the Bahamas. American clairvoyant Edgar Cayce, otherwise known as the "Sleeping Prophet," claimed he could foretell the future during hypnotic trances. In 1934, he predicted that the sunken portion of Atlantis lay near Bimini, off the coast of Florida, and would be discovered between 1968 and 1969.

In 1968, after Bimini fishermen reported they saw large flat rocks on the ocean floor in Bimini, marine technology expert Dimitri Rebikoff investigated the site and discovered what is now known as the Bimini Road. According to Rebikoff, "The Road," covered by 15 feet of water, was made of hundreds of flat rocks laid out in two straight parallel rows. He felt the right angles of the rocks were not possible in nature and must be from a buried civilization. A few later scientists have disputed this, saying that the placement of the rocks may have resulted from erosion, but that story isn't nearly as interesting!

In 1974, Dr. David Zink, archeological director for the Bahamas, determined the profile of the structure was horizontal, unlike the normal sloped ocean floor. Zink also found two ancient artifacts, a tongue-and-groove building block and a stylized marble head near the sunken road that had to have been imported. Most recently, in 1997, an extensive aerial survey of the site and further sampling was completed. Bill Donato, American anthropologist and archaeologist, found unnatural features on the stones, such as a perpendicular cut from top to bottom. We don't know if the road is part of Atlantis, but we can guarantee it to be a fun snorkel trail.

The **Sand Mounds of Bimini** offer more mystery. Large sand dunes that appear in the shape of a shark, a cat and a sea horse lie in North Bimini. They are so vast they can only be recognized from the air. The mounds appear on early maps of the island that were drawn by natives. However, these natives did not have the capability to fly over the island, so they never actually saw the mounds. The origin of these formations remains unknown.

Bimini north end features an intricate labyrinth of narrow tunnels, one of which is connected to a creek that has earned the name the **Healing Hole**. At

Bahamas

high tide, the tunnels fill with water rich in mineral content and empty into the creek. This water is said to have mystical healing powers.

Getting to Bimini

Bimini lies just 60 miles off Florida's coast and may easily be reached by boat or plane. From Miami, fly into North Bimini Airport via Chalk's International Airlines (☎ 305-653-5572, 800-348-4644), a popular seaplane service. From there take a water taxi or the Bimini Bus to your hotel. A short ferry ride connects North and South Bimini.

Best Dives of Bimini

Reefs along Bimini's shore range from 35 to 100 ft, with healthy fish populations and vibrant corals. A nice shore-entry snorkeling reef sits off the beach at the **Bimini Beach Club & Marina** (☎ 242-359-8228, fax 954-725-0918) on the south end of North Bimini.

☆☆☆ **The Nodules** are a fascinating web of coral structures: ledges, tunnels, overhangs, caverns, swim-through chimneys, and towering coral heads, lavish with gorgonians, sea fans, sponges and invertebrates. Schools of copper sweepers, sergeant majors, grunts, groupers, snappers and lobster inhabit this reef. Average depth 70 ft. For experienced divers. Boat access.

☆☆☆ **Tuna Alley** is a special coral passageway frequented by migrating tuna, along with large groupers, angelfish, and stingrays. Fabulous visibility. Average depth is 50 ft. Boat access.

Best Snorkeling Sites of Bimini

☆☆☆ **Sunshine Reef** hosts crowds of butterfly fish, angels, parrot fish, lobsters, moray eels, grunts. At noon, the sun's rays sparkle waves of pink and ruby light across the corals. This is a good spot for photos. Average depth runs 15 ft. Boat access.

☆☆☆☆ **The Road to Atlantis** at 15-ft depths offers fun snorkeling adventure. Located at the north end of Bimini, it makes for endless après-dive, tale-swapping opportunities. Boat access. (See details preceding page.)

Dive Operators of Bimini

Bill and Nowdla Keefe's Bimini Undersea has complete dive/accommodation packages with the Bimini Big Game Fishing Club, Blue Water Resort, Seacrest and Diver's Dorm. PADI, NAUI affiliations. All are within a five-minute walk of the dive shop. This operation has been around for 17 years and offers a variety of dive and snorkeling trips, including one to a wild spotted dolphin pod. Retail shop sells snorkel gear, clothing accessories. Rental gear too. ☎ 800-348-4644 or 305-653-5572, fax 305-652-9148. E-mail: info@

biminiunderseaadventures.com. Website: www.biminiundersea.com. PO Box 693515, Miami FL 33269.

Scuba Bimini at the South Bimini Yacht Club & Marina features wreck dives, wall and reef dives. No special trips for snorkelers; although they may join the dive trips, many spots are too deep. Complete vacation packages available with the Yacht Club (see resort listing below). ☎ 800-848-4073 or 954-359-2705, fax 954-462-4100. E-mail: beth@nealwatson.com. Write to 1043 S.E. 17th St., Fort Lauderdale FL 33316.

Bimini Accommodations

Rates subject to change. Call for current rates.

The South Bimini Yacht Club features 25 spacious rooms with two queen beds, private bath and air-conditioning. There is a full-service water taxi to North Bimini for nighttime activities. Scuba Bimini on property. Resort restaurant serves breakfast, lunch and dinner daily. Rates for divers are from $493 for five days, four nights, including three boat dives each dive day (not day of arrival or departure), room, taxes and service charges, parking at the Ft. Lauderdale Executive Airport, night dives Wednesday or Saturday. Nondivers pay from $175. Airfare supplement $110, plus US departure taxes. ☎ 800-848-4073 or 954-359-2705, fax 954-462-4100. E-mail: beth@nealwatson.com.

Bimini Big Game Fishing Club & Hotel has 49 air-conditioned rooms, cottages and penthouses that cater to fishermen. Restaurant. Diving and snorkeling trips are arranged with Bill and Nowdla Keefe's Bimini Undersea Shop. Many shops and island bars nearby. Resort rates year-round for a room are from $154 per day, cottages from $200 per day. Packages. ☎ 800-737-1007 or 242-347-3391 or 3393, fax 242-347-3392. Website: www.bimini-big-game-club.com.

Cat Island

Cat Island is a sparsely populated, hilly and largely undeveloped 50-mile-long island just south of Eleuthera. Pink and white sand beaches rim its perimeter. For centuries Cat Island was called San Salvador and some believe this is where Columbus first landed. However, in 1926, a nearby island was designated San Salvador (as it is known today) and the name Cat Island was revived here.

A single road runs the island's length, making it difficult to get lost while exploring. Appropriately called Main Road, it begins at Arthur's Town in the north and ends at Port Howe in the south. Along the way, visitors will spot residents engaged in traditional activities such as straw plaiting (weaving) hats and bags.

The island's historical sites are easily accessible from the Main Road too. At Port Howe, one can see the ruins of the **Deveaux Mansion**, a two-story whitewashed building formerly used as a cotton plantation and now overrun with wild vegetation. The mansion was once the home of Col. Andrew Deveaux of the US Navy and was given to him as a reward for recapturing Nassau from the Spaniards in 1783.

Mt. Alvernia, the highest point on Cat Island and in the Bahamas, rises 206 feet through a pine forest. The **Hermitage**, a small monastery built by Father Jerome, an Anglican seminarian turned Catholic priest, sits at the summit.

Many Cat Island residents lead a primitive existence, without electricity or stoves. Obeah, a counterpart of Voodoo from Haiti, is still practiced here. Practitioners believe that one can interact with the spirit world, and those using the power of Obeah can protect their property and cast or prevent a spell from being cast on other people. Island inhabitants hang bottles from trees with salt minerals sprinkled below to protect them and their families from evil spirits (don't touch them).

For divers and snorkelers seeking total seclusion and who want to explore miles of underwater wilderness, this is a terrific spot. Twelve miles of wall diving sites lie along the southern coast, with depths starting at 50 feet. Shallow reefs off the Greenwood Resort beach range from 15 to 40 ft. Up-to-date facilities exist for both private pilots and boaters.

Cat Island Accommodations

Greenwood Beach Resort offers 20 rooms on eight miles of pink beach. Rooms feature private baths, king-size beds and patios. Ceiling fans and sea breezes keep you cool. Their oceanfront restaurant and lounge has satellite TV and provides a nice spot to swap fish tales. Good food. Diving and snorkeling off the beach. On-premises Cat Island Dive Center offers full scuba services. Room rates are $85 from May 15th to November 1, $99 in winter, plus service charges. Dive packages for five nights are $482 in summer, $780 in winter, including, room, meals and diving. ☎ 800-688-4752 or 242-342-3053. Website: www.hotelgreenwoodinn.com.

Fernandez Bay Village is a small, family-run resort offering six lovely beachfront villas with kitchens and six cottages. Great hospitality. Good restaurant serves native seafood specialties, fresh fruit. Terrific snorkeling exists off the resort beach in three to six feet of water. Good for children. Scuba trips are arranged with the nearby Greenwood Beach Resort. Winter rates start at $220 per day, summer from $215 per day. Includes two meals per day. ☎ 800-940-1905, or 954-474-4821, fax 954-474-4864. E-mail: fbv@ batelnet.bs. Website: www.fernandezbayvillage.com.

Hawk's Nest Resort & Marina features a marina and an airstrip. They rent 10 guest rooms with ceiling fans, new king-size beds, private baths, and patios. Fridges available. Clubhouse restaurant and bar offers food and drinks. Nice snorkeling beach. They do not have a full-service dive shop, but they do have a compressor and will take guests out to the reef or rent you a dinghy. Informal, but fun. Rates year-round start at $270 per night for two and include continental breakfast and dinner. They also rent a two-bedroom house, which sleeps six, for $370 per day or $2,200 per week. ☎ 800-688-4752, direct 242-342-7050.

Crooked Island

This remote islet, 380 nautical miles from Ft. Lauderdale, offers unexplored reefs and spectacular beaches where you can walk for miles without seeing another soul. It is fabulous for snorkeling and diving. The reef starts at the shoreline, slopes to 40 ft, then plunges steeply to 600 ft in the Crooked Island Passage. Snorkelers can walk in just about anywhere on the island. Divers opt for the wall dives, which start about 300 yards offshore, with the top at 45 ft. The sole resort, Pittstown Point Landing accommodates all watersports.

Crooked Island Dive Operator & Accommodations

Pittstown Point Landing, a comfortable 12-room beachfront resort, overlooks Bird Rock Lighthouse. Its close proximity to neighboring Colonel Hill Airport makes it a popular spot for private pilots. It offers personalized service to snorkelers and experienced divers. ☎ 800-752-2322 or 242-344-2507, fax 704-881-0771. Website: www.pittstown.com.

Getting to Crooked Island

Bahamasair has two flights per week to Crooked Island. The one resort provides transportation from the airport. Private pilots can land at either Colonel Hill Airport or Pittstown Point Landing Strip.

Bahamas

Eleuthera Island

Eleuthera, a long, narrow arc, stretches from New Providence for 110 miles to Cat Island. Spanish Wells, tiny Harbour Island, and a small cay called Current are considered part of Eleuthera. Together they offer some of the most famous and interesting shallow wrecks and dive sites in all of the Bahamas.

The name Eleuthera, which means freedom in Greek, was bestowed by British Puritans who settled the island in 1648. Seeking religious freedom, they lived in caves and developed the land for farming. Their fine produce became known throughout the islands and coastal US as far as New England. Even today, despite a coral and limestone surface, the land they tilled is considered one of the prime agricultural areas in the Bahamas. Hilly farmlands in the center of the island have a rich, red soil that is ideal for producing pineapples, tomatoes and vegetables. In the late 1800s Eleuthera dominated the world's pineapple market with its sweet fruit.

Best Dives of Eleuthera

☆☆☆☆☆ **Current Cut**, a narrow ocean channel between Eleuthera and Current Island, serves as the major link between Eleuthera Sound and the open sea. Tide changes cause millions of gallons of seawater to whip through this narrow gap at speeds of seven to 10 knots, with visibility ranging from 50 to 80 ft. Divers "shooting the cut" can join schools of horse-eye jacks, eagle rays and barracudas as they sail by at exhilarating speeds. Depth in the center is 65 ft, with sharp, smooth, vertical walls on both sides and large potholes lining the bottom. Not for the timid! Boat access. Experienced divers.

☆☆☆ **Egg Island Lighthouse Reef**, located due west of Egg Island in 60 ft of water, features 35-ft coral heads rising from a sandy bottom. Reef regulars include groupers, squirrel fish, glasseye snappers, crevalle jacks, amberjacks, blue chromis, wrasse, parrot fish, and surgeon fish. The reef is pretty, with varied corals, pastel sponges and good visibility. A photographer's paradise.

☆☆☆☆ **The Gardens**, a favorite reef for photographers, sits about one mile west of the Cut. Diverse corals and sponges provide a home to large schools of surgeon fish, parrot fish, blue chromis, queen and French angels, butterfly fish, goatfish, porgies, margates and snappers. Crabs, shrimp and lobster are abundant and giant manta rays are frequently sighted here.

☆☆☆ **Miller's Reef**, off the east coast of Harbour Island, forms a maze of coral archways, canyons, caves and pinnacles at depths from 50 to 100 ft. Schools of grunts, hogfish, turtles, angels, barracuda, lobsters, chubs, and jacks along with mini-critters reside in the reef.

Snorkeling & Shallow Dives of Eleuthera

Five shore-entry sites exist off the **Cove Eleuthera Beach**. A nice reef parallels the shore just 20 yards off the beach side of the island in **Governor's Harbour**, **Hachet Bay** and **Palmetto Point**. **Rock Sound** also has some nice shore snorkeling.

✩✩ **Mystery Reef**, located three miles outside of Current Cut in the direction of Egg Island, has six coral heads in 25 ft of water. The heads, which sit in the middle of a sprawling sand patch, are 10 to 20 ft high. Swarms of small fish provide endless entertainment and can be hand-fed. Great photo opportunities. Visibility 70 ft.

✩✩✩ **Freighter Wreck**. Approximately five miles from Current Cut lies the rusting hull of a 250-ft Lebanese freighter that caught fire and was purposely run aground. The wreck sits perfectly upright in 20 ft of water with most of her structure above the surface. Her keel is broken at mid-ship, making salvage an unlikely prospect. Although the propeller was removed by scrap-metal salvors, furnishings and ship's parts are scattered around the hull. Large parrotfish, glasseye snappers, and watchful angels are attracted to the wreck.

✩✩✩ **Devil's Backbone**, north of Spanish Wells island, is a long stretch of shallow coral reefs. Great clumps of razor-sharp elkhorn coral rise to the surface and are often awash at low tide. This treacherous barrier reef is a graveyard for ships, but a paradise for divers and snorkelers. Boat access.

✩✩✩✩ **Train Wreck**. Perhaps the most unusual shipwreck in all the Bahamas is the remains of a steam locomotive lying in 15 ft of water. Still in the barge, which sank during a storm in 1865, it was part of a Union train believed captured by the Confederacy and sold to a Cuban sugar plantation. The wreck site also contains three sets of wheel trucks believed to be part of the same locomotive, as well as wood beams half-buried in the sandy sea floor. The wreckage, which is slowly settling in a garden of elkhorn and brain coral formations, offers some great opportunities for wide-angle photography.

✩✩✩✩ *Cienfuegos* **Wreck**. Just a few hundred yards away from the Train Wreck lies the *Cienfuegos* wreck, the twisted remains of a passenger steamer that sank in 1895. Part of the Ward Line of New York, this 200-ft-long steel-hulled ship crashed into the reef during a bad storm. All passengers on board survived and her cargo of rice was salvaged. The remaining wreckage lies in 35 ft of water with some sections at a mere 10 ft. Prominent features are two giant heat exchangers, a big boiler and the main drive shaft. The wreck, looking much like an undersea junk yard, with jumbled steel plates, broken ribs and twisted steel beams, makes for a fascinating dive.

✩✩✩ **Potato & Onion Wreck**. The *Vanaheim*, an 86-ft coastal freighter, was carrying a cargo of potatoes and onions when she crashed into Devil's

Backbone in February, 1969. The force of the heavy seas during the storm pushed her over the barrier reef into 15 ft of water – an easy dive. Surrounding the wreck are very pretty reefs. Boat access.

Eleuthera Dive Operators & Accommodations

The Cove Eleuthera sprawls over 28 acres with two beautiful ocean beaches, 24 ocean- or garden-view rooms and a fine restaurant featuring Bahamian and continental specialties. Friendly staff. Terrific close-in snorkeling exists off the beach. Scuba is arranged with Valentine's Dive shop. There is a charge for the 30-minute cab ride each way, but the dive shop waives the gear rental fees for guests. Winter (December 18 to April 28) rates for a double start at $129. Summer rates from $109. ☎ 800-552-5960 or 242-335-5338, fax 242-335-5338. E-mail: george@thecoveleuthera.com. Website: www.the coveeleuthera.com.

Cambridge Villas, located in Gregory Town, provides free transportation to and from the beach for snorkelers. Diving is arranged with Valentine's, requiring a cab ride to and from the dive shop. Accommodations are apartments with fully equipped kitchenettes, standard and superior double, triple and quad rooms with private baths. Air-conditioned. Saltwater pool. Winter weekly rates for a two-bedroom are $950 for a superior double; in summer, rates are $913.50. Includes taxes, gratuities and MAP. ☎ 800-688-4752 or 242-335-5080, fax 242-335-5308. The resort has a five-passenger airplane for island hopping.

Rainbow Inn offers miles of deserted beaches, great snorkeling from the shore and rooms with refrigerators, microwave ovens, coffee makers, air-conditioning and sundecks. They also offer one-, two-, and three-bedroom villas. (Closed from September through November 15.) A full-service marina is two miles away. Near to shops. ☎ 800-688-0047 or 242-335- 0294, fax 242-335-0294.

Harbour Island

Getting to Harbour Island

Fly into North Eleuthera Airport, then take a taxi to the water taxi for Harbour Island. It docks at Valentine's Yacht Club.

Harbour Island Dive Operator & Accommodations

Valentine's Yacht Club and Dive Center features a complete dive shop, scuba and snorkeling tours, fishing charters and 21 air-conditioned rooms, convenient to Dunmore Town. They also offer 39 boat slips for craft up to 160 ft in their deep-water facility. Closed from September through December 3.

The resort's English-style pub and an outdoor bar serve fresh seafood and local produce. Their dive shop offers free snorkel lessons every day with a video show, booklet and pool practice. A nice reef outside the dive shop is good for all levels of snorkelers.

Winter rates (December 21 to April 13) for six days, five nights are from $592 per person for a double with three boat dives per day (except on days of arrival and departure). Boat night dives and trips to Current Cut are extra. No credit or refunds for unused package features. Summer (April 27 to December 19) dive package rates for six days, five nights start at $520 per person for a double. MAP add $35 per adult, $20 per child under 12 per day. ☎ 800-323-565, 502-897-6481 or 242-333-2309. Hotel direct: ☎ 242-333-2142, fax 242-333-2135.

The Exumas

Three hundred sixty-five islands and cays strung out over 120 miles of ocean from New Providence to Long Island make up the Exumas. The 3,600 residents live on Great Exuma or Little Exuma, the two largest islands that connect by a short bridge. They earn a living by fishing or by farming onions, tomatoes, pigeon peas, guavas, papayas and mangoes.

Some of the fields still have wild cotton growing, a testament to the islands' history. Lord John Rolle, who imported the first cottonseeds in the 18th century, had more than 300 slaves on Great Exuma. The slaves, following the custom of the day, adopted their master's surname. When cotton proved to be a failure and the prospect of emancipation loomed, he deeded 2,300 acres of land to his former slaves. This land, in turn, has been passed on to each new generation and can never be sold to outsiders. Today almost half of the residents go by the name Rolle.

In the heart of the Exuma Cays lies the **Exuma Cays Land and Sea Park**, a 176-square-mile nature preserve that is home to coral reefs, exotic marine life and the Bahamian iguana – some of which grow over two feet long.

Renowned as a cruising spot for live-aboard dive boats and private yachts, the Exumas boast 200 miles of robust coral reefs. Depths average 35 ft, making them ideal for divers of all skill levels as well as underwater photo enthusiasts. Snorkelers will find many shallow spots, especially around Stocking Island.

Bahamas

History buffs will enjoy a tour to the **Hermitage** plantation house at Williams Town, Little Exuma. The plantation house is from the Loyalist years (1783-1834). Cotton plantations flourished on Exuma during this period, sending regular cargo ships directly from Elizabeth Harbor to England. The Hermitage is one of the few reasonably preserved houses (perhaps the only one) from this period. Cotton was profitable for about 15 good years before poor management and the chenille bug laid waste to the industry. The "cotton" islands are Exuma, Long and Cat islands, where wild cotton grows.

Getting to the Exumas

Fly into Exuma International Airport. Taxi to the hotel.

Best Dives of the Exumas

☆☆☆☆ **Coral Reef** and **Sting Ray Reef**, off Uly Cay, lie just north of Stocking Island. Elkhorn and soft coral patches shelter hordes of trumpet fish, barracuda, turtles, large schools of grunts and yellowtail. Depths range from 20 to 40 ft. Boat access. Good for scuba and snorkeling.

☆☆☆ **Conch Cay** is a northern dive area offering shallow walls and wide ledges for easy exploration with scuba or just a mask and snorkel. Marine life is the big attraction here – huge turtles, rays and occasional sharks. The shallow reef's depths range from six to 20 ft. Boat access.

☆☆ **Long Reef**, sitting at the southern tip of Stocking Island, encompasses a maze of staghorn and elkhorn coral thickets. Residents include queen triggerfish, grey and French angelfish, grunts, hogfish and turtles. Depths are 25 to 60 ft. Snorkel or scuba. Boat access.

☆ **Lobster Reef**, situated in the Eastern Channel just north of Man of War Cay, features huge coral masses teeming with lobster, hogfish, snappers, angels, sergeant majors and morays. Scuba. Boat access.

☆☆☆ **Crab Cay Blue Hole** (aka Crab Cay Crevasse) lies south of George Town. Starting at a depth of 35 ft, this mysterious blue hole provides a sensual diving experience. The unusual current in the area creates a twirling drift dive with fish and critters racing by. Scuba. Boat access.

Exuma Dive Operators

Exuma Dive Center tours all the best dive sites of Exuma and Stocking Island and has packages in conjunction with the Peace and Plenty Hotel, Coconut Cove, Two Turtles and Regatta Point. Friendly, experienced staff. They also offer bonefishing, deep sea fishing, boat and motoscooter rentals. Dive trips start at $60, including tank and weight belt. Snorkel trips $35. Rental of a 17-ft Polar Craft with Bimini top is $80 per day plus a $100 security deposit. NAUI, IDEA, IANTD instruction. Equipment rentals. ☎ 800-874-7213 or

242-336-2390, fax 242-336-2391. E-mail: exumadive@bahamasvg.com. Website: www.webcom.com/cdk/exumadive.html.

Exuma Accommodations

In 1783, Lord Denys Rolle sailed to Exuma on the English trading ship *Peace and Plenty*. The name passed on to a cotton plantation, to a sponge warehouse and then to a huge resort complex.

Club Peace and Plenty in George Town on Great Exuma offers 35 recently renovated accommodations, an indoor-outdoor dining room, tropical gardens, private balconies, and a wealth of water sports. The resort shuttles guests twice daily to nearby Stocking Island, where you can snorkel surrounding reefs, sunbathe or explore the island's caves. Snack bar service. Dive trips are arranged with nearby Exuma Divers who will arrange transportation to and from the resort. Their Eco-Dive package includes round-trip air from Ft Lauderdale or Miami, two dives per day, weights and tanks, transfers from the airport, daily ferry to Stocking Island, air-conditioned suite, gratuities and resort tax. For six days and five nights (eight tanks) $750 per person. Room only starts at $155 per day for a double. ☎ 800-525-2210. E-mail pandp@ peaceandplenty.com. Website: www.peaceandplenty.com.

Coconut Cove Hotel features 11 beachfront or beach-view rooms with terraces. Two are air-conditioned. All have ceiling fans and queen-sized beds. Meals are prepared to the diner's specifications. Pool. Dive and snorkeling trips with nearby Exuma Dive Center. Year-round rates range from $140 to $250 for a double. ☎ 800-688-4752 or 242-336-2659, fax 242-336-2658.

Regatta Point has six spacious apartments on a beautiful, small island near George Town's shops and restaurants. Dive and snorkeling trips with Exuma Dive Center. Winter room rates are from $128 per day for a one-bedroom apartment, double occupancy. Summer from $104 per day. ☎ 800-310-8125 or 242-336-2206, fax 242-336-2046.

Two Turtles Inn features 14 rooms overlooking George Town shops and restaurants. Guest rooms are all air-conditioned with TV. Some have kitchenettes. Diving and snorkeling with Exuma Dive Center. Winter rates start at $98 per day for a double. Summer from $78. ☎ 800-688-4752 or 242-336-2545, fax 242-336-2528.

Long Island

Long Island, home of the Stella Maris dive community, is world-renowned as a mecca for reef explorers. At 80 miles long and four miles wide, Long Island is also one of the most scenic hideaways in the Bahamas. The island is divided by the Tropic of Cancer and is bordered on each side by two contrasting

Bahamas

coasts, one with a soft white beach, the other with rocky cliffs that plunge into the sea. Inland, the island varies from sloping hills in the northeast to low hill-sides and swampland in the south.

Snorkelers can bike, hike or boat to the dive sites. Divers find walls, reefs and wrecks within a short distance of the Stella Maris docks.

No one is quite certain when the name Long Island took hold. The island was originally named "Yuma" by the Lucayan Indians, then renamed "Fernandina" by Christopher Columbus upon his third landfall in the New World. In 1790, Fernandina was settled by Loyalists from the Carolinas and their slaves. They built large plantations and produced sea island cotton until the abolition of slavery, which made them unprofitable.

Today, the plantations are overgrown and non-productive, though agricul-ture is still a very important part of life. Pothole farming, which is a method that uses fertile holes in the limestone where topsoil collects, yields much of the food supply for the other islands, including peas, corn, pineapples and ba-nanas. Raising sheep, goats and pigs is also popular among islanders.

Their pace of life has not changed much from the past. A carriage road, built more than a century ago, connects the island's major settlements of Burnt Ground, Simms, Wood Hill, Clarence Town, Roses and South Point, all situ-ated around the island's harbours and anchorages. Snorkelers can bicycle from spot to spot.

Getting to Long Island

Fly into Stella Maris Airport. Take a taxi to either hotel. ($40 for two to Cape Santa Maria Beach Resort, $3.50 per person to Stella Maris. Stella Maris of-fers its own commuter service from Nassau, George Town and other destina-tions.)

Best Dives of Long Island

☆☆☆☆☆ **Stella Maris Shark Reef** was the first shark dive in the Baha-mas and it is still one of the best, with dependable shark appearances. Upon entering the water, divers are greeted by seven to 14 sharks, who stay with the divers for the entire dive. Among them are gray-tipped reef sharks, bull sharks and a very tame nurse shark. A single hammerhead makes an occasional ap-pearance. The drill is simply to sit still on the ocean floor and watch Stella Maris divemasters feed the sharks. The sharks stay in the "circus ring," but there are unmatched photo and video opportunities for the viewers. Divers are warned not to travel about during the dive nor visit the reef without the guides. Sea conditions are sometimes choppy. The depth is about 30 ft. The boat trip takes roughly 30 minutes. Suggested for experienced ocean divers.

☆☆☆☆☆ **Cape Santa Maria Ship's Grave Yard.** This is a deep reef with a drop-off where the prime attraction is the wreck of **MS Comberbach**, a 103-ft steel freighter at 100 ft that was especially prepared for safe diving before it was sunk. The hull is intact and sits upright on its keel so the interior can be easily explored. Divers enter through the front hatch, then swim through the freight hold into the engine room to the control stand, with escape outlets open in every section. The wreck itself offers fantastic still and video possibilities. Super visibility. Divers are greeted by extremely tame oversized groupers. The reef, which spreads over three-quarters of a mile with a 50-ft wall drop-off to another 50-ft wall, is covered with enormous sponges of all types and colors. The

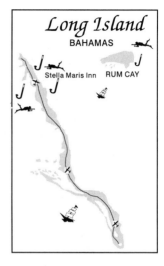

seas are generally calm. Located just one mile from shore. Recommended for experienced divers. Boat access.

☆☆☆☆☆**Conception Island Wall** is one of the most beautiful reefs in the Bahamas. Gigantic coral heads climb from a depth of 90 ft to 55 ft and the wall, which drops in straight ladder-steps, is covered with a lush carpet of corals and fantastic sponges. Caves and tunnels invite novice and experienced divers alike. The site sits just 300 ft from the beach, with depths from 45 ft to bottomless. Conception Island, off the northeast tip of Long Island, is an underwater park and a bird and turtle breeding area. Boat access.

☆☆☆ **Flamingo Tongue Reef** takes its name from the thousands of flamingo tongue shells along its bottom. It's located six miles from Stella Maris Marina within a half-mile of the shore – a 15-minute boat ride. It is a great spot for beginners since the reef is only 25 ft below the surface and the seas are almost always calm. Large moray eels, groupers, and schooling fish abound. Caves and cuts add a touch of mystery. Good snorkeling.

Snorkeling Long Island

☆☆☆ **West Bar Reef**, a lovely, pristine coral garden in the shape of a bar some 600 ft long and 300 ft wide, lies within half a mile of two beautiful beaches. The reef has a superb variety of brain and staghorn corals along with soft corals and towering pillar corals, all at a depth of 15 ft. It is in the lee of the island, protected from wind, waves, and strong currents. Visibility is excellent. Boat access.

☆☆☆☆ **Southampton Reef** is the site of a wrecked ocean freighter that sank some 80 years ago. The 300-ft hull has been flattened by time and the

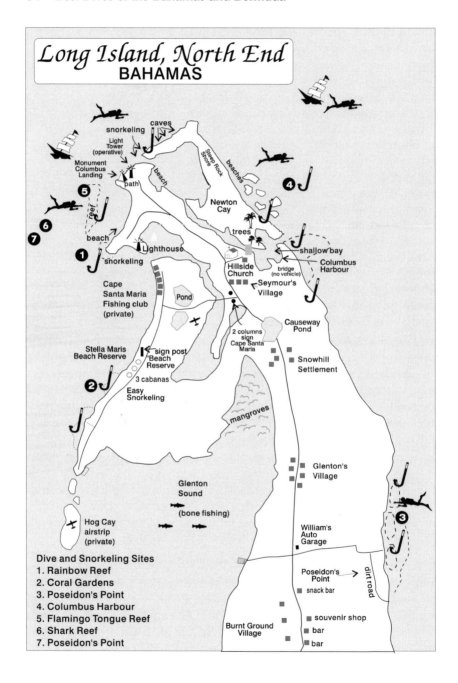

Long Island, North End
BAHAMAS

snorkeling

caves

Light Tower (operative)

Monument Columbus Landing

path

beach

Steep Rock Shore

beaches

Newton Cay

trees

reef

beach

Lighthouse

snorkeling

Hillside Church

shallow bay

Columbus Harbour

bridge (no vehicle)

Seymour's Village

Cape Santa Maria Fishing club (private)

Pond

Causeway Pond

2 columns sign Cape Santa Maria

Stella Maris Beach Reserve

sign post

Beach Reserve

3 cabanas

Easy Snorkeling

Snowhill Settlement

mangroves

Glenton Sound

(bone fishing)

Glenton's Village

Hog Cay airstrip (private)

William's Auto Garage

Poseidon's Point

dirt road

snack bar

Dive and Snorkeling Sites
1. Rainbow Reef
2. Coral Gardens
3. Poseidon's Point
4. Columbus Harbour
5. Flamingo Tongue Reef
6. Shark Reef
7. Poseidon's Point

Poseidon's Point

Burnt Ground Village

souvenir shop

bar

bar

ebb and flow of water, yet it still offers dramatic photo possibilities. Prominent are huge engine boilers, the shaft, propellers, and anchors and lots of ship's debris. Thickets of elkhorn and staghorn surround the wreck, providing refuge for huge groupers, sleeping nurse sharks, and large parrot fish. Depths range from five ft to 100 ft, with the average about 25 ft. Sea conditions range from dead calm to rough. One major drawback to this dive is the three-hour boat ride from Long Island (Stella Maris dock).

☆☆☆☆ **Coral Gardens** and **Poseidon's Pint** are two beautiful snorkeling reefs accessible from the beach or by boat (a three- or four-minute ride from the Stella Maris docks). Access depends on the weather. The gardens sparkle with dramatic displays of massive brain, elkhorn, and staghorn coral. Eagle rays, sand rays, tarpon and crawfish are in residence here. Depths range from three to 30 ft.

☆☆ **Rainbow Reef**, terrific for snorkeling, has three easy entries from Cape Santa Maria Beach. It lies 20 yards from shore and is completely protected in most weather situations (except northwest winds). Encrusting corals and sponges cover the rocky bottom, which is inhabited by a good mix of reef fish. Passing eagle rays are frequently sighted. Some large stingrays bury themselves in the sand. Beach or boat access.

Long Island Dive Operators & Accommodations

Stella Maris Inn, a dive and snorkeling plantation-style resort, offers rooms, cottages and luxury villas all situated high atop the hillcrest of the island's east shoreline and featuring breathtaking views of the ocean. The dive operation is top-notch, offering guided reef and wreck tours. Non-divers and snorkelers get special attention too with a wide choice of beaches, cycling, cruises, and even a glass bottom boat. Guided day and night snorkeling tours. Complimentary shuttle bus service to different shore-entry snorkeling spots. Great dive packages available. Reef, bone and deep-sea fishing. Winter dive package rates for eight days and seven nights start at $860 per person, double occupancy. Included are deluxe hotel room, welcome drink, six days of scuba diving (two-three dives per day), weekly cave party, slide shows. Add $45 per person, per day, for breakfast and dinner. ☎ 800-426-0466 or 954-359-8236 or 242-338-2050, fax 954-359-8238. E-mail: smrc@stellamarisresort.com. Website: www.stellamarisresort.com.

Cape Santa Maria Beach Resort offers only snorkeling tours aboard their catamaran. Guests stay in beachfront cottages overlooking four miles of white sand beach. Snorkeling reef off the beach. Fly fishing off the flats. Winter rates are from $245 for a one-bedroom villa. For three meals per day add $65 per person, per day, $35 per child. ☎ 800-663-7090 or 250-338-3366, fax 250-

Bahamas

598-1361. E-mail: obmg@pinc.com. The cab ride from the Stella Maris Airport to this resort will cost $40 for two.

San Salvador Island

Miles of virgin shallow reefs, walls and new wrecks are yet to be explored in the waters around San Salvador, truly one of the diving jewels of the Bahamas. It is so remote that the Riding Rock Inn feels they must point out in their promotional material that it is *not in South America*. On shore, visitors delight in miles of white sand beaches, including the site where Christopher Columbus first set foot in the New World.

The island's several name changes reflect its checkered past. The Lucayan Indians initially named the island "Guanahani." Then, in 1492, Columbus made his first landfall in the New World on the island. He named it San Salvador or "Holy Saviour" and noted in his travel journal that "the beauty of these islands surpasses that of any other and as much as the day surpasses the night in Splendor." Today, four separate monuments mark the spots where he came ashore, although it is generally thought that he landed at Long Bay, where a large stone cross stands. Centuries later British pirate Captain George Watling took over the island, making it his headquarters and naming it "Watling Island" after himself. The island retained this name until 1925, when it was renamed San Salvador.

Besides diving and snorkeling, visitors to the island enjoy touring the plantation ruins, climbing to the top of the old kerosene-operated lighthouse and exploring the archeological sites of the Lucayan Indians.

Getting to San Salvador

Regularly scheduled Riding Rock Inn charter flights depart from Ft. Lauderdale each Saturday morning at 10 am (☎ 800-272-1492). Bahamasair flies from Nassau and Miami to the island. The full-service marina accommodates large and small vessels.

Best Dives of San Salvador

Most of San Salvador's dive sites lie off the leeward coast, sheltered from wind and high waves. Currents are usually light. Depths range from shallow to 130 feet, with enough variety to suit most skill and interest levels.

☆☆☆☆ **Hole in the Wall** at the end of Gardiners Reef, on the southwest side of the island, offers dramatic topography. Two deep crevices inhabited by king crabs and big lobsters cut through the wall from 50 to 110-120 ft. Resident schoolmaster snappers hover around a big black coral tree at 90 ft. Large pillar corals crown the rim of both crevices. Locals include schools of horse-

*Monument to Columbus,
San Salvador, Bahamas.*

© Bahamas Tourist Board

eyed jacks. Occasional hammerhead sharks and manta rays spin by the blue water off the wall.

⭐⭐⭐⭐ **Telephone Pole** is the classic San Salvador wall dive. It starts on a sand bottom at 40 ft, then slopes off into a large "well lit" cave. Swimming near the roof you can pop out on the face of a straight drop-off at 70 ft. Turn right to see a magnificent large purple tube sponge usually inhabited by several brittle starfish.

⭐⭐⭐⭐⭐ **Dolittle's Grottos**, located off the southwest corner of the island, is popular for its big barrel sponges, variety of corals, caves and grottos. Three main caves cut into the wall at 50 ft come out at 80-90 ft. These are not true caves, but more like tunnels or chutes with holes in the roofs.

South of the caves, a sand "causeway" starts at 70 ft, rises to 60 ft, then gently plunges to great depths. Coral walls 15 to 20 ft high flank the causeway on both sides. The top of the wall is shallow, 30 to 35 ft, with large stands of pillar coral and lots of micro subjects. Boat access.

⭐⭐⭐⭐⭐ **Double Caves** in French Bay is locally known as the "wall to end all walls." A constant current washes the area with nutrients that feed a huge variety of soft and hard corals. Every inch of wall is splashed with vibrant color. The big attraction is two "well lit" caves. The first is entered from a large crevice that cuts through the wall beginning on sand at 60 ft. Like Dolittle's, they are really chutes or tunnels with big holes in the roofs rather than actual caves.

Coral walls tower above the diver by 25 to 30 ft. As you follow the line of the crevice, you come to a large hole where you can swim through an A-shaped cave that opens up at 110 ft. Leaving the cave, you see two big black coral

Bahamas

Riding Rock Inn, San Salvador, Bahamas.

trees. Schools of hammerheads, eagle rays and manta rays are frequently sighted along the wall.

Enter the second cave through an arch at 110 ft, then up the wall to a sand hole at 60 ft. From here, you can ascend to the top of the wall at 40 ft or go through another crevice that leads back to the wall. Good for experienced ocean divers. Boat access.

☆☆☆☆ **The Hump**, a large mound of coral 80 ft long, 40 ft wide and 20 ft high, lies just two minutes by boat from the Guanahani Dive boat docks. A favorite spot for night dives, the Hump shelters thousands of critters in its many cracks and crevices. Big spiny lobsters and Caribbean king crabs hang out under the ledges. A spotted moray eel or chain moray eel might be seen peeking from a hole. Flamingo tongues graze the sea fans. Beware the scorpion fish. At night hundreds of red shrimp emerge, small octopus cruise the top of the reef and the rare orange ball anemone appears.

Snorkeling San Salvador

Snapshot Reef, a short ride from the resort, packs in schools of angelfish, groupers, parrot fish, trumpetfish, damsels, blue chromis, tangs, tarpon, and invertebrates – all waiting for a handout. Boat access.

The Frescate, a 261-ft freighter resting at 20 ft, hit the reefs in 1902 and its wreck has since attracted throngs of lobsters, silversides and barracuda. Outstanding visibility. Boat access.

The prettiest beach-entry sites lie about three miles south of the resort. You can reach them by bicycle or rental car. There is also nice snorkeling off the

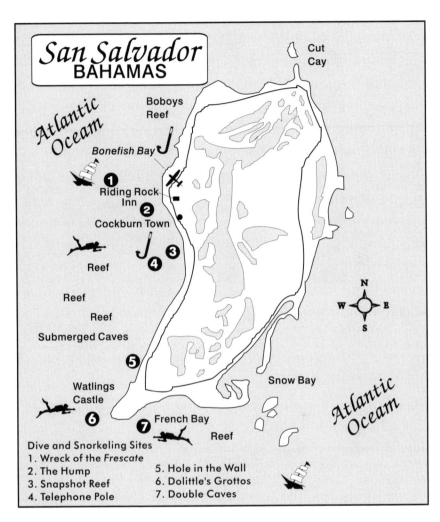

San Salvador
BAHAMAS

Cut Cay

Atlantic Ocean

Boboys Reef

Bonefish Bay

1 Riding Rock Inn

2 Cockburn Town

3

4 Reef

Reef

Reef

Submerged Caves

5

Watlings Castle

6

7 French Bay

Reef

Snow Bay

Atlantic Ocean

N W E S

Dive and Snorkeling Sites
1. Wreck of the *Frescate*
2. The Hump
3. Snapshot Reef
4. Telephone Pole
5. Hole in the Wall
6. Dolittle's Grottos
7. Double Caves

Bahamas

end of the runway. Climb down a small slope to get there or swim north from the Riding Rock Inn Beach.

Dive Operator & Accommodations

Rates subject to change.

Riding Rock Inn offers divers all the comforts of home in a relaxed, casual atmosphere. This plush resort has 12 standard air-conditioned rooms and 30 deluxe oceanfront rooms, conference center, pool, restaurant, and marina. Standard rooms, single or double, are from $110, deluxe from $136. Children under 12 (one per adult) are free. Meals are about $55 per person

The Nekton
*floating dive
resort.*

Courtesy
Nekton Diving
Cruises

per day, or $35 per child per day. Bike and car rentals available. Drivers must be 25 years or older. ☎ 800-272-1492, 954-359-8353, fax 954-359-8254. E-mail: ridingrock@aol.com. Website: www.ridingrock.com. Write to: Out Island Service Company, Inc., 1170 Lee Wagener Blvd., Suite 103, Ft Lauderdale FL 33315-3561.

Club Med on Columbus Isle offers all-inclusive dive vacations starting at $1,120. ☎ 800-CLUBMED. You can book direct, but it might be easier to book through your travel agent.

Guanahani Divers Ltd., based at the Riding Rock Inn, is well equipped with a large photo center featuring daily E-6 film processing, camera and video rentals and a resident pro skilled in both video and still photography. They operate three fast V-hulled boats that have a sun deck, camera work area with freshwater rinse, and large swim platform with ladder and safety gear. Snorkeling available. Rental gear. Two dives on the morning trip cost $60, one dive, $40. Beginners' resort course (gear/dive included) is $105, snorkel trip $20, finish-up scuba course with dives $100, refresher course $65. ☎ 800-272-1492 or 954-359-8353. On-island 331-2631.

Bahamas Live-Aboards

Note: passport needed.

Touring the Bahamas by boat offers access to remote reefs and wrecks normally out of cruising area for land-based dive operations. The downside is the trade-off of living space for being on the water. Snorkelers are welcome but pay the same price and will find some areas too deep.

Blackbeard's Cruises offer a relaxing week of sailing, snorkeling and diving through the Bahama islands, including one night ashore. Three 65-ft passenger monohulls are available, each crewed by two captains, a first mate, dive instructors, cook and crew. Guests choose single- or double-space bunks. Cabins are fully air-conditioned. Shared heads. Trips include all meals, beverages, bedding, fishing tackle, tanks, back packs and weight belts for certified divers. Main divng areas are Bimini, Victories, Cat Cay, shark areas, Grand Bahama, Nassau, Exuma and the Berries. Topside excursions. Cost is $729 per person, plus $55 port tax. Recommended for diehard divers and sailing fans. Snorkelers welcome. Dress is casual. Boarding in Miami. ☎ 1-800-327-9600 or 305-888-1226, fax 305-884-4214 or write to PO Box 66-1091, Miami Springs FL 33266. E-mail: sales@blackbeard-cruises.com. Website: www.blackbeard-cruises.com.

Sea Fever Diving Cruises tour remote Bahama areas – Cay Sal Banks, Shark Blue Hole, Exuma Cays, Berries, Little Bahama Bank and Dolphin Grounds. Captain Tom Guarino, one of the best in the islands, has 26 years' experience navigating these areas.

The 90-ft aluminum-hulled *Sea Fever* has air-conditioning throughout. Passengers share two heads. Rates for a six-day, five-night trip run from $1,099 per person, seven days from $1,299, plus port taxes. Tanks, weights and belts supplied. Drinks extra. E-6 processing, video editing, shore excursions, waterskiing, Nitrox, Nitrox instruction. ☎ 800-44-FEVER or 305-531-DIVE. Write: Captain Tom Guarino, PO Box 21725, Ft. Lauderdale FL 33335. E-mail: seafevr@gate.net. Website: www.seafever.com.

Bottom Time Adventures operates a first-class floating dive resort, *The Bottom Time II.* This 86-ft luxury catamaran tours remote out-island destinations as well as familiar dive spots around the Exuma Cays, Cat Cay, and Eleuthera. ☎ 800-234-8464 or 954-921-7798. Website: www.bottom time2.com.

Nekton Diving Cruises caters to scuba divers and snorkelers. Their staff of 11 includes seven instructors who offer guided reef or wreck tours daily. A special 17-ft tender on board the 78-ft yacht is dedicated to carrying snorkeling guests to the best shallow spots.

The unique twin-hulled design of the yacht eliminates the rocking that causes most seasickness. Cabins are nice rooms. E-6 processing, complete audio/visual capabilities, spa, private baths and elevating dive platform. Departs from Ft. Lauderdale, Georgetown and Great Exuma. Tours include Cay Sal Banks and snorkeling with wild spotted dolphins.

The boat tours alternate between Belize and the Bahamas. Rates for seven nights, six dive days range from $1,295 to $1,495 plus taxes. Call for current schedules. ☎ 800-899-6753 or 954-463-9324, fax 954-463-8938. Website: www.nektoncruises.com.

MV Ballymena transports dive and snorkeling groups from reef to wrecks in pure luxury. The 124-ft modern yacht features roomy air-conditioned cabins with CD players. Higher-priced staterooms have TV and VCR. Two custom tenders – 22 ft and 31 ft – take divers and snorkelers to all the top spots, which are listed on their Website. The main diving areas are Exumas, Andros, Cat Island, San Salvador, Conception, Long Island and Crooked Island. E-6 processing, A/V, kayaks, Sailfish, Sunfish. Capacity 20 passengers. Whole-boat, all-inclusive charters are offered at $6,000 per day for up to eight passengers; $6,250 for 10; $6,500 for 12; $7,500 for 13 to 20. ☎ 800-241-4591 or 242-394-0951, fax 242-394-0948. E-mail: balymena@bahamas.net.bs. Website: www.ballymenacruise.com.

Cruise Ships' Private Island Retreats

Several cruise lines operating in the Caribbean call at their own private islands, including the **Disney Cruise Line, Holland-America, Norwegian Cruise Line, Premier Cruise Lines, Princess** and **Royal Caribbean International**.

Each island is equipped with snorkeling facilities, Bahamian craft shops, food pavilions, at least one local bar and miles of white-sand beach. Most of the ships anchor offshore and shuttle passengers via small boats, or "tenders," to the island.

Disney Cruise Line's Bahamian retreat, **Castaway Cay**, is 1,000 acres of sand and sun. There are separate activities for children and adults. This is the only island cruise retreat that is equipped with a cruise ship pier. Diving is arranged with Nassau shops. Snorkeling is possible at the island.

Princess cruises' home-away-from-home, **Princess Cay**, lies on the southwest coast of Eleuthera. Princess Cay touts 1.5 miles of lovely beach. Their New Waves program with PADI offers instruction, dive and snorkeling excursions.

Holland America's **Half Moon Cay**, near Eleuthera, is a 2,400-acre island with fine snorkeling beaches, nature trails, bone fishing, water sports center and even a wedding chapel.

Norwegian Cruise Line's **Great Stirrup Cay** was the first private island to be developed by a cruise ship company. The island is part of the Berry Islands,

Snorkeling off Exuma
photo © Jean-Michel Cousteau's Out Islands Snorkeling Adventures

between Nassau and Freeport. Great Stirrup Cay boasts six beaches, two of which are maintained. Snorkeling around the island is superb.

Royal Caribbean International's **Coco Cay** is adjacent to Great Stirrup Cay and is a 140-acre island in the Berry Islands. The island's most unusual attraction, especially to divers, is the underwater sunken airplane, not to mention a nice coral reef and a sunken replica of Bluebeard's flagship, *Queen Anne's Revenge*, waiting to be explored.

Premier Cruise Line's **Salt Cay** lies three miles northeast of Paradise Island and can be reached by tender from Prince George's Dock in Nassau. The destination has earned fame as the filming location for *Gilligan's Island*. Diving and snorkeling excursions are arranged with Nassau shops.

Facts

Recompression Chamber: Located on Lyford Key in Nassau. The chamber in Nassau is privately owned by Bahamas Hyperbaric Center Limited, ☎ 242-362-5765, fax 242-362-5766. A second chamber operated by UNEXSO on Grand Bahama Island was not operational at press time (☎ 242-373-1244). Dr. John Clements, based at the Lucayan Medical Center (☎ 242-373-7400) on Grand Bahama, specializes in dive-related injuries. UNEXSO transports divers to Florida if necessary. The trip is two-three hours. A third chamber is operated by Club Med on San Salvador for their guests.

Getting There: Daily flights service Nassau International Airport and Freeport from most US gateway cities. Freeport and the Out Islands are scheduled daily from South Florida by Bahamasair, ☎ 800-222-4262; American Eagle, ☎ 800-433-7300 and Chalk's International Airlines, ☎ 305-653-5572, 800-346-4644. Some of the Out Island resorts arrange their own charters from Fort Lauderdale or Nassau. Check with individual resorts for details.

Private Planes: More than 50 airstrips serving light planes are scattered throughout the Bahamas. Some are paved and lighted with instrument approaches, some are no more than patches of crushed coral along a beach. Private aircraft pilots are required to obtain a cruising permit before entering Bahamas airspace and should contact the Bahamas Private Pilot Briefing Center at ☎ 800-32-SPORT-USA. Excellent plotting services and charts are also available through AOPA, ☎ 800-USA-AOPA.

A 500-page annually updated book, *The Pilot's Bahamas and Caribbean Aviation Guide*, is published by Pilot Publications, PO Box 88, Pauma Valley CA 92061 (☎ 800-521-2120) and contains every airport in the Bahamas, Turks & Caicos, Hispaniola, Puerto Rico, USVI, Jamaica and the Eastern Caribbean islands. Cost is $44.95 plus $6 shipping.

Driving: On the left. You may drive on your own license for up to three months. Those staying longer must obtain a Bahamian license. If you drive a motor scooter a helmet is required.

Documents: United States law now requires citizens to carry a current passport to re-enter the US. To enter the Bahamas, US citizens and Canadians need proof of citizenship and a return ticket.

Customs: Current United States regulations allow each visitor to return home with up to $600 worth of merchandise duty-free, provided the resident has been out of the United States for at least 48 hours and has not claimed the exemption within 30 days. Each adult may bring back two liters of spirits, but one must be a product of the Bahamas or another Caribbean Basin country. Up to $1,000 beyond the $600 will be assessed at 10%. If you carry expensive cameras, electronics or dive gear, it is best to register them with customs before your trip.

Canadians may take home US $100 worth of purchases duty-free after 48 hours and up to $300 worth of goods after seven days.

Each person leaving the Bahamas must pay a $15 departure tax.

Vaccinations: Certifications for smallpox and cholera shots are needed for persons coming from an endemic area.

Currency: The Bahamian dollar is the monetary equivalent of the US dollar. The $3 Bahamian bill, square 15¢ pieces and fluted 10¢ pieces are popular among souvenir hunters.

The US dollar is also considered legal tender, but Canadian dollars are not generally accepted. Travelers checks and major credit cards are widely accepted.

Climate: Average year-round temperatures range from 70 to 85°F. The rainy season lasts from early June through late October. Islands toward the south end of the arc have warmer weather.

Clothing: Casual. A light jacket or sweater is needed in the evening, especially during winter months. You may want to dress up in the evening for some hotels, restaurants, and casinos in Nassau and Freeport. The Out Islands are very casual. For diving, a light wetsuit or lycra wetskin is desirable in winter.

Time Zone: The Bahamas are on Eastern Standard Time (EST) from the last Sunday in October to the last Saturday in April, and Eastern Daylight Time the rest of the year.

Electricity: 120 volts, 60 cycles. No adaptors necessary for US electrical products.

Service Charges: The standard tip is 15%. Some hotels and resorts add a service charge to cover gratuities.

Religious Services: Houses of worship for many faiths minister to visitors in Nassau. Check with your hotel for individual island services.

Weddings: Couples wishing to marry in the Bahamas may now do so after only one day. Marriage license $40. ☎ 888-NUPTIALS or 800-BAHAMAS.

Additional Information: For general information about all the Bahama Islands, ☎ 800-4-BAHAMAS. Website: www.gobahamas.com.

For Nassau and Paradise Island, ☎ 800-327-9019, 800-866-DIVE (3483) or 305-931-1555, fax 305-931-3005. Or write to Bahamas Tourist Offices in the US at 150 E. 52nd St, 28th Fl, New York NY 10022 or at 19495 Biscayne Blvd, Suite 242, Aventura FL 33180.

For Grand Bahama, ☎ 800-448-3386. Website: www.grand-bahama.com.

Out Island Promotion Board, ☎ 800-688-4752 or 954-359-2429, fax 954-359-2428. E-mail: boipb@ix.netcom.com. Website: www.bahama-out-islands.com.

Bahamas

Harbour Island, Eleuthera

Turks & Caicos

Despite a rapid and huge growth in dive tourism during the past 10 years, the Turks & Caicos remain one of the last great diving frontiers, with miles of vast reefs and wrecks yet to be explored. In fact, some of the finest and oldest coral communities in the Western Hemisphere fringe the shores.

Located well off the beaten path, at the southeastern tip of the Great Bahama Bank, most of these islands are sparsely populated. Topside, the terrain and vegetation resembles the Bahamas – flat with scrub brush and tall cactus, edged by pink and white sand beaches.

The Turks consist of two main islands: Grand Turk and Salt Cay, which are separated from the Caicos by a 22-mile-wide deep-water channel, the Turks Island Passage. The Caicos group consists of six principal islands: West Caicos, Providenciales, North Caicos, Grand Caicos, East Caicos and South Caicos. All are flanked by small uninhabited cays.

Providenciales' posh hotels, casino gambling and direct flights from Miami attract most dive tourists. Grand Turk, on the other hand, has fabulous diving too, but lacks the posh resorts and takes a little more effort to get to.

History

Soon after Ponce de Leon discovered the Turks & Caicos during the 1500s, word of the islands' vast salt flats spread quickly. Bermudians came first to rake salt and stayed to become the first European occupants of the islands. They converted salinas (salt ponds) on Grand Turk, Salt Cay and South Caicos into workable salt mines and developed an export trade of salt and slaves to the American colonies. Fortunes were made from this "white gold." Lavish houses and churches that they built can still be seen in the islands.

As demand for the sea salt grew, so grew governments' interest in the islands. After a few hostile bouts, the islands went to Spain, then France, then the Brits, who governed the islands until the 1700s, when the Turks & Caicos were declared an extension of the Bahamas. Between 1848 and 1962, Jamaica ruled. Presently they are a British dependency. Through all these power shifts, the islands' peaceful waters churned into a haven for pirates who preyed on the West Indies merchant ships.

The Great Depression and World War II ruined the salt industry. By the 1960s salt sales had severely diminished. All the islands suffered and many islanders migrated to the Bahamas, Miami and New York. British Government aid provided a substandard economy for those who remained.

Fortunately, the advent of flights to the islands, the Cold War and Space Exploration rejuvenated the national economy and enabled the introduction of tourism. The American Navy, NASA and the Coast Guard built bases that caused an economic, social and cultural revolution. The first tourists were private pilots en route to the West Indies during the 1960s who fell in love with the islands. They invested in three small hotels and established a domestic air service which linked all the inhabited islands to each other and the US.

Their efforts paid off. By the 1970s the islands were growing in popularity with scuba divers and leisure travelers. In 1978 scheduled jet service was introduced from Miami and the 1980s, following construction of the Club Med village on Providenciales, was a decade of continued tourism investment and growth.

When to Go

A substantial annual rainfall during the late summer and early fall almost dictates that you visit the Turks and Caicos in late winter, spring or early summer. Generally, the high season runs a week later than most Caribbean islands and at many establishments lower hotel prices prevail until mid-December.

Grand Turk

Grand Turk, the seat of the Turks & Caicos government, has about 4,300 permanent residents, not counting street chickens or the dive-tourist crowd. Aside from Front Street, the main road along the western coast, most of the island's streets are fairly narrow, bordered by low stone walls. Grand Turk is home to the **National Museum**, where exhibits of the oldest European shipwreck are displayed.

Cockburn Town, the main municipality, reflects the islands' history in its colorful homes. Some, over 100 years old, are either brightly painted wood frame construction or made from Bermudian stone brought in as ballast by ships seeking salt. Donkey carts clatter through the streets.

Best Dives of Grand Turk

Superb diving and snorkeling exist all along Grand Turk's western coast. The reef starts shallow just 300 yards off shore, then drops to about 35 ft for a quarter-mile. Then the wall drops 7,000 ft into the Turks Island Passage, an expressway for every imaginable creature in the sea. Schools of manta rays come in to feed on the shallow reefs during spring, a period when the waters are rich with a bloom of plankton – free-swimming micro-organisms that are a food source for many species of marine life. Bottlenose dolphins pass through the dive areas and, occasionally in late winter, humpback whales do as well.

Dolphin Dive off Grand Turk.

Several shallow areas entice snorkelers. Good shore diving exists off Governor's Beach on the south end.

☆☆☆☆ **The Gardens** start at 35 ft, then slope off to channel depths. Marine life is so abundant along this section of the Grand Turk wall that the magnificence of the animals often overshadows the reef's exquisite beauty. Residents include giant Nassau groupers, oversized parrots, rock beauties, and Spanish hogfish, as well as schools of large barracuda. During springtime, manta rays come in to feed. Tiny cleaner shrimp and octopi inhabit the crevices. Mini-critters hide in the vase sponges and gorgonians that grow from the wall. Farther down you'll find immense barrel sponges and black corals. Visibility is usually excellent except during the plankton "blooms," which create a soupy cloud over parts of the reef.

☆☆☆☆☆ **The Tunnels**, just south of the Gardens, are swim-through chutes between 50 and 75 ft. Reef life is similar to the Gardens. Six-ft mantas arrive during spring migration. At 60 ft there's a big sandy bowl where our researchers surprised a number of spotted and Nassau groupers. Big and small jacks, trunk fish and enormous file fish sway with the light current. Spotted and green morays poke their heads out from the crevices.

☆☆☆☆ **The Anchor**, one of the prettiest sections of the Grand Turk wall, features huge pastel sea fans, dense thickets of soft and hard corals, and some enormous tube and barrel sponges. Black coral is found in the deeper

Photo © Cecil Ingham, Sea Eye Diving

sections. Like most of the wall, the reef starts at about 40 ft and drops off to channel depths. Unusual coral sculptures provide superb photo compositions.

Snorkeling Grand Turk

Good beach snorkeling is found off the **Sitting Pretty Hotel** (formerly the Kittina), the **Arawak Hotel, Guanahani Beach Resort** and the **Salt Raker Inn**, where juvenile reef fish (angels, barracudas), shells, and small turtles blast by shallow coral heads.

☆☆**South Dock** at the south end of Grand Turk is a virtual junkyard of lost cargo from ships, inhabited by a flirty community of frog fish, sea horses, batfish, eels, shrimp and crabs. Sponges cover the pilings. Check with the dockmaster before entering the water.

☆☆☆☆ Snorkeling trips take off to **Round Cay** and **Gibbs Cay**, two out islands surrounded by elkhorn reefs. Bright sponges and colorful gorgonians abound. At Gibbs, friendly stingrays greet you in the shallows off the beach. They will pose for your pictures while you pet and handfeed them.

Dive Operators of Grand Turk

Rates subject to change.

Sea Eye Diving, in Cockburn, picks up from most Grand Turk resorts. Owner Cecil Ingham has been diving Grand Turk for many years and is a trustworthy dive operator and superb underwater photographer. The shop offers PADI and NAUI courses from resort to instructor, including Nitrox training. Sea Eye boats tour the wall and reefs, with special trips to the HMS Endymion Wreck and Salt Cay. They also offer Sunset cruises and whale watching in season. Rate for a single dive is $30, two-tank dive $50, night dive $35. Gibbs Cay snorkeling, beach barbecue and stingray encounter is $40. Six skiffs carry eight to 10 divers. Average trip time is 10 minutes. The shop's 41-ft dive boat visits areas out of the immediate cruising range. ☎ 800-810-3483 or 649-946-1407, fax 649-946-1408. E-mail: ci@tciway.tc. Website: www.reefnet.on.ca/grandturk. Write to: PO Box 67, Duke St., Grand Turk, Turks & Caicos Islands, BWI.

Blue Water Divers in Cockburn Town at the Salt Raker Inn offers guided reef trips to the Grand Turk Wall as well as to some of the small uninhabited cays south of Grand Turk. The shop offers a complete line of rental gear, including 35mm cameras. Open year-round, they offer terrific hotel-dive packages with the Salt Raker Inn. Single-tank dives cost $30, two-tanks $55, night dive $35. Dive packages drop the cost per dive down to $25. Snorkelers are welcome to join the dive boat for $10 with their own gear or for $15 with rental equipment. Snorkel-sightseeing trips to the cays cost $20. ☎ 649-946-1226.

E-mail: mrolling@tciway.tc. Website: www.microplan.com/bluerake.htm. Write to: Blue Water Divers, PO Box 124, Grand Turk, Turks & Caicos Islands, BWI. Complete dive/accommodation packages available.

Oasis Divers offer wall and reef tours, a full line of rental gear, dive computers, cameras and video recorders. They also have E-6 processing. PADI certifications and training through Divemaster. Nitrox courses. The PADI shop provides towels and refreshments on board and does complete gear handling and set-up. They offer daily afternoon and night dives. One-tank dive $30, two-tank dive $50, snorkel trip $20. Whale watching trips with Captain Everette Freites are offered during January, February and March.

Hotel-dive packages with Arawak Inn for seven nights start at $685 per person, with unlimited beach diving, tanks and weights, airport transfers, six days of two single-tank dives per day and continental breakfast. Similar packages with the new eight-room Island House are from $682 to $829; with Turks Head Inn from $682 to $929 per person; Salt Raker Inn from $670 to $855; Guanahani Beach Resort or Sitting Pretty from $665 per person. ☎ 800-892-3995 or 649-946-1128. Write to PO Box 137, Grand Turk, BWI. E-mail: oasisdiv@tciway.tc. Website: www.oasisdivers.com.

Grand Turk Accommodations

For additional resorts and accommodations contact the Turks & Caicos Tourism Office, ☎ 800-241-0824. E-mail: tci.tourism@tciway.tc. Website: www.turksandcaicostourism.

The Arawak Inn & Beach Club has the best beach snorkeling on Grand Turk. Numerous coral heads buzzing with fish dot the shallows, all close to the shore. The resort features 15 air-conditioned rooms, a restaurant, phones, TV and pool. Room rates start at $125 per night. ☎ 800-725-2822, 800-577-3872. Direct: 649-946-2277, fax 649-946-2279.

Guanahani Beach Resort offers 16 spacious, oceanfront rooms with air-conditioning, TV, phones, a gift shop and convenient dive facility with storage and rinse area on the beach. Snorkeling off the beach. Excellent restaurant. Room rates start at $137. (Undergoing renovation at press time.) ☎ 800-725-2822, 800-577-3872 or 649-946-1459, fax 649-946-1460.

The Sitting Pretty Hotel has 24 simple beachfront rooms with air-conditioning, some with kitchenettes. TV and phones. Diving with Sea Eye. Native restaurant, beach bar, sand beach, and freshwater pool. $137. (Undergoing renovation at press time.) ☎ 800-577-3872 or 649-946-2232, fax 649-946-2668.

The Salt Raker Inn, a 150-year-old Bermudian shipwright's home, features 10 lovely guest rooms and three suites that open onto the sea or gardens.

Turks & Caicos

TURKS ISLANDS

GRAND TURK
Cockburn Town
GIBB CAY
LONG CAY
⑧
⑨ ⑩ ⑪
COTTON CAY
⑫ SALT CAY
BIG SAND CAY

Christopher Columbus Passage

Drum Pt

Atlantic Ocean

MIDDLE CAICOS

EAST CAICOS

Ocean Hole

SOUTH CAICOS

LONG CAY

⑦
SIX HILL CAY

BUSH CAY

SEAL CAYS

NORTH CAICOS

PARROT CAY
WATER CAY
④ ⑥
PINE CAY
FORT GEORGE CAY
② ①
⑤
③
PROVIDENCIALES
South Bluff

AMBERGRIS CAYS

CAICOS ISLANDS

FRENCH CAY

WEST CAICOS

Caicos Passage

Dive and Snorkeling Areas
1. Smith's Reef, Grace Bay
2. The Bight Reef, Grace Bay
3. North West Point
4. Eagle Ray Run
5. Wheeland Cut
6. Fort George's Cut
7. Long Cay, South Caicos
8. The Wall at Grand Turk
9. The Library
10. Coral Gardens
11. South Dock
12. Point Pleasant, Salt Cay

Air-conditioning and ceiling fans. Good restaurant. ☎ 800-548-8462 or 649-946-2260, fax 649-946-2817. E-mail: blueraker@aol.com.

Turks Head Inn, an 1860s mansion, once served as a US consulate, then a governor's private guest house. Seven rooms all have original antique furnishings (four-poster beds, rocking chairs), air-conditioning, TV and balconies. One apartment has a kitchenette. Outstanding restaurant features local and European specialties. Expensive. ☎ 649-946-2466, fax 649-946-2825, or book through your travel agent.

Salt Cay

Salt Cay, the most remote of the inhabited islands, lies seven miles southeast of Grand Turk. It features 101 friendly residents, one dive shop, outstanding diving and a rich heritage dating back to the 1700s when Salt Cay flourished as one of the world's largest salt exporters. The salt industry died during the 1960s, but you can still tour the Salinas (salt ponds) and windmills where the salt was mined and stored. Lovely churches and grand plantation homes – many converted to inns – attest to the prosperity of those days.

Today's wealth lies in Salt Cay's magnificent diving and snorkeling. Pristine walls packed with fish, spectacular corals and sponges bathe in the rush of sea water passing through the outlying channel. Because the island is remote and tricky to reach few divers make the trek, but those who do are rewarded with fine diving. Topside, miles of deserted beaches make for terrific shelling and bird watching.

During January, February and March, Salt Cay transforms into Humpback Whale Headquarters, as the island sits directly in the Columbus Passage, the byway for whales migrating to Silver Banks.

Nightlife is limited to stargazing and moonlight dives. Two restaurants and one café provide fresh-caught seafood and steaks.

Best Dives of Salt Cay

The wall dives start at 35 feet, dropping to 7,000 ft. Salt Cay Divers tour the Grand Turk sites as well.

☆☆☆☆ **The HMS Endymion** is a favorite shallow wreck at depths from 15 to 30 feet. There's actually not much left of the wreck, just the cannons and anchors, but it's worth a trip for the abundant fish life. The trip from Salt Cay takes between 40 and 50 minutes. Sea conditions vary.

☆☆☆☆ **Point Pleasant**, the Turks and Caicos' best snorkeling and shallow-dive spot off the northern tip of Salt Cay, will leave you in awe with massive vertical brain corals, giant elkhorn and staghorn gardens – all in 15 ft of water. You can swim side-by-side with big turtles, stoplight parrot fish, pompano, and eagle rays. This fabulous spot is always calm with no currents. Visibility exceeds 100 ft. Beach or boat access.

Salt Cay Dive Operator

Debbie Manos at **Salt Cay Divers** will handle your entire Salt Cay dive vacation with stays at a choice of inns converted from the old plantation homes or in the Castaways Beach House cottages. If you pass up their sumptuous meal and plan to cook for yourself, they will stock your cottage with foods from your own pre-arranged menu. The fully equipped PADI dive shop runs skiffs to the walls. Most sites are a few minutes from shore. The dive shop also rents kayaks and offers sailing cruises. ☎ 649-946-6906, fax 649-946-6940. E-mail: scdivers@tciway.tc. Website: www.saltcaydivers.tc.

Salt Cay Accommodations

Castaways Beach House offers six simple beachfront guest rooms at moderate rates. ☎ 315-536-7061, fax 315-536-0737; direct 649-946-6921, fax 649-946-6922.

Mount Pleasant Guest House has eight comfortable beachfront rooms with TV. ☎ 649-946-6927 for voice and fax.

For a list of 20 guest houses and dive-package rates (from $974 to $1,114 per person for a week), contact **Salt Cay Divers** at ☎ 649-946-6906, fax 649-946-6940. E-mail: scdivers@tciway.tc. Website: www.saltcaydivers.tc.

The Caicos

The Caicos' six principal islands and their surrounding small cays offer superb wall diving. Along the barrier reef surrounding them you'll find iridescent sea anemones, huge basket sponges and dense gardens of elkhorn coral. Closer to shore are patches of coral swarming with reef tropicals. Miles of beautiful swimming beaches attract families and non-divers as well.

All island activities center around the resorts. Most Provo (short for Providenciales) dive sites require a 35-minute boat ride from the dive shops.

Best Dives of Providenciales Island & North Caicos

☆☆☆☆☆ **West Wall** comprises hundreds of sites along a vertical edge of the continental shelf. A few favorites are Grand Canyon, Black Coral Forest and Carol's Wall. Drop-offs begin at 25 ft and bottom at 6,000 ft. Divers exploring this ledge encounter huge fish, schooling eagle and manta rays, sharks and dolphins. During winter months, humpback whales pass by.

Spectacular gigantic barrel sponges, tube sponges and anemones grow from the ledges, providing cover for arrow and spider crabs, sea cucumbers, Spanish lobster, barber shrimp, green and spotted moray eels. Forests of black coral start as shallow as 60 ft.

Visibility is always excellent, with sea conditions dependent on the winds and weather. Recommended for experienced divers.

☆☆☆☆ **The Pinnacles** on the northeast coast of Provo near Grace Bay, range in depth from 35 to 60 ft. This spur and groove reef shelters Nassau groupers, sea turtles, snappers, sergeant majors, basslets, and schooling grunts. Clump plate corals dotted with purple and orange sponges make bright homes for moray eels that surprise divers by emerging during daylight hours. Visibility is exceptional. Usually calm, though seas vary with the winds.

☆☆☆ *Southwind* **Shipwreck**, an 80-ft freighter off Provo's north coast, provides dramatic backgrounds for fish and diver portraits. Sunk during 1985, the wreck's denizens include several tame groupers and barracudas, Spanish hogfish, French angels, horse-eye jacks, damsels, schools of sergeant majors and yellowtails. The wreck sits on the sand at 60 ft. Visibility is usually good. Seas vary, usually light chop.

☆☆☆ **Grouper Hole**, off the north shore, is a wide sand hole encircling a large coral head. Mammoth groupers and jewfish circle the area. Seas are generally calm. Light current may occasionally be encountered.

Snorkeling Provo

The Turks and Caicos National Trust has established snorkeling trails on Smith's Reef and Bight Reef in Providenciales' Grace Bay. Both are close to the shoreline. The marked trails display 24 tile signs with directions and tips on reef preservation. Beach signs direct visitors to points of entry.

☆☆☆ **Smith's Reef**, located north of Turtle Cove off Bridge Road at the beginning of Grace Bay, has a reef trail that runs along a shallow shelf through flourishing elkhorn and staghorn corals, vase sponges and pink-tipped anemones. Depths run from eight to 25 ft, with the majority at eight to 10 ft. Residents include three turtles, parrot fish, yellow and blue-headed wrasses, queen angels and lots of juvenile fish. There is also a *huge* green moray who pops his head out from the coral now and then, as well as stingrays, small eagle rays and nurse sharks. A large barracuda hangs out and adores getting close to snorkelers. Beach access. If you can't find the entry point, stop in at Provo Turtle Divers in Turtle Cove for directions.

☆☆☆ **The Bight Reef** is in the Grace Bay area known as the Bight, just offshore from a large white house. A public footpath leads to the beach and two marker buoys indicate both ends of the snorkel trail. This trail has 11 signs that describe corals and how they grow. Depths range from three to 15 ft. Daily denizens are yellow-tailed snappers, big jolthead porgies and sand sifting mojarras. Calm. Beach entry.

✩✩✩ **Eagle Ray Run**, off Fort George Cay, features sun-splashed elkhorn corals, large eagle rays, turtles, spotted groupers and crustaceans. The reef pierces the surface in some spots with deeper areas to about 20 ft. Good Visibility. Beach entry.

✩✩✩✩ **Wheeland Cut**, on the northwest point just off Navigation Light, shelters schools of grunts and sergeant majors, turtles, barracudas, an occasional small shark and a host of critters amidst a dense elkhorn reef. Vase sponges and gorgonians thrive in the light current. Boat access.

✩ **Fort George's Cut**, on the northeastern end of Provo just off Fort George Cay, is very shallow and a good place for beginning divers. The bottom is strewn with patches of coral and some old cannons inhabited by juvenile barracudas that peek out from the shadows.

Caicos Islands Dive Operators

Art Pickering's Provo Turtle Divers offers reef trips from their Ocean Club location. Use of gear included. Friendly and helpful service. Cost for a one-tank dive is $40, two-tank dive $70. Average boat trip is 45 minutes. Hotel pick-up service available. Snorkeling trips. Hotel-dive packages with Comfort Suites (from $891 for six nights, five dive days), Erebus Inn (from $975 for seven nights, five dive days), Ocean Club (from $1,285 for seven nights, five dive days) and Turtle Cove Inn (from $707 for seven nights, five dive days). ☎ 800-833-1341 or 649-946-4232, fax 649-941-5296. Write to Box 219, Providenciales, Turks & Caicos, BWI. E-mail: Provoturtle divers@provo.net. Website: www.provoturtledivers.com.

Caicos Adventures specializes in diving West Caicos and French Cay. Maximum 12 divers. Day trips include lunch, sodas, water and snacks. Dive-hotel packages available. ☎ 800-513-5822 or 649-941-3346, fax 649-941-3346. E-mail: divucrzy@tciway.tc. Website: www.caicosadventures.tc.

Flamingo Divers offers guided reef trips aboard two 29-ft custom Delta dive boats, NAUI and YMCA instruction, resort courses and rental gear. Hotel-dive packages available. They also offer cheaper hostel-style rooms and stays at Provo Marine Biology Centre. One-tank dives cost $40, two-tank, $70. ☎ 800- 204-9282 or 649-946-4193, fax 649-946-4193. E-mail: flamingo@ provo.net. Website: www.provo.net/flamingo. Write to: PO Box 322, Providenciales, Turks & Caicos, BWI.

Dive Provo provides a complete range of services, including a full-service, photo-video operation. Besides dive gear, they rent ocean kayaks, Laser sailboats and windsurfers. Snorkeling tours. Dive Provo offers complete vacation packages. Winter rates are for seven nights, five dive days. Hotel-dive packages with the Allegro Resort (from $1,739 pp), Comfort Suites Hotel (from $1,011 pp), Le Deck Hotel (from $1,081 pp), Crystal Bay Resort Condominiums (from $1,466 pp), Erebus Inn (from $941 pp) and Ocean Club ($1,264 pp). Two-tank dives cost $75. Dive areas include Grace Bay, Northwest Point, Pine Cay and West Caicos. ☎ 800-234-7768 or 649-946-5029. E-mail: diveprov@gate.net. Website: www.diveprovo.com. Write to: PO Box 350, Providenciales, Turks and Caicos Islands, BWI.

Photo Service

Fish Frames photo service rents a wide variety of cameras and offers one- or two-day photo courses, E-6 processing, personalized video or stills of your snorkeling or dive tour. ☎ 649-946-5841.

Providenciales Accommodations

Note: The all-inclusive resorts are easiest to book through a travel agent. A few Turks and Caicos' hotels close during summer months. For additional information, contact the tourist board. ☎ 800-241-0824 or 649-946-2321/2, fax 649-946-2733.

Allegro Resort Turks & Caicos recently completed a major renovation. The 400-room property on Grace Bay offers two restaurants, two pools, bar and a children's (four-12)activity program and indoor club. PADI five-star facility on premises. Dive packages. Room rates for two are from $390 ($195 per person). Rate does not include scuba trips. ☎ 800-858-2258, Website: www.allegroresorts.com.

Beaches Turks & Caicos, an all-inclusive luxury resort on Grace Bay, features 390 rooms with satellite TV, air-conditioning, minibar, coffee maker, hair dryer and in-room safe. Two freeform pools, a childrens' pool and a scuba training pool ensure sufficient wetness between dives. The resort dive shop has fast boats and visits the best dive and snorkeling spots. Winter rates start at $1,790 per person for six nights. ☎ 800-BEACHES. Website: www.beaches.com.

Erebus Inn, one of Provo's first hotels, sits on Turtle Cove, with 28 rooms overlooking the Turtle Cove Marina. All have air-conditioning, cable TV, mini-bars and direct-dial phones. The resort, in walking distance of snorkeling sites, offers a free shuttle or boat to a private beach. The inn features a pool, tennis, miniature golf, a bar, restaurant, and sundeck. Room rates are from $115. ☎ 649-946-4240, fax 649-946-4704.

Turtle Cove Inn features a dive center and marina, 32 guest rooms and one suite. Each room has a porch or balcony, air-conditioning, cable TV and phones. Pool with waterfall. Two restaurants feature indoor or outdoor seating and a nice selection of Caribbean lobster dishes, pastas and sauces. Swim or snorkel to Smiths Reef off the beach. The resort also has a beach shuttle, fresh-water pool, cycle, jeep and scooter rental. More restaurants within easy walking distance. Winter room rates are from $120 per night. Dive packages include accommodations, airport transfers, tanks, weights, belt, guide boat. They start at $328 per person for two two-tank dives, $581 for four two-tank dives, $834 for six two-tank dives. ☎ 800-887-0477, direct 649-946-4203, fax 649-946-4141. Website: www.provo.net/turtlecoveinn.

Club Med Turkoise, on Grace Bay Beach, features all-inclusive packages from $1,299 per person for seven days. Diving costs from $160 for five days. If you haven't stayed at Club Med before, they charge a $30 initiation fee and a $50 annual membership fee. The 298-room resort offers all water sports, lounge, disco and restaurant. Golf nearby. ☎ 800-258-2633, direct 649-946-5500, fax 649-946-5501. Website: www.clubmed.com.

Treasure Beach Villas offers 18 deluxe beachfront suites. Near beach snorkeling sites. ☎ 649-464-4325, fax 649-946-4108.

Ledeck Hotel & Beach Club, a 25-room hotel on a lovely stretch of Grace Bay beach, features a Creole restaurant and freshwater pool. Air-conditioned guest rooms have color TV. Diving arranged with nearby Dive Provo. ☎ 800-528-1905 or 649-946-5547, fax 649-946-5770. Write to Box 144, Grace Bay, Providenciales.

Grace Bay Club, a posh, all-suite resort, features 22 air-conditioned suites and penthouses. Balconies overlook the sea. All have cable TV, ceiling fans, safes, washer/dryer. Daily rates run $355 to $1,255. ☎ 800-946-5757.

The Comfort Suites Turks & Caicos Islands, adjacent to the Ports of Call shopping Village and across the street from Grace Bay Beach, offers 99 junior suites with either a king-size bed or two twin beds, sofa bed and fridge. Winter room rates from $190 per day. Off-season, from $135. Dive packages with Provo Turtle Divers. ☎ 800-992-2015 or 305-992-2015; direct 649-946-8888, fax 649-946-5444.

The Sands at Grace Bay features 39 luxurious one-, two- and three-bedroom suites. All have air-conditioning, floor-to-ceiling windows and contemporary furnishings. They also have fax and Internet access, cable TV, kitchenettes with microwave, in-room safe and direct-dial phones. Oceanfront cabana restaurant and bar, dune deck, easy beach access, free-form pool, tour desk and vehicle rentals. Dive packages that include tanks, weights, transfers, taxes and accommodations are with Calypso Adventures. Package rates start at $495 for three nights, $1,230 for seven nights. ☎ 877-77-SANDS (toll free). Website: www.thesandsresort.com.

The Prospect of Whitby Hotel, on North Caicos, neighbor island to Providenciales, features a secluded beachfront location, spacious, air-conditioned rooms with phones and TV. Restaurant, bar and lounge, dive shop, baby-sitting, travel services. Dive-hotel packages. Room rates range from $120 to $205 per day. ☎ 649-946-7119, fax 649-946-7114.

South Caicos

Countless snorkeling coves and miles of shell-lined beaches make this island a beachcomber's paradise. It is also ideal for those wishing a quiet escape from telephones, television and newspapers. A herd of wild horses roams the Eastern Ridge.

Diving and snorkeling on the nearby reefs and uninhabited cays is magnificent. There is excellent snorkeling on the western shores.

Best Dives of South Caicos

☆☆☆☆☆ **The Arches Reef**, beautiful by day, is also a favorite choice for night dives. On one evening exploration, *Best Dives* diver Dr. Susan Cropper made friends with two enormous angel fish and saw many large sleeping parrot fish. Glass-eyed snappers, brittle stars, blue tangs, big puffers, banded butterflies and a bevy of critters line a huge coral-encrusted arch, which itself is covered with finger corals, gorgonians, and red and orange sponges. Stands of elkhorn and brain corals offer a nice photo background.

☆☆☆☆ **The Plane**, actually the remains of a Convair 340, houses six-ft nurse sharks, eagle rays, huge coral crabs, schools of grunts and some big barracudas that like to follow divers around. The fuselage sits on the edge of a wall and makes an interesting video subject. Seas are generally calm.

☆☆☆☆ **Amos' Wall** dive centers around a huge cut in the wall between 65 and 130 ft. This spot shelters many "cleaning stations" where barracudas and other fish line up to have "barber" or "cleaning" shrimp pick parasites from their teeth and scales. Both lavender and clear shrimp have also been observed. Huge eagle rays, sea turtles, big groupers, queen angels, and Spanish hogfish abound. A super dive.

☆☆☆ **Anchor Alley**, a junkyard for lost anchors, is also a byway for huge spotted gray angels, a number of Nassau groupers, spotted morays, and king-size jacks. The coral heads rise from the sand at 70 ft to within 40 ft of the surface. Abundant sea cucumbers. Seas vary with wind conditions.

☆☆☆ **The Point**, a favorite night dive, sits off the south end of South Caicos. Numerous lobsters, butterfly fish, crabs, spotted cowfish, morays and parrots rove the reef. Shrimp and sea cucumbers comb the ledges.

Turks & Caicos

South Caicos Accommodations

Club Carib Harbour & Beach Resorts has two locations, one overlooking Cockburn Harbour and one at the Beach. The Harbour is good for scuba divers, while the Club Carib Beach Resort is the choice of snorkelers. Choose from eight rooms cooled by ceiling fans (no air-conditioning) or a two-room, air-conditioned villa with a kitchen. During high tide the water ranges from three ft inshore to six ft 200 yards offshore. There are small reefs in this area with plenty of marine life. A two-minute boat ride from the harbour will take you to the marine park. The 16-room resort features a restaurant and bar. Horseback riding. Color TV. Dive shop on premises operates four boats. ☎ 800-241-0824 or 649-946-3444, fax 649-946-3446. Book through Caradonna Tours, ☎ 800 328 2288.

Live-Aboards

(rates subject to change)

Peter Hughes Diving operates the 120-ft luxury dive yacht ***Wind Dancer*** between April 10 and December 31 and 110-ft ***Sea Dancer***, which departs Providenciales every Saturday. Seven nights aboard *Wind Dancer* or *Sea Dancer* costs between $1,195 and $1,495, varying with your choice of stateroom. The lower-end rooms have upper and lower bunks, while the more expensive master stateroom has a queen bed, private head/shower, TV, VCR and porthole view. Both vessels have air-conditioning to all areas, E-6 processing, Nitrox, video and camera rental, photo instruction, an accommodating crew, good food and up-to-date navigation and safety equipment. ☎ 800-932-6237 or 305-669-9391, fax 305-669-9475.

Newly refurbished ***Turks & Caicos Aggressor*** accommodates 14 divers in six staterooms, five with double and single berths and private baths. The sixth cabin is a roomy quad for four divers with private head and shower outside the door. There is also a new Nitrox system. January through March, this yacht offers humpback whale-watching charters from Grand Turk. April through December, she offers scuba charter from Providenciales. The yacht provides breakfast to order, maid service, all meals, on-board film development, a video lounge. Week-long stays are from $995 for the quad, from $1,495 pp, double occupancy, for the stateroom. ☎ 800-348-2628 or 504-385-2628, fax 504-384-0817. E-mail: diveboat@aol.com or diveboat@compuserve.com. Website: www.aggressor.com.

Facts

Recompression Chamber: Providenciales.

Getting There: American Airlines (☎ 800-433-7300) provides twice-daily service from Miami to Providenciales. Beaches Champagne Express offers nonstop service Sundays from New York and Philadelphia to Providenciales.

Bahamasair (☎ 800-222-4262) flies from Miami to Grand Turk Thursdays and Mondays. Service between the islands is available on Turks & Caicos Airways (☎ 649-946-4255), Inter-Island Airways (☎ 649-941-5481), and SkyKing (☎ 649-941-KING). Flying time from Miami to Providenciales is 80 minutes.

Island Transportation: Taxis. Car rentals available on Grand Turk and Providenciales.

Driving: Traffic moves on the left side of the roads.

Documents: US and Canadian residents require proof of citizenship such as a passport, birth certificate or voter registration card and photo identification, plus a return ticket.

Customs: Cameras and personal dive equipment do not require any special paperwork. No spear guns are allowed on the islands.

Currency: The US dollar is legal tender.

Climate: 70 to 90°F year-round. Water temperature never below 74°F. Possibility of storms and heavy rainfall July through November. Credit cards and personal checks are not welcome in some Turks and Caicos establishments.

Clothing: Lightweight, casual. A lightweight lycra wetskin is a good idea for winter snorkeling or to prevent coral abrasion.

Diving: All divers must present a valid C-card before they will be allowed to dive. Spearguns and Hawaiian slings are not permitted in the Turks and Caicos. Treasure hunting is forbidden.

Electricity: 110 volt, 60 cycle.

Time: Eastern Standard Time.

Language: English.

Tax: There is a $15 departure tax. Hotels may add a 15% service charge and a 7% government accommodation tax.

Religious Services: Roman Catholic, Anglican, Baptist, Methodist, Seventh Day Adventist, Church of God.

For Additional Information: Turks and Caicos Tourist Board, PO Box 128, Grand Turk, Turks and Caicos Islands, ☎ 800-241-0824, 649-946-2321, fax 649-946-2733. E-mail: tci.tourism@tciway.tc. Website: www.turksandcaicostourism.com.

Turks & Caicos

Snorkeling boat, Bermuda.

Bermuda

Sitting hundreds of miles from anywhere, or more precisely 650 miles off the coast of North Carolina, Britain's oldest colony is known for its natural beauty. Everyone who's been to Bermuda understands why Mark Twain once said: "You go to heaven if you want – I'd rather stay here in Bermuda."

Geographically, Bermuda consists of 181 hilly islands and countless cayes that swing from northwest to southwest in a fish-hook shape. Its 21-mile stretch of islands is connected by several bridges and causeways. Town Hill, the highest point, rises 260 feet above sea level. There are no rivers or freshwater lakes. Residents depend solely on rainfall for drinking water.

Bermuda is divided into nine parishes – once known as tribes. The boundaries still remain as they were drawn on the original maps in 1622, and the original names from the principal shareholders have been retained: Hamilton, Smith, Devonshire, Paget, Warwick, Sandys and St. Georges. About 58,460 people live on 20 of the islands.

Surrounding Bermuda is one of the largest fringing reef systems in the entire world. Despite a continuous influx of tour boats, the dive operators' installation and use of 20 permanent moorings, along with adherence to smart buoyancy control measures, has kept the reefs in pristine condition.

History

Though the islands were first discovered in 1503 by Juan de Bermudez, a Spaniard who left his name and sailed away, the first visitors to stay in Bermuda were British travelers shipwrecked when Admiral Sir George Somers' flagship *Sea Venture* came to grief on Bermuda's reefs in 1609. En route to the Jamestown Colony, they ran aground on the shallow reefs that ring the island.

Bermuda Today

The natural beauty of this tiny island, both above and below the sea, is well guarded by preservation laws. Visitors are often surprised to find a noticeable lack of neon signs, tall buildings or strip malls. Many areas of the island have been kept exactly the same as when the first shipwrecked settlers arrived. The quality of life is high in Bermuda – no pollution, no unemployment and no illiteracy.

When to Go

March through December are prime months for divers to visit Bermuda, though some operators dive all year. Annual rainfall is 57.6 inches, with October being the wettest month. Snorkeling is best during summer when the waters of the Gulf Stream reach 85°F. In winter, the main flow of warm water moves away from Bermuda, causing local temperatures to drop as low as 60°F. This annual cold spell prohibits the growth of delicate corals and sponges, but heartier corals, such as brain, star, sea fans, soft corals, pillar corals and some long purple tube sponges thrive. Overall, Bermuda's reefs are very lush with marine growth. The predominant soft corals swaying in the surges impart a garden-like quality to the reefs.

Although Bermuda is an undisputed paradise for shallow-water wreck diving, coral formations along Bermuda's south shore offer divers another amazing treat. Nature has provided a coral architecture of canyons, caves, grottoes, labyrinths, and tunnels – which may make you entirely forget about Bermuda's singular claim to fame, her hundreds of shipwrecks.

In Peter Benchley's story, *The Deep*, two vacationing divers enlist the aid of a seasoned Bermuda treasure hunter, supposedly modeled after real life treasure-hunting celebrity, Teddy Tucker, and they find a cache of golden artifacts from a lost treasure galleon. Experts agree that many of Bermuda's treasure galleons are yet to be found.

Bermuda law requires that all diving be done with a government-licensed guide. Most dive operators will pick you up at your hotel and transport you and your equipment to and from the dive boat. No car rentals exist on Bermuda and the taxi and horse-drawn carriage operators have not yet demonstrated any fondness for divers piling loads of dripping gear in the back seat.

The Shipwrecks of Bermuda

Three centuries of sunken ships lie at rest in Bermuda's briny deeps. To protect them while still allowing recreational and commercial access, the Bermuda Government has created a special department – "The Receiver of Wrecks." This agency is responsible for issuing licenses to individuals for the excavation of newly discovered shipwreck sites in Bermuda waters. Despite modern navigational aids and numerous safety precautions, ships still wreck occasionally on Bermuda's reefs.

The Government officially acknowledges the existence of as many as 400 wrecks. These have been charted, more or less identified, properly worked, and most of them left alone. Some of the older and more historically important wrecks are protected sites and divers are forbidden to visit them.

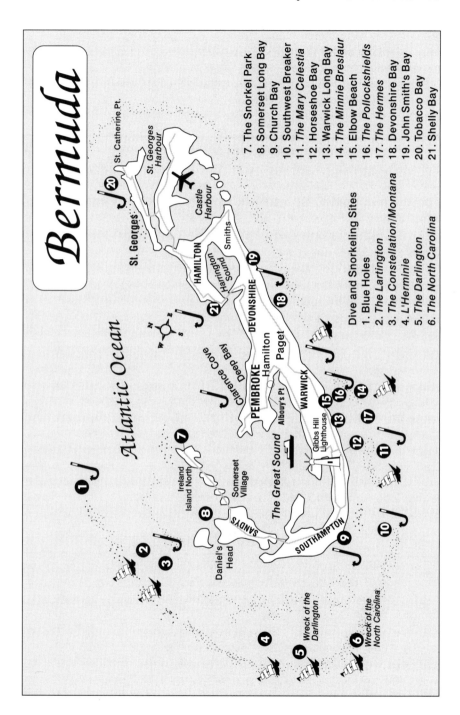

Bermuda

Atlantic Ocean

St. Catherine Pt.

St. Georges Harbour

St. Georges

Castle Harbour

HAMILTON

Smiths

Harrington Sound

DEVONSHIRE

Ireland Island North

Somerset Village

SANDYS

Daniel's Head

Clarence Cove

Deep Bay

Albouy's Pt

PEMBROKE   Hamilton

Paget

WARWICK

Gibbs Hill Lighthouse

The Great Sound

SOUTHAMPTON

Wreck of the Darlington

Wreck of the North Carolina

Dive and Snorkeling Sites

1. Blue Holes
2. *The Lartington*
3. *The Constellation/Montana*
4. *L'Herminie*
5. *The Darlington*
6. *The North Carolina*
7. The Snorkel Park
8. Somerset Long Bay
9. Church Bay
10. Southwest Breaker
11. *The Mary Celestia*
12. Horseshoe Bay
13. Warwick Long Bay
14. *The Minnie Breslaur*
15. Elbow Beach
16. *The Pollockshields*
17. *The Hermes*
18. Devonshire Bay
19. John Smith's Bay
20. Tobacco Bay
21. Shelly Bay

Robert Marx, in one of his books, remarks that there are at least 1,500 ship-wrecks and possibly 2,000 in Bermuda waters. His estimates come from personal research, including original photographs of ships that sank in the past 100 years or so and drawings of older ships or their sister ships. Local divers agree that figure may not be an exaggeration.

The waters around Bermuda have given up a great deal of what most call treasure to eager and diligent treasure hunters. Most notable of the Bermudian treasure hunters would certainly be Mr. Teddy Tucker. Teddy has developed numerous innovative methods to search for wrecks, including riding in a hot air balloon towed behind a power boat. His innovations have proved to be very successful and he has recovered more than any other Bermudian treasure hunter.

The greatest single find from Bermuda waters must be the "Tucker Treasure," discovered after many years of working the same site. This find produced numerous gold bars, gold cakes, pearl-studded golden buttons, and a magnificent emerald cross. It also netted numerous artifacts depicting life at the time of the wreck (1595), which is often called one of the most important finds of the century. Others of Teddy's wrecks have yielded considerable gold and silver and, even though he is now getting on in years, he is still out in the reefs looking for new wrecks or working on those he has already registered.

Another legendary Bermuda treasure hunter is Mr. Harry Cox, who has found a nice-sized collection, as he prefers to call it. It consists of a quantity of gold coins, bars and circlets, a pearl cross and a gold ring with a space for a large stone. Ironically, almost one year from the day of discovering the ring, one of Harry's crew came up with a three-karat emerald. It fit perfectly into the space in the ring. But the best find of this particular collection must be the 15-ft-long double-braided gold chain. Each link is gold, created using the lost wax process common in the Middle Ages, but unknown to modern jewelers and goldsmiths until the 20th century. Harry believes this collection to be the personal property of a merchant who may have fallen overboard or been cast off a ship.

Best Dives of Bermuda

Unless otherwise noted, Bermuda's wreck dives are all boat access.

☆☆☆☆☆ **The *Constellation/Montana*,** a few miles off the northwestern coast of Bermuda, consists of two ships that sank on exactly the same reef, although 80 years apart. The *Montana* was an English paddlewheel steamer on her maiden voyage as a Confederate blockade runner during the American Civil War. She was a very sleek vessel, 236 ft in length and with a beam of 25 ft. Her steam engines and twin paddle wheels were capable of turning out some 260 hp. She ground to a halt in shallow reefs 5½ miles from the Western end of Bermuda on December 30, 1863. As she was an iron-hulled ship, a great deal of her hull and boilers are remarkably intact and make for an excellent dive. Numerous reef fish and some rather large schools of barracuda make the *Montana*, also known as the *Nola, Gloria* and *Paramount,* their home. Literally overlapping the *Montana* are the remains of the *Constellation*. This four-masted, wooden-hulled schooner sank on the Bermuda reefs en route from New York to Venezuela on July 31, 1943. Hers was a general cargo, but on her deck she carried 700 cases of Scotch whiskey, an assortment of drugs and hundreds of bags of cement which, when washed with seawater, solidified into concrete and so remain to this very day. The *Constellation* is often referred to as the "Dime Store" or "Woolworth" wreck because of the wide variety of artifacts that can be seen. After perusing the *Constellation*, a diver might think he had been diving at Woolworth's. She was carrying all sorts of goods to be sold in Venezuela, including red glass, cut glass, china, glasses, tea and coffee cups and saucers, tickets to Coney Island (in Spanish), yo-yos, 78-rpm records by RCA (with labels in Spanish), cases of pistachio nuts, radios, parts for radios, religious artifacts, devotion altars of pewter, crucifixes, cosmetic supplies by Mennen and Elizabeth Arden, cold cream, Vaseline, and pharmaceutical products, including at least eight different types of drug ampules, which provided Peter Benchley with the premise for *The Deep*. This is a very enjoyable dive and all in 30 ft of water. The site is about five miles offshore and is recommended for both snorkelers and divers. Some areas of the reef are as shallow as eight feet. The sea conditions vary with the wind direction and speed. Dive boat captains vigorously discourage taking bottles and artifacts from the *Constellation*.

☆☆ **The *Cristobal Colon***, a 480-ft, three-story Spanish luxury liner, is Bermuda's largest known shipwreck. She ran aground on October 25, 1936 after hitting a reef between North Rock and North Breaker. The ship sat on the reef for some time while furniture, art and other valuables were salvaged. The following year Captain Stephensen of the Norwegian steamer *Aristo* mistook the stationary wreck of the *Colon* as a ship underway and "followed" her onto the reefs. Following that tragedy, the Bermuda government dismantled the *Colon's* mast and funnel to prevent other ships from mistaking her for an active vessel. Today, the *Cristobal Colon* lies in 15 ft (at the bow) to 80 ft (at the stern) with her remains scattered across 100,000 square ft of seafloor. Divers and snorkelers will find plenty of fish hiding beneath the propellers, drive shafts and boilers lying on the bottom.

☆☆ The 250-ft steamship ***Aristo*** (aka *Iristo*) sank under tow during a rescue effort. Her general cargo included a vintage fire truck that sits off the forward deck, gasoline drums and a steamroller. Rocks and coral rubble surround the hull. Visibility varies. Seas calm. Depths to 50 ft but the bow comes to within 18 ft of the surface.

☆☆☆☆ *Lartington*. Long listed on the Bermuda wreck chart as an unidentified 19th-century wreck, the *Lartington* was often referred to as the *Nola* until one of Blue Water Divers' young divemasters discovered her name under the port side of her partially intact bow. After writing to Harland & Wolf, a builder of this type of vessel during the 19th century, we learned that this kind of sailing steamer was very common in the late 1800s.

The Lartington *gave rise to the expression, "tramp steamer," because every time the coal-burning engines were fired up, she belched out a cloud of coal dust, liberally coating everything and everyone aboard with black soot. Then everyone resembled railroad hobos, or tramps, and the name stuck!*

The *Lartington's* saturation steam boilers are visible amidships and, at the stern, the driveshaft and propeller. The steering controls located on the fantail are now encrusted with over 100 years of coral growth. The bow, partially destroyed, lies a few feet above the 30-ft-deep sand bottom. There is an air pocket inside the bow, but it is oxygen-poor and dangerous to breathe.

A lovely reef, honeycombed with small caves and tunnels, surrounds the wreck. Depths are shallow enough to snorkel, within 10 ft of the surface at some spots. The entire length of the wreck is visible from the surface. She lies facing almost due south, as if heading into Bermuda. This site is recommended for snorkelers and divers, both novice and expert. Sea conditions vary with the wind.

☆☆☆☆ **Southwest Breaker**. This massive breaking reef, the cause of at least one wreck along Bermuda's south shore, rises from a 30-ft bottom and actually protrudes above the surface, casting up considerable whitewater even on the calmest days. Through the center of the breaker is a massive tunnel, large enough to drive a boat through. The tunnel is often occupied by two to four black groupers and a resident barracuda who is not shy of photographers. In early summer, clouds of fry or glass-eye minnows feed in the nutrient-rich and oxygenated waters here. They draw others and then more still until the breaker is home to more fish than you can count. The surrounding reef is very colorful and appears quite lush, with many smaller non-breaking heads known locally as "blindbreakers." These are carved with numerous ledges and caves. This area, a favorite for night dives, is excellent for snorkelers and novice and experienced scuba divers. It is particularly interesting to photograph. Surface swells are encountered here.

☆☆☆ *Mary Celestia*. After making at least five round trips to Wilmington, NC successfully, running the Northern blockade of Confederate ports, the

Mary Celestia ran aground on the "Blind Breakers" and sank on September 13, 1864, only nine months after her sister ship, the *Montana*, was wrecked on the northern reefs. The story, as reported in the *Royal Gazette* a week later, states that her captain, knowing the waters of Bermuda, warned the navigator about the breakers. The navigator remarked with certainty, "I know these waters like I know my own house!" He apparently hadn't spent much time at home, for within minutes the *Mary Celestia* struck bottom. She was towed off the reef the next morning and reportedly sank within 10 minutes, the seas rushing in through a great hole torn in her underside.

The only loss of life on the Mary Celestia *was the ship's cook, who returned to salvage his frying pan or some piece of personal equipment. The remainder of the crew made it safely to shore, where most of them died of yellow fever, which was ravaging Bermuda at the time.*

Today, the *Mary* sits quietly in just under 60 ft of water as if she were still steaming along. More than 120 years' accumulation of sand covers most of her hull, but her two rectangular steam boilers and engine machinery lie upright and perfectly visible. Both of her paddle wheels stand upright. The entire wreck is surrounded by a high reef, honeycombed with caverns, canyons and cuts that open onto the sand bottom. Dive boats normally anchor on the shallow top of the reef, allowing for a gradual descent onto the sand hole housing the wreck, then spend part of the dive moving about the cuts and tunnels. The anchor of the wreck lies in about 30 ft of water, just on the edge of the drop-off from the shallow to the deeper sand pocket.

Very large schools of parrot fish are frequently sighted here. The reef, which starts at 15 ft and drops off to 60 ft, is lush with hard and soft corals. Surface swells are common to this area; visibility varies. Large black groupers inhabit the wreck during spring, fall and winter. It's a terrific night dive site when visibility is good.

☆☆☆ The British merchant ship **Minnie Breslaur** sank in the 1870s after striking the Southwest Breaker reef. Her stern lies in a sand pocket at 70 ft; her bow, totally collapsed on a flat coral reef at 40 ft, points out to sea. Her midships section, steam boilers and engine mechanism lie angled upward from a sandy bottom at 70 ft to the flat reef top at 40 ft. Several old torpedo-shaped bottles, Belfast and marble bottles (made by pinching the neck around a clear marble) have been recovered from her hull, and several small black coral trees can be found on the site, with one growing right above the propeller on the stern of the wreck. The adjacent reef consists of numerous small caves and tunnels and in the mounds of high reef just inshore of the stern a honeycomb of tunnels works its way through the reef formation. It is not uncommon to see schools of large jacks or several large barracudas on this dive. Where she rests, near deep water, visibility is often incredible, sometimes exceeding 150 ft. Sea fans and small brain corals surround the wreck. Visiting the *Minnie Breslaur* requires some previous diving experience. Large surface swells are generally encountered at this location.

☆☆☆☆ **The *Hermes*,** a Disney-like shipwreck, was intentionally sunk in May, 1985, by the Bermuda Diving Association. Much of the work that had gone into her cleaning and final sinking was performed by Ross Menses, a Bermuda dive tour operator. Her sinking was perfect; she sits on the bottom as if she were still steaming along. Her stern is wedged between two large coral mounds at 80 ft, her deck at 50 ft and her mast structure in less than 30 ft of water. Since her sinking, the powerful swells have moved her slightly closer to shore, but this has helped to better secure her position into the reef. Visibility is often exceptional on this site. The *Hermes* is 167 ft long, yet visibility is so good that you might see past the stern while standing on the bow. A surface swell is to be expected here, but generally does not affect underwater conditions. Some scuba experience recommended.

☆☆ **The *Xing Da* Wreck,** a 325-ft freighter, was confiscated off Bermuda by a US Marine patrol in 1996 when they discovered a cargo of illegal immigrants. The immigrants were deported and the ship was given to the Bermuda government for use as an artificial reef. She now lies at depths from 40 to 110 ft. Visibility is excellent. Residents include groupers, lobsters, barracudas and grunts. Expect a stiff surface current. For experienced divers.

☆☆☆ ***L'Herminie*,** a huge French ship carrying 495 crew members, sank on a flat calm day in 1838. En route back to France after seeing action against Maxmillian in Mexico, she ground to a halt on the shallow flats of Bermuda's western ledge. The reef in this area is rather bland, visibility is rarely in excess of 60 to 80 ft, and the water always has a slightly greenish tone, but it is a very exciting dive! Even though this site was thoroughly worked by three of Bermuda's finest wreck hunters, it still boasts over 40 cannon, easily visible atop the sand or reef. There were originally 60 of these huge 12-pounders, but the others lie beneath the sand.

The wreckage is scattered over a vast area, indicative of the immense size of the ship. Her anchor and armory section lie at one end of the sand flat, the anchor standing straight up, flukes spread across the bottom and rising at least 15 ft from the bottom. The armory section has yielded numerous 12- and 32-pound cannon balls, chain shot, bar shot, musket balls, ball molds, canister shot with cotton wadding still intact, numerous copper sheathing nails and many more interesting artifacts. In the middle of the sand flat lie the crossed cannons and two large guns just touching each other. Her windlass, capstan

Snorkeling Bermuda
Courtesy Bermuda Tourism

Wreck of the Benwood, *Key Largo, Florida* © Jon Huber 2000

Bermuda Shipwreck © Bermuda Tourism

Wall Dive, Andros Bahamas
Photo © Small Hope Bay Lodge

Squirrel Fish © Jon Huber 2000

Castle Islands Nature Reserve, Bermuda © Bermuda Tourism

Snorkeling in Exuma
Photo © Jean Michel Cousteau's Out Islands Snorkeling Adventures

African Queen, *Key Largo* © Florida Keys TDC

Marble Grouper © Jon Huber 2000

Dolphin Swim, Marathon, FL © Florida Keys TDC

Sunset Celebration, Key West © Florida Keys TDC

Elkhorn Corals, Bahamas © Bahamas News Bureau

Christ of the Abyss, Key Largo, Florida © Jon Huber

and several other cannon are also visible around the sand flat. Across a low piece of reef lies the galley section and stern, where large square iron boxes thought to be water casks can be found. Also visible are bricks from the oven, many still in the original formation, numerous cannon in neat rows along the reef, piles of cannon balls and bits and pieces of glass fragments, pottery and copper nails and sheathing.

Divers occasionally discover very valuable artifacts from *L'Herminie*. One example is a pair of matching black glass rum bottles, embossed across the bottom "H. Ricketts Bristol," a major bottle-maker of that time. Another amazing find was a clear glass figural bottle in the form of a maiden with a water jug above her head. Still another diver found a perfectly intact pewter mug with handle still in place. Weights for measuring scales, olive oil bottles and embossed labels are found as well. Depths average 30 ft. Good for snorkeling.

☆☆☆ The *North Carolina,* a late 19th-century wreck, sits off the south shore of Southampton. Although broken into two distinct sections, she remains pretty much intact. The bow section is perhaps one of the eeriest pieces of wreckage in the sea. Her bowsprit looms rather menacingly, covered with algae and rustcicles; the sides of her hull hold the riggings for her sail fittings, called dead-eyes due to their resemblance to the death's head – two holes for the eye sockets and a third that represents the mouth. Given the silt and murkiness of the water in that area, the *North Carolina* is a little spooky. The reef here is storm-damaged and not terribly prolific (fish life tends to be a bit mundane), but the *North Carolina* ranks as one of the most photogenic wrecks. Maximum depth 45 ft.

☆☆☆ The *Darlington*, located off the western end of Southampton, sank in the 1870s, running straight into Long Bar, one of the shallowest stretches of reef in Bermuda. This long, shallow flat is now marked by channel stakes and the Chub Head Beacon, which warns ships of the reefs.

The *Darlington* was a sailing steamer. Her huge cylindrical steam boilers lie amidships with the stern pulpit rising to within three ft of the surface, making for an impressive photo in late afternoon. Ironically, right next to the *Darlington* lies an ancient bit of wreckage unknown as to date of origin. She has given up several bronze hull spikes, copper sheathing that is very brittle and almost crumbles upon touch, lots of old wood and numerous copper sheathing nails much smaller than those found on other early 1800s wrecks. Contributor John Buckley found a section of an amphora or pottery jug complete with handle, which has been tentatively dated to the late 1700s in style. But there are no large timbers, cannon or riggings to aid in further definition of this "Ghost Wreck." The *Darlington* lies in no more than 25 ft of water and is often done as a second dive with the *North Carolina* on a two-tank dive trip.

Bermuda

☆☆☆ **Rita Zovetta**, a 360-ft Italian cargo steamship piloted by Captain Fortunato de Gregant, ran aground during a hurricane on February 11, 1924. The ship, en route to Baltimore with a cargo of manganese ore, went down near St. David's Island off Bermuda's east end. The hull rests between 20 and 70 ft. Semi-penetrable, with some nice swim-throughs. Good visibility. Expect some surface swells.

Other notable reef and wreck sites include **The Caves**, **Kevin's Wreck** (probably the **Lord Donegal**, 1822, and featured in a Jacques Cousteau special); **Tarpon Hole**, a coral reef dive near Elbow Beach off the south shore, **The Catacombs** (the reefs behind the *Virginia Merchant* site, 1620, located off Warwick Long Bay on the South Shores), **Smuggler's Notch** and **Champagne Breaker**. These sites are similar in nature, all having a common high reef that starts at the surface and drops down to depths of 45-50 ft. The reef is honeycombed with caves, caverns, tunnels, cuts, canyons, crevices and labyrinths. Divers find 50-ft pinnacles breaking the surface here and huge cathedral arches of coral with innumerable snappers and other reef fish.

☆☆ **The Taunton**, a 228-ft Norwegian cargo steamer, hit Bermuda's northeast reefs during fog on November 24, 1920. Her remains are widely scattered, but her boilers and engine compartment lie intact and upright. The Gibb's Hill Lighthouse Museum displays the ship's bell. The *Taunton* rests in 20-ft depths; her bow comes to within 10 feet of the surface.

☆☆☆ **Blue Holes**. Not to be confused with the real blue holes of the Bahamas or Belize, these are deep sand pockets surrounded by exceptionally shallow reef – in some places as shallow as four ft – which drop straight down into an iridescent teal blue, reaching a maximum depth of nearly 70 ft. The reef here is incredibly lush with sea fans, soft corals and black coral bushes. There are two holes directly adjacent to each other and joined at the bottom by a series of tunnels where one can often find a school of huge tarpon. An occasional enormous (150-200 lb) grouper can also be found on the reefs. There are many of the colorful reef fish that inhabit all of Bermuda's dive sites. Exceptional visibility. The Blue Holes area offers five different dive sites at depths from 30 to 70 ft. When conditions are right, this is a must-see spot for every diver. Terrific snorkeling exists in the shallows.

Additional good sites frequented by the shops are the **Caraquet**, a 200-ft British mail steamer at 40 ft, the **Madiana**, a 160-ft passenger liner that ran aground in 1923, depth 40 ft, and the "**Airplane Wreck**," a B-29 bomber that took off from Bermuda and went down due to a fuel problem, with no injuries to the pilot or crew.

Beach Snorkeling

Snorkeling tours to the offshore wrecks and reefs are offered at every hotel desk. New swimmers and beginning snorkelers should test their skills at sheltered Devonshire Bay, Jobson's Cove or Shelly Bay before heading offshore.

★★ **The Snorkel Park** at The Royal Naval Dockyard (fort) is adjacent to the Maritime Museum, a short walk from the cruise ship dock, ferry and bus stops. It's open daily from 10:30 am to 6 pm.

The park, a protected coral reef preserve, has well-marked reef trails, floating rest stations and a helpful staff, including experienced lifeguards. Depths are shallow and the seas calm. Bottom terrain consists of plate corals and gorgonians. Schools of grunts, doctor fish and parrot fish roam about. Several historic cannons dating back to the 1500s are marked off. Look along the base of the fort for ceramic shards, musket miniballs and insulators dating from the fort's use as a radio station in WWII.

Rental equipment is available on-site, including flotation vests, masks and snorkels. ☎ 444-234-1006, fax 441-292-5193. E-mail: bic@ibl.bm.

★★★ The reef at **Elbow Beach** starts 10 yards from the shoreline, then stretches seaward for a mile. If you are not staying at the Elbow Beach Hotel, be sure to enter the water from the public beach to the west of the resort and swim east toward the restaurant.

★★★ A 300-yard swim from Elbow Beach seaward takes you over the wreck of the **Pollockshields**, a 323-ft German-built steamer. The swim out takes 10 to 15 minutes. A strong surge makes this a bad choice on windy or choppy days. For advanced snorkelers only.

★★★ **Church Bay**, a terrific spot when seas are calm, may be entered anywhere along the beach. Park along the road above the beach and climb down the steep stairway.

★★★ **John Smith's Bay**, on the beautiful south shore, is handicapped-accessible and has a lifeguard from April through October. A 50-yard swim brings you over a shallow reef. Usually calm, with exceptional visibility.

★★ **Tobacco Bay's** grassy terrain shelters soft corals and schools of juvenile fish. A rocky breakwater separating the bay from the ocean keeps this area calm. Depths run from three to 10 ft.

★ **Somerset Long Bay**, on Bermuda's southwest end, appeals to first-time snorkelers with calm, shallow water and a wealth of marine life. Nice spot for a picnic.

The rocks encircling **Devonshire Bay**, on the south shore, harbor an abundance of fish and invertebrates.

Bermuda

☆ On a calm day, **Shelly Bay** on the north shore features easy access and impressive marine life. Avoid this spot on windy days unless you want to go board sailing. The parking lot and surrounding area are accessible to people with disabilities.

Dive Operators of Bermuda

One-tank dives average $50, two-tanks $70, snorkeling $40 with gear. Tanks and weights are included, but additional scuba equipment rental costs extra. Night dives are $60, excluding equipment. Resort courses cost about $100.

Blue Water Divers & Watersports, Bermuda's oldest full-service dive center, now has three shops, located at Somerset Bridge, Marriott's Castle Harbour Hotel and Elbow Beach Hotel. Their fast boats visit all the best wrecks plus the Airplane Wreck and the *Pollockshields*, a shore dive off Elbow Beach that is explored with underwater scooters (DPVs).

For those not certified, they offer beginner/resort instruction and great snorkeling from the dive boat.

Trips depart at 9 am for 16 to 18 scuba divers and 1:30 pm with a mix of 20-22 certified and beginner divers and snorkelers. The shop's three boats are outfitted with a dive platform, ladder, tank racks, oxygen, toilets and showers. Instructors and guides are on all excursions.

The Elbow Beach location offers shore diving and pool instruction. One night dive per week is scheduled. PADI courses, CPR and first aid.

During March, April and May they offer full- and half-day whale watch charters. ☎ 441-234-1034, fax 441-234-3561. E-mail: bwdivers@ibl.bm. Website: www.divebermuda.com. Write to: PO Box SN 165, Southampton, SN BX, Bermuda.

Fantasea Diving & Snorkelling Ltd., a five-star PADI facility, can be reached by a 10-minute ferry, taxi or scooter ride from the city of Hamilton, the cruise ship terminal or from the central hotels.

The shop employs internationally qualified PADI and NAUI instructors. Two custom dive boats carry 18 and 30 divers to the favorite wrecks and reefs. Snorkelers welcome. Large snorkeling groups travel aboard a custom 55-ft catamaran, *Aristocat*. The shop offers whale watching in April, parasailing, sunset and dinner cruises aboard the catamaran, gear and camera rentals, with all levels of instruction. Accommodation-dive packages, ☎ 800-637-4116. Dive and snorkel reservations and information, ☎ 888-DO-A-DIVE or 441-236-6339, fax 441-236-8926. E-mail: info@fantasea.bm. Website: www.fantasea.bm.

Nautilus Diving Ltd. Located at the Southampton Princess Hotel, this PADI five-star IDC Center offers one-tank reef dives in the morning and a shallow wreck dive in the afternoon. The 40-ft *Cracklin Rosie* cruises at 15 knots, has a dive platform with a ladder and carries up to 30 divers. Snorkelers welcome, with gear provided. Resort courses in hotel pool followed by an ocean dive on a shallow reef. Certification courses, referrals and Discover Scuba courses are conducted daily. Referrals. Rental gear, including kayaks, floats, dive and snorkeling equipment. ☎ 441-238-2332 or 295-9485, fax 441-234-5180. E-mail: nautilus@ibl.bm. Website: www.bermuda.bm/nautilus.

Nautilus Diving Ltd. In Hamilton at the Princess Hotel, they carry up to 20 divers to favorite sites off the west, north and east side of the island. Their 40-ft custom dive boat, *Cante Libra*, has a dive platform and ladder. Rental gear. PADI five-star facility, IDC. ☎ 441-295-9485 or 441-238-2332 ext 4371, fax 441-234-5180. E-mail: nautilus@ibl.bm. Website: www.Bermuda.bm/ nautilus.

South Side Scuba, at the Sonesta Beach Hotel, Southampton, offers a resort course in the hotel pool, then a shallow dive on the reefs. Includes all dive gear. Scuba excursions to the south shore reefs. Packages available. Local, ☎ 441-238-1833, fax 441-238-3199. Accommodations, 800-SONESTA. E-mail: sonetab@ibl.bm.

Scuba Look, located at the Grotto Bay Beach Hotel, Hamilton Parish, visits the reefs on the east end and south shores of Bermuda. Snorkelers welcome. Resort course in hotel pool. Open March through November. All equipment provided. Local, ☎ 441-292-1717 or 441-235-1427, fax 441-295-2421. E-mail: scubluk@ibl.com. Website: www.diveguideint.com/p0078.htm.

Snorkeling Tours & Rentals

Snorkeling cruises cost from $25 for a short tour to $50 for a half-day.

Blue Water Divers and Watersports offers a Guided Snorkel Certificate Program for all ages and abilities. They teach mask defogging, clearing and adjustment, removing and replacing the mask on the surface, swimming in waves and surf, surface exit and entry techniques, surface breathing, clearing the snorkel, submerging, exploring, resurfacing and regaining position, use of a snorkel vest, first aid, free dive techniques, use of weight belt, basic knowledge of marine life, fish and coral identifying. ☎ 441-234-1034, fax 234-3561. E-mail: bwdivers@ibl.bm Website: www.divebermuda.com.

Bermuda Barefoot Cruises Ltd. departs Darrell's Wharf, Devonshire for snorkeling and sightseeing aboard the 32-ft *Minnow*. Equipment and instruction provided. Complimentary refreshments on return trip. ☎ 441-236-3498.

MV Bermuda Longtail **Party Boat** operates a 65-ft motor catamaran that carries 200 people. Tours depart Flag Pole, Front St., Hamilton. Snacks and drinks sold on board. ☎ 441-292-0282, fax 441-295-6459.

Bermuda

Bermuda Water Tours offers both glass-bottom and snorkeling cruises aboard the 50-ft, 75-passenger *Bottom Peeper*. Tours depart near the Ferry Terminal, Hamilton. Gear provided. Full bar and changing facilities on board. Refreshments on return trip. Operates from the end of April 1 to November 30. ☎ 441-236-1500, fax 441-292-0801.

Bermuda Water Sports departs St. Georges for half-day snorkel cruises aboard the 100-passenger glass-bottom boat, *Sun Deck Too*. Anchors in waist-high water on an island beach. Guides feed and identify fish and corals. Instruction and equipment provided. Full bar and snack bar on board. May to November. ☎ 441-293-2640 or 441-293-8333 ext. 1938.

Fantasea Diving and Snorkeling, at Darrell's Wharf on the Warwick Ferry Route, takes snorkelers with scuba divers to the favorite wrecks and reefs. ☎ 441-236-6339, fax 441-236-8926, 888-DO-A-DIVE. E-mail: fantasea@ ibl.bm. Website: www.bermuda.com/scuba.

Hayward's Cruises' 54-ft, 35-passenger snorkeling and glass-bottom boat, *Explorer*, departs next to the Ferry Terminal in Hamilton. Bring swim suit and towels. Snorkeling gear provided. Instruction. Changing facilities on board. Cameras available for rent. Complimentary swizzle on return trip. May to November. ☎ 441-292-8652.

Jessie James Cruises aboard the 57 ft, 40-passenger *Rambler* and 48-ft, 75-passenger *Consort* depart Albouy's Point, Hamilton. Pick-ups at Darrell's and Belmont wharves. ☎ 441-236-4804, fax 441-236-9208.

Pitman Boat Tours' snorkeling and glass-bottom boat trip departs Somerset Bridge Hotel dock and cruises five miles northwest to the perimeter reef. Snorkeling instruction on ancient shipwrecks and coral reefs. Gear supplied. Changing facilities on board. No children under five years. ☎ 441-234-0700.

Salt Kettle Boat Rentals Ltd., Salt Kettle, Paget, offers snorkeling cruises to the western barrier reef and shipwrecks. Refreshments. ☎ 441-236-4863 or 441-236-3612, fax 441-236-2427.

Sand Dollar Cruises are aboard the 40-ft, 189-passenger Bristol sloop *Sand Dollar*, departing Marriott's Castle Harbour dock, Hamilton. Gear provided. This boat may be chartered. ☎ 441-236-1967 or 234-8218.

Nautilus Diving Ltd., at the Southampton Princess Hotel, offers morning and afternoon reef and wreck tours. All equipment provided. Snorkeling is from a 40-ft boat to reefs within 10 minutes of shore. Group charters available. ☎ 441-238-2332 or 441-238-8000 ext. 6073.

Tobacco Bay Beach House on Tobacco Bay, St. George's. Snorkeling and underwater cameras for rent. Ideal for beginners. ☎ 441-293-9711.

St. Peter's Church, St. George's.

Other Activities

Helmet Diving is fun for all ages. No lessons needed. Depth 10 to 14 ft. Does not get your hair wet. Available at **Hartley's Helmet**, Flatt's Village Smith's, ☎ 441-292-4434, or **Greg Hartley's Under Sea Adventure**, Village Inn dock, Somerset. ☎ 441-234-2861.

Horseback Riding along scenic beach and shore trails is available year-round. Law requires that all rides be supervised. Both experienced and inexperienced riders are welcome at **Lee Bow Riding Centre**, Tribe Road # 1, Devonshire, ☎ 441-236-4181, or **Spicelands Riding Centre**, Middle Road, Warwick. ☎ 441-238-8212 or 238-8246.

Golf is one of Bermuda's most popular year-round attractions. Golf courses are located at **Belmont Golf Club**, Warwick (☎ 441-236-6400, fax 441-236-0120); **Castle Harbour Golf Club**, Hamilton Parish (☎ 441-298-6959, fax 441-293-1051); **Mid Ocean Club**, Tucker's Town (☎ 441-293-0330, fax 441-293-8837); **Ocean View Golf & Country Club**, Devonshire (☎ 441-295-9093, 295-6500, fax 441-295- 9097); **Port Royal Golf Course**, Southampton (☎ 441-234-0974, 295-6500, fax 441-234-3562); **Southampton Princess Golf Club**, Southampton (☎ 441-239-6952, fax 441-238-8479), **Riddells Bay Golf & Country Club**, Warwick (☎ 441-238-1060, 238-3225, fax 441-238- 8785); and **St. George's Golf Club**, St. George's Parish (☎ 441-297-8353, 295-6500, fax 441-297-2273).

Para-Sailing can be arranged at the **Bermuda Island Parasail Co**, Darrell's Wharf (☎ 232-2871 or 297-1789), **St. George's Parasail**, Somers Wharf (☎ 297-1542), St. George's, or **Skyrider Bermuda** at the Royal Naval Dockyard (☎ 234-3091).

Nature Walks at Spittal Pond, Smith's Parish, take you through a 64-acre reserve and park. The sanctuary is a major habitat for waterfowl and shorebirds and is situated along the rugged coastline bordering the Atlantic Ocean to the south. Here visitors can see Bermuda's only two wild flamingoes.

Sightseeing

Taxis sporting blue flags are driven by qualified tour guides who know all about the island and usually throw in a few local anecdotes for good measure. Particularly interesting visits include **Hamilton**, the island's capital, **Flatts Village** for a tour of the **Government Aquarium, Natural History Museum and Zoo**, with its superb collection of marine life, gaily colored exotic birds and relics of Bermuda's history.

While in Hamilton, don't miss a stop at the **Underwater Exploration Institute** on East Broadway, which features interactive exhibits, including a simulated journey to the bottom of the ocean, films, treasures from the sea, a neat gift shop and restaurant. Open daily from 10 am to 6 pm. ☎ 441-292-7219, fax 441-236-6141.

St. George's, the historic former capital, is another must-see, with the pillory and stocks in King's Square, as is **St. Peter's Church,** with its glistening white facade and Bermuda cedar interior. It is the oldest Anglican church in the Western Hemisphere.

In Southampton, stop in at **Bermuda Triangle Brewing** on Industrial Park Road for a microbrewery tour. Tours start at 4 pm, Monday-Friday from March to October, Saturdays from November to March. ☎ 441-238-2430, fax 441-238-1759.

Several reminders of both American and Bermudian history are found in St. George's, notably the replica of the *Deliverance,* the tiny ship that Sir George Somers and his shipwrecked crew built from natural Bermuda cedar and what could be salvaged from the shipwreck of the *Sea Venture.* Nearby **Fort St. Catherine**, at Bermuda's eastern end, houses dioramas of the colony's history and replicas of the Crown Jewels. The fortification lends itself to exploration. Other notable sites include the **Crystal Caves** or **Leamington Caves,** with their superb stalactite and stalagmite formations and impressive illuminations.

Dolphin Quest at Southampton Princess.

For a more leisurely look at the islands, try a horse-drawn carriage tour (sans wetsuits) through the blossom-lined streets and lanes. Helicopter tours are offered by **Bermuda Helicopters, Ltd.**, Southampton. ☎ 293-4800, 295-1180 or 238-0551.

Shopping

Bermuda shopping offers great savings on imports from Great Britain and Europe. Most large shops are in the City of Hamilton, with branches in St. George's, Somerset, Royal Naval Dockyard and several major hotels.

Local "buys" include island-made sherry peppers, black rum and local liqueurs, rum cakes, jams, jellies, soups and dressings, as well as cookbooks featuring island recipes. Lilies, passion flowers, cedar, allspice, bay laurel and island limes go into locally produced perfumes and fragrances.

Accommodations

All room rates fluctuate and are subject to 7.25% Bermuda Government Hotel Occupancy Tax, service charges and a resort levy. Contact individual properties or dive shops for dive-accommodation packages. Prices below are for summer – the high season on Bermuda. They are per room for a double and do not include taxes or service charges. Rates are subject to change.

Bermuda

Accommodations range from ultra-luxurious resorts to inexpensive house-keeping cottages and charming small hotels. Call ☎ 800-223-6106 (US), 416-923-9600 (Canada) or 071-734-8813 (England) for a list.

Elbow Beach, on the south shore in Paget Parish, has Blue Water Divers on-site. The hotel features an immense pink sand beach, three restaurants, a heated pool, shopping arcade, tennis courts and 50 acres of lush gardens. Guests stay in the main hotel or suites in the out buildings. Rooms have telephone, radio, remote 25-channel TV, safe, robes, slippers, hairdryer and air-conditioning. Rooms are from $385 per night, suites from $485. Rates drop between November and March. ☎ 800-344-3526 or 441-236-3535, fax 441-236-8043. Write to PO Box HM 455, Hamilton, HM BX, Bermuda.

Southampton Princess Hotel features a three-acre lagoon in East Whale Bay that houses several friendly dolphins. The lagoon opens to the sea and has an underwater fence. Marine mammal specialists offer several interactive "Dolphin Quest" programs for children and adults. Southampton guests get priority bookings, but non-guests may sign up on a space-available basis. Packages for the dolphin encounter are available.

The resort sits on one of the highest points in Bermuda, with panoramic views from all 600 rooms. Air-conditioned. Nautilus Diving on premises. Amenities include six restaurants, two pools, private beach and beach club, 18-hole par-three golf course, 11 tennis courts, health club, game room, shops and beauty salon. Room rates per day in summer run from $329 to $629 for a petite suite. ☎ 800-223-1818 (US) or 441-238-3000, 800-268-7176, fax 441-238-8968. Write to PO Box HM 1379, Hamilton HM FX, Bermuda.

The Reefs sits on a cliff overlooking Christian Bay, Southampton. Built around the ruins of a 1680 farmhouse, this luxury resort features 67 rooms and suites plus eight two- and three-bedroom cottages, two bars, three terrific restaurants, two tennis courts and a fitness center. Good snorkeling for all skill levels exists over the patch reefs just off the beach. Dive trips are arranged with Blue Water Divers. MAP Summer rates which include breakfast and lunch or dinner start at $358 for a room (double), $398 for a cottage, $658 for a two-bedroom cottage plus a service charge of $17 per day. The Reefs participates in a carousel dining program with other hotels that gives guests an opportunity to try other restaurants. ☎ 800-742-2008 or 441-238-0222, fax 441-742-8372. E-mail: reefsbda@ibl.bm. Website: www.bermuda.bm. Write: South Road, Southampton SN 02, Bermuda.

Sonesta Beach Hotel & Spa is a modern luxury resort hotel with 25 acres of picturesque grounds. SouthSide Scuba and Snorkelling, Inc. on premises. Summer room rates are from $340 to $440 per night. ☎ 441-238-8122 or 800-SONESTA (US), fax 441-238-8463. Write to PO Box HM 1070, Hamilton HM EX, Bermuda.

Grotto Bay Beach Hotel & Tennis Club sits on 21 acres of beachfront gardens in Hamilton Parish with two underground grottos, deep-water dock, a freshwater pool with swim-up bar, and outdoor hot tub. Bus stop at door. Scuba Look dive shop on premises offers dive and snorkeling tours. A private beach features two small coves in an enclosed bay and a 500,000-year-old cave to explore. Deep-water dock. All rooms have private balconies and panoramic sea views, cable TV, phone, coffeemaker, safe, mini-fridge and hairdryer. Air-conditioned. All-inclusive packages available. Summer room rates start at $205. ☎ 800-582-3190 (US) or 441-293-8333, fax 441-293-2306. E-mail: gro@bspl.bm. Write to: 11 Blue Hole Hill, Hamilton Parish CR 04, Bermuda.

Marriott's Castle Harbour Resort, adjacent to the world-renowned Castle Harbour Golf Club, now features Blue Water Divers & Watersports on their property. This classic Bermuda resort sits on a hilltop amidst 250 manicured acres and touts two private beaches, one being the largest resort beach in Bermuda. Guest rooms overlook the gardens, fairways, pool or Castle Harbour and Harrington Sound, many with balconies or terraces. All have individual climate control, ironing board, iron, hairdryer. The resort is convenient to the airport. Room rates start at $289 per night. ☎ 800-223-6388 or 441-293-2040, fax 441-293-8288.

Dining

Bermuda menus cater to every taste and pocketbook with more than 100 restaurants and fast-food eateries. Prices for two range from $10 at a fast-food restaurant to more than $200 for gourmet cuisine. Traditional dishes of Bermuda are mussel pie, fish chowder laced with black rum and sherry peppers, spiny Bermuda lobster (September to April), Hoppin' John (blackeyed peas and rice) and a Sunday morning breakfast of codfish and potatoes. The island drinks are a Rum Swizzle, a mixture of four colors of rum and fruit juices, and "dark and stormy," an interesting blend of black rum and ginger beer. The small eateries may offer delicacies such as conch stew, fritters or hashed fish. A 15% gratuity charge is added to the bill at most restaurants. Most accept Amex, Visa and MC.

For informal dining in Hamilton Parish, try the **Landfall Restaurant** on North Shore Road. Open Monday from 9 am to 9 pm, seven days a week, this restaurant serves lunch and dinner and offers salads, appetizers and sandwiches starting at $3. Dinner entrées include sweet & sour chicken, filet mignon and barbecued spare ribs. ☎ 293-1322.

Local favorites and fine coffees are found at **Kathy's Kaffee**, on Front Street in Hamilton. Kathy's serves fish chowder, curry chicken, codfish cakes and hamburgers in a café-style atmosphere. From $4. Monday-Friday, 7:30 to 4 am. Saturday, 8:30 to 4 am. ☎ 295-5203.

The Pubs of Hamilton are popular for rehashing the day's dive and enjoying island dinner specialties. Try **The Hog Penny**, Bermuda's oldest English style pub and restaurant at 5 Burnaby Hill, Hamilton, ☎ 292-2524, the **White Horse Tavern**, at 8 King's Square, St. George, ☎ 297-1838, **North Rock Brewing Co.** at 10 South Road, Smiths Parish, ☎ 236-6633, **The Swizzle Inn** on Blue Hole Hill, Bailey's Bay, or **The Frog & Onion** on Freeport Road at the Royal Naval Dockyard for creative entrées. Meals start at $20.

Bouchées Waterfront Bistro on 36 Water St., St. Georges, serves French and Mediterranean cuisine. Open for lunch and dinner. Entrées average $40. ☎ 297-2951.

Pasta Basta at 1 Elliott St., Hamilton (☎ 295-9785) and 14 York St (☎ 297-2927), St. George, offers Italian lunch and dinner specialties from $10. No credit cards.

Tuscany Restaurant, Bermuda House, 95 Front St., Hamilton (☎ 292-4507), **Tio Pepe** at 117 South Road, Southampton (☎ 238-1897) and **La Trattoria** on 22 Washington Lane, Hamilton (☎ 295-1877), feature formal Italian entrées from $25.

Mediterranean and Continental haute cuisine are offered by **The Harbourfront,** 21 Front St. West, Hamilton (☎ 295-4207, closed Sundays), **Ascot's** at the Royal Palms, 24 Rosemont Ave, Pembroke (☎ 295-9644) and the **Waterlot Inn** at the Southampton Princess, Southampton (☎ 239-6967). All from $50.

Most large hotels offer elegant dining as well as nightly entertainment with steel bands, limbo and calypso groups or international stars. There is no gambling in Bermuda.

Be sure to stop for tea at the **Gibbs Hill Lighthouse Tea Room** on Lighthouse Road Southampton (☎ 238-0524).

Facts

Recompression Chamber: Located at King Edward Memorial Hospital, Point Finger Road, Paget. Drs. Charles Schultz and Carol Ferris. ☎ 236-2345 ext 1592.

Getting There. Daily direct flights leave from most US East Coast gateway cities aboard American (☎ 800-433-7300), Continental, USAir, Air Canada, or British Airways.

Island Transportation: There are no rental cars available to visitors. Taxis, pink buses, ferries, bicycles or mopeds offer a variety of transportation methods. Traffic is on the left side of the roads at a speed limit of only 20 mph. Moped drivers must be at least 16 years of age and wear safety helmets.

Documents: Passports are the preferred documents when entering Bermuda. Visitors from the United States are required to have one of the following: a passport, or a birth certificate with a raised seal along with a photo ID. Canadians need either a valid Canadian passport, a Canadian certificate of citizenship, proof of their landed immigrant status or a birth certificate and photo ID.

Currency: Legal tender is the Bermuda dollar, which is equal to $1 US. Travelers' checks and major credit cards accepted in most establishments.

Climate: Bermuda is a semi-tropical island. Rainfall is distributed evenly throughout the year. Average temperature during the period April to November ranges from the mid-70s to mid-80s. Cool months: December-March, 65-70°F.

Clothing: Conservative. Bathing suits, abbreviated tops and short shorts are not acceptable except at beaches and pools. In public, beach wear must be covered. Casual sportswear is acceptable in restaurants at lunch time and in fast-food restaurants any time, but some upscale restaurants require gentlemen to wear a jacket and tie in the evenings.

Electricity: 110 volts, 60 cycles AC throughout the island.

Time: Atlantic Standard (Eastern standard + 1 hr.)

Tax: A 7.25% hotel tax is payable upon checkout. Airport departure tax, $20.

For Additional Information: *US*, Suite 201, 310 Madison Avenue, New York NY 10017. ☎ 800-BERMUDA, 800-223-6106 or 416-923-9600. *United Kingdom,* Bermuda Tourism, BCB Ltd., 1 Battersea Church Road, London SW11 3LY, England. ☎ 071-734-8813. Websites: www.bermudatourism.com or www.bermuda.bm.

Bermuda

The Florida Keys

Once a favorite hunting ground of ruthless pirates like Black Caesar and Blackbeard, the Florida Keys now attract scuba divers and snorkelers from around the world.

A necklace of islands that begin just south of Miami, the Florida Keys are connected by the Overseas Highway's 42 bridges – one seven miles long – over the Atlantic Ocean and Gulf of Mexico. The area is divided into five regions: Key Largo, Islamorada, Marathon, Big Pine Key and Key West. Most dive and snorkeling vacations center around Key Largo, Big Pine Key and Key West.

The entire 125-mile chain, including its shallow water flats, mangrove islets and coral reefs, has been designated the Florida Keys National Marine Sanctuary.

Key Largo, the jumping-off point to the Florida Keys and the area's most popular diving, lies 42 miles south-southwest of Miami. The largest of the island chain, Key Largo's star attraction is **John Pennekamp Coral Reef State Park** – the first underwater preserve in the United States – and the adjacent **Key Largo National Marine Sanctuary**. These two refuges, part of the Keys Marine Sanctuary, feature 55 varieties of delicate corals and almost 500 species of fish.

Islamorada is the centerpiece of the "purple isles." Spanish explorers named the area "morada" (purple) either for the lovely violet sea snail, *janthina janthina*, found on the seashore here, or for the purple bougainvillea flowers in the area.

Known as the Sportfishing Capital of the World, Islamorada features the Keys' largest fleet of offshore charter boats and shallow-water "back country" boats.

Marathon, home to the Seven Mile Bridge, is the heart of the Florida Keys, centrally located between Key Largo and Key West. It features the **Dolphin Research Center**, one of four Keys facilities that provide visitors an opportunity to swim and interact with the playful mammals.

Big Pine Key and the Lower Keys straddle the **Looe Key National Marine Sanctuary**, a terrific shallow-water dive spot also popular for kayak-snorkeling trips.

Just west of Looe Key, the 210-foot island freighter **Adolphus Busch Senior** rests on the sea floor as an artificial reef. Endangered miniature Key deer and a few alligators rove Big Pine's wooded areas.

Key West, the nation's southernmost city, marks the final stop on the Overseas Highway. Situated closer to Havana than Miami, Key West exerts a charm all its own, with quaint, palm-studded streets, century-old gingerbread mansions and a relaxed citizenry of self-styled "Conchs." Offshore lies *Stargazer*, an undersea living work of cosmic art created by sculptor Ann Labriola.

 Key West's legendary treasure hunter Mel Fisher, who died in December 1998, recovered more than $400 million in gold and silver from the ship Nuestra Señora de Atocha, *a 17th-century Spanish galleon that sank 45 miles west of Key West. Fisher, who spent 16 years of his life searching for the booty, established the* **Mel Fisher Maritime Heritage Society Museum,** *where visitors may view, touch and even buy some of the riches of the* Atocha *and the* Santa Margarita.

Plush resorts, mom and pop motels, marinas, restaurants and shopping areas pave the route from Key Largo to Key West.

Diving

Spectacular coral reefs, offshore from Florida's Keys, attract nearly a million sport divers each year. Patches of finger-like spur and groove reefs parallel the islands from Key Biscayne to Key West and are inhabited by over 500 varieties of fish and corals. Shallow depths, ideal for underwater video and still photography, range from just below the surface to an average maximum of 40 feet. All the sites require a 15- to 25-minute boat ride.

Snorkeling trips depart from Pennekamp Park, the Holiday Inn docks in Key Largo and from booths along the main streets in Key West. Many dive boats will carry snorkelers if space permits.

During summer, water temperatures climb to 85°F, making a wetsuit unnecessary. A safe-second regulator is encouraged, but not mandatory. Standard gear – buoyancy compensators, weight belts, weights, mask, knife, snorkel, camera and video equipment – may all be rented at most dive shops. Boaters will find small craft for rent at the marinas.

Weather

Good diving on the Florida Keys shallow reefs (most 45 ft or less) depends on good weather conditions. High winds that churn up surface swells also stir up the sandy bottom. You might plan a dive the morning after a storm and find

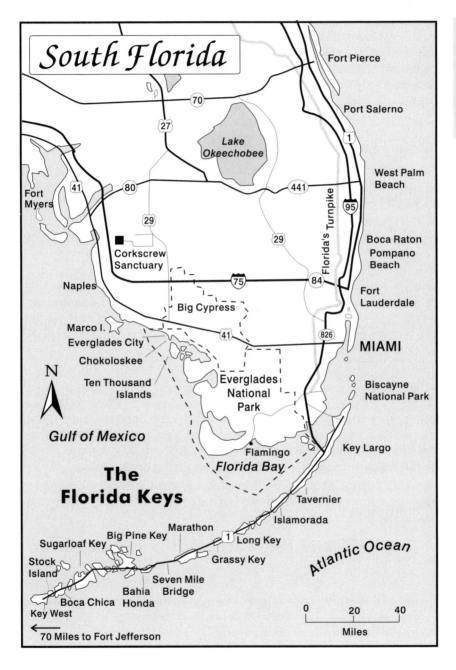

visibility as low as 25 ft, yet return in the afternoon to calm seas and visibility in excess of 100 ft. October through June offer the best weather conditions. Because the reefs are fairly shallow, winds that churn up the seas may cause lowered visibility.

When storms rule out trips to the outer reefs, visit the Content Keys, a sheltered area which is almost always calm, located on the Gulf side of Marathon.

The Florida Keys National Marine Sanctuary

After three freighters grounded on the reefs in 1989, destroying acres of the tiny coral reef organisms, President Bush signed into law a bill designed to protect a 3,000-square-mile stretch of Florida Keys land and sea. The area, known as The Florida Keys National Marine Sanctuary, contains the entire strand of Keys barrier reefs on the Atlantic and Gulf sides of the islands. Freighter traffic close to shore is prohibited, providing a safe "cushion" area between keels and corals.

The sanctuary, managed by the National Oceanographic and Atmospheric Administration, also encompasses, and dwarfs, two previous federal preserves in the Keys, the Looe Key National Marine Sanctuary and the Key Largo National Marine Sanctuary. In contrast to the new 3,500-square-mile sanctuary, the Looe Key Sanctuary is 5.32 square miles and the Key Largo Sanctuary is 100 square miles. Within the sanctuaries, spear fishing, wearing gloves and anchoring on the coral are prohibited.

On the ocean reefs, replenishment reserves are being set up to protect and enhance the spawning, nursery or permanent resident areas of fish and other marine life. Some sections will restrict fishing, will allow diving, but will be "no-take" areas. Prime areas are shallow, heavily used reefs. Check with local dive or bait shops for current information before diving on your own.

Dive shop signs and billboards offering reef trips line the highway throughout Key Largo. Boat trips to the best dive sites takes from 15-30 minutes, depending on sea and wind conditions.

Best Dives of Key Largo & the Upper Keys

☆☆ The park's most popular dive, underwater wedding site and perhaps the one which symbolizes the area is "the statue," a nine-foot bronze replica of **Christ of the Abyss**, created by sculptor Guido Galletti for placement in the Mediterranean Sea. The statue was given to the Underwater Society of America in 1961 by industrialist Egidi Cressi.

The top of the statue is in 10 feet of water and can be seen easily from the surface. The base rests on a sandy bottom, 20 feet down, and is surrounded by huge brain corals and elkhorn formations. Stingrays and barracudas inhabit the site. A buoy marks the statue's location, but small swells make it difficult to

Reef Etiquette

• Do not allow your hands, knees, tank or fins to contact the coral. Just touching coral causes damage to the fragile polyps.

• Spear fishing in the sanctuary is not allowed. This is one reason the fish are so friendly that you can almost reach out and touch them.

• Hand-feeding of fish is discouraged, especially with food unnatural to them. Besides the risk of bodily injury, such activity changes the natural behavior of the fish.

• Hook-and-line fishing is allowed. Applicable size, catch limits and seasons must be observed.

• Spiny lobsters may be captured during the season except in the Core Area of the Looe Key Sanctuary. Number and size regulations must be followed.

• Corals, shells, starfish and other animals cannot be removed from the Sanctuary.

• Regulations prohibiting littering and discharge of any substances except chum are strictly enforced.

• Fines are imposed for running aground or damaging coral. Historical artifacts are protected.

• The red-and-white dive flag must be flown while diving or snorkeling. Boats must go slow enough to leave no wake within 100 yards of a dive flag.

pinpoint. If you are unfamiliar with navigating in the park, join one of the commercial dive trips. Extreme shallows in the area provide outstanding snorkeling areas, but make running aground a threat.

☆☆ More easily found is **Molasses Reef**, marked by a huge, lighted steel tower in the southeast corner of the park. Noted as the area's most popular reef dive, it carries the distinction of having had two shiploads of molasses run aground on its shallows.

The reef provides several dives, depending on where your boat is moored. Moorings M21 through M23 are for diving. M1 through M20 are shallow and better for snorkeling.

High profile coral ridges form the perimeter of a series of coral ridges, grooves, overhangs, ledges and swim-through tunnels. In one area, divers see huge silver tarpon, walls of grunts, snappers, squirrel fish and Spanish

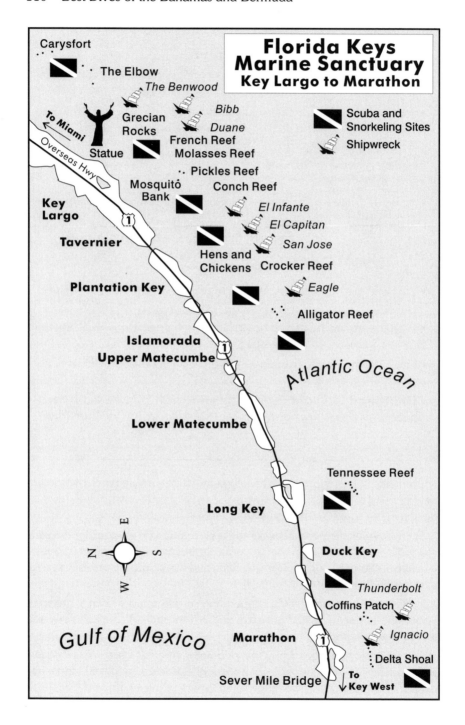

Carysfort

The Elbow

The Benwood

**Florida Keys
Marine Sanctuary
Key Largo to Marathon**

Bibb

Grecian
Rocks

Duane

Scuba and
Snorkeling Sites

Shipwreck

French Reef
Molasses Reef

Statue

Pickles Reef

**Key
Largo**

Mosquito
Bank

Conch Reef

El Infante

El Capitan

Tavernier

San Jose

Hens and
Chickens

Crocker Reef

Plantation Key

Eagle

Alligator Reef

**Islamorada
Upper Matecumbe**

Atlantic Ocean

Lower Matecumbe

Tennessee Reef

Long Key

Duck Key

Thunderbolt

Coffins Patch

Gulf of Mexico

Marathon

Ignacio

Delta Shoal

Sever Mile Bridge

**To
Key West**

hogfish. In another, divers swim over an ancient Spanish anchor. Visibility often exceeds 100 ft.

Be sure to check the current at Molasses before entering the water since an occasional strong flow makes the area undiveable. Depths vary from very shallow to approximately 40 ft.

☆ Slightly northeast of Molasses stands **French Reef**, an area many consider the prettiest in the park, with swim-through tunnels, caves, and ledges carpeted in pink and lavender sea fans, tube sponges, soft corals and anemones. Shallow depths range from the surface down to 45 ft.

☆ North of French Reef lies the wreck of the **Benwood,** a 300-ft freighter hit by a German submarine during World War II and later sunk by the Coast Guard when it became a navigational hazard.

Presently under guard by throngs of sergeant majors, grunts, and yellowtails, the wreck sits on a sandy bottom at 45 ft. Lobsters, huge morays and sting rays peek out from beneath the hull as huge groupers and turtles blast by. During summer, swirls of glass minnows hover over the wreck.

☆☆☆ Despite pristine reefs and a robust fish population, a long boat ride prevents most dive operators from frequenting **Carysfort Reef**, located in the northeast corner of the park.

If you are fortunate enough to catch a trip out to Carysfort Reef, expect a good display of fish and the possibility of one huge resident barracuda, tamed by a local divemaster, swimming up to within an inch of your mask. This unique, engaging plea for a handout makes the toothy guy tough to ignore, but sanctuary officials greatly discourage fish feeding, so try to resist sharing your lunch.

Instead, explore the reef's healthy display of staghorn, elkhorn and star corals at depths varying from very shallow to 65 feet. Normally calm waters make Carysfort a good choice for novice and experienced divers, but beware the dramatic overhangs that top the walls. We discovered some the hard way – by surfacing without first looking up.

☆☆☆ Just south of Carysfort Reef lies **The Elbow**, a crescent-shaped, spur-and-groove reef littered with the twisted remains of two steamers – the *City of Washington* and the *Tonawanda*. Near the wrecks lie ballast and the frail remains of a wooden ship known as the Civil War wreck. Depths average 40 feet. Visibility is usually good, with an occasional strong current. Friendly barracudas and tame moray eels await.

Key Largo's Artificial Reef

In November, 1987, two vintage Coast Guard cutters were sunk off Key Largo by a team of Navy divers. The 1930s-era sister cutters **Bibb** and **Duane**, whose careers took them from the Caribbean and Cape Cod to duties in the North Atlantic, Pacific and Mediterranean, were towed to their final resting site following cleaning and removal of potential hazards for divers.

The *Bibb* sits on her side in 125 ft of water, while the *Duane* sits upright at 130 ft. The top of the *Duane* can be viewed at 75 ft. They rest seven miles offshore and one mile south of Molasses Reef. This area is a buffer zone around the Key Largo National Marine Sanctuary. Both ships have attracted huge groupers, schooling tropicals, barracudas, eels and rays. An occasional hammerhead or nurse shark makes an appearance.

The ships, now camouflaged with a thin layer of coral, were part of a seven-vessel "Secretary" class built by the Coast Guard in the late 1930s, with their original role as long-range rescue ships, according to Dr. Robert Scheina, a Coast Guard historian. "The vessels were also built to prevent poaching by Japanese fishing boats in Alaskan waters. And there was a third purpose – one quite familiar to today's Coast Guard. There was a problem with opium smuggling from the Orient to various outlets on the West Coast of the United States. The vessels were utilized for drug interdiction back then."

*John Pennekamp
State Park,
Key Largo.*

Courtesy Monroe
County Tourism

With spare parts for the *Bibb* and *Duane* difficult to obtain and with excessive maintenance costs, the Coast Guard decommissioned the ships in 1985 and turned them over to the US Maritime Administration for disposal.

The **Speigel Grove**, Key Largo's newest dive site and artificial reef, measures a whopping 510 ft. The wreck of this amphibious boat transport sits at 124 ft, the top at 40 ft.

☆☆ South of Pennekamp Park lies **Pickles Reef**, a shallow area rich with marine life, sea fans and boulder corals. Near Pickles is **Conch Reef**, a wall dive that drops off to more than 100 feet, and the wreck of the **Eagle**, a 287-foot freighter, sunk intentionally to create an artificial reef. Residents include parrot fish, schools of grunts, sergeant majors, moray eels and angels.

☆☆ Another popular site frequented by Islamorada dive shops is **Alligator Reef**, home to walls of grunts, parrot fish and groupers and an occasional nurse shark. There are some nice stands of elkhorn and brain corals.

More spectacular, though, are the reefs surrounding the **Marquesas Islands**, 30 miles from Key West and the Dry Tortugas, 70 miles off Key West.

Key Largo & Upper Keys Dive Operators

The following operators provide guided reef and wreck trips. Prices include tanks and weights, unless otherwise stated (all subject to change). Many offer dive and accommodation packages, though some will not refund unused dives, even if they cancelled the trip. Check with the individual dive shop's cancellation policy before buying a package.

Admiral Dive Center, a full-service PADI shop operating since 1985, offers dive and snorkeling trips to the best sites in Pennekamp and the marine sanctuary. Divers and snorkelers ride on the same boats. Two-tank dives cost $50, snorkeling $30. Nitrox and Nitrox instruction available.

Owners Captains Susan and Bill Gordon also offer three-, five- and seven-night live-aboard dive and fishing trips aboard the 65-ft *Admiral I*, which sleeps 12 (two heads). Destinations include the Keys, Cay Sal Banks and Bahamas. ☎ 800-346-3483 or 305-451-1114, fax 305-451-2731. E-mail: info@admiralcenter.com. Website: www.Admiralcenter.com. Write to them at MM 103.2, Key Largo FL 33037.

American Diving Headquarters, the Keys' oldest dive shop, operates three fast custom dive boats. They visit the best sites in Pennekamp Park and the marine sanctuary. Gear rentals. Snorkelers welcome. ☎ 800-634-8464, fax 305-451-9291. E-mail: amdiving@aol.com. Write to them at MM 105.5, Bayside, Key Largo FL 33037.

Amy Slate's Amoray Dive Center, Inc., at the Amoray Dive Resort, operates a fast dive/snorkel boat to Pennekamp and the marine sanctuary. The resort, bayside, is conveniently located next to a cut from the bay to the ocean that leads to Pennekamp Park. Dive trips cost $54.50, snorkeling $25 without equipment. Accommodation packages. ☎ 800-AMORAY or 305-451-3595, fax 305-453-9516. E-mail: amoraydive@aol.com. Website: www.amoray.com. Write to: 04250 Overseas Hwy, MM 104, Bayside, Key Largo FL 33037.

Aqua Nut Divers, at Kelly's Motel, offers dive and snorkeling tours aboard two 42-ft custom dive boats. Dive trips cost $54.50. Night dives. Nitrox. E-6 processing. Courses. NAUI, PADI, SSI and equipment rentals. ☎ 800-226-0415 or 305-451-1622, fax 305-451-4623. E-mail: kellysmo@aol.com. Website: www.florida-keys.fl.us/kellys.htm.

Captain Slate's Atlantis Dive Center has three 40-ft dive boats with showers, camera tables, new heads and decks. The shop offers dive and snorkeling tours of Pennekamp Park and the marine sanctuary. Dives cost $55 with tanks and weights, $39.50 without. Snorkelers join the trips for $26.50, equipment included. Night dives. E-6 processing. Nitrox. Courses and referrals – CMAS, NASE, NAUI, PADI, SSI, YMCA. ☎ 800-331-3483, fax 305-451-9240.

Captain Slate is pictured on many Keys postcards feeding a barracuda a piece of fish from his mouth.

Caribbean Water Sports at the Sheraton Resort offers a variety of watersports, including scuba and snorkeling trips. Divers pay $40 for a one-tank dive, $60 for two-tanks. Snorkelers pay $30; $25 for children. Stop in at the beach shack behind the Sheraton Resort. ☎ 800-223-6728 or 305-852-4707, fax 305-852-5160.

Conch Republic Divers offers dive and snorkeling trips. ☎ 800-274-3483 or 305-852-1655, fax 305-853-0031. Write to: 90311 Overseas Hwy, Tavernier FL 33070.

Ocean Divers at the Marina Del Mar Resort operates two 48-ft dive boats. Reef trips cost $55 for two tanks. Snorkelers pay $35, with equipment $39. Nitrox. Night dives. E-6 processing. ☎ 800-451-1113, 305-451-1113, fax 305-451-5765. E-mail: info@oceandivers.com. Website: www.oceandivers.com. Write to: 522 Caribbean Drive, Key Largo FL 33037.

Quiescence Diving Services, Inc., on the Bay at MM 103.5, offers personalized service with no more than six divers on a boat. They visit the popular sites and some off-the-beaten-track areas. Trips cost $38, with tanks and weights $55; snorkelers pay $30, $35 with equipment supplied. The shop operates three fast boats, has Nitrox and Nitrox training, underwater photo courses, referrals. PADI, SSI, PDIC, NASDS, and IDA. The shop is next to the cut that leads to Pennekamp. ☎ 305-451-2440, fax 305-451-6440. E-mail: info@keylargodiving.com. Website: keylargodiving.com. Write to them at MM 103.5, Key Largo FL 33037.

Sea Dwellers Dive Center, Inc. operates a custom dive boat from the Holiday Inn docks. They offer resort through dive master courses. Referrals for most agencies. Rates for a two-tank dive are $39.50, with tanks and weights $57.50. Snorkelers pay $25, $33 with equipment supplied. ☎ 800-451-3640 or 305-451-3640, fax 305-451-1935. E-mail: sdwellers@aol.com. Website: www.sea-dwellers.com.

Seafarer Dive Resort runs snorkeling and scuba tours for their resort guests. The PADI shop offers courses and referrals for most agencies. ☎ 800-

*Wreck Dive,
Key Largo.*

Courtesy Florida
Keys Tourism

599-7712 or 305-852-5349, fax 852-2265. E-mail: seafarer@terranova.net.
Website: www.keysdirectory.com/seafarer. Write to: PO Box 185, Key Largo
FL 33037.

Sharky's Dive Center operates both a scuba and snorkeling boat from the
Holiday Inn docks. Stop by their booth to sign up or ☎ 305-451-5533. For
schedules call 800-935-DIVE, fax 451-0124. Write to: 106240 Overseas
Hwy, Key Largo FL 33037.

Sun Divers is an all snorkeling operation. Great for new snorkelers, they offer trips for $24.95 and equipment rentals for $5. Dry snorkels available. Sign
up at the Best Western Resort in Key Largo or ☎ 800-4-KEY FUN, fax 305-
451-1211.

Pennekamp State Park Dive Center operates a 16-passenger dive boat
and three snorkeling boats – the *Sea Garden, El Capitan* and the *Snorkel Ex-*

press. They also offer sail- snorkel cruises aboard the catamaran *Sea Dancer*. Rentals and certifications. ☎ 305-451-1621. For information about the park in general ☎ 305-451-1621 or 305-451-1202.

Islamorada & Lower Key Largo Dive Operators

Bud 'n Mary's Dive Center operates a glass-bottom dive/snorkel boat. Their morning dives are for scuba only and visit 40- to 60-ft reefs, deeper wrecks. Afternoon tours visit shallow areas for scuba, snorkeling and glass-bottom viewing. Scuba trips cost $48.50, sometimes less if more divers are on board. Snorkelers pay $25 without equipment, $35 with. They also offer fishing trips. ☎ 800-344-7352 or 305-664-2211, fax 305-664-5592.

Caribbean Water Sports at Cheeca Lodge, offers scuba, snorkeling and parasailing. Two-tank dive trips with lead and tanks cost $60. Snorkelers join the dive trips for $30; add $6 for equipment. ☎ 888-SEA REEF or 305-664-9547, fax 305-852-5160. E-mail: divecws@aol.com.

Florida Keys Dive Center has two-tank morning and afternoon dives aboard a 36- or 42-ft dive boat. Cost for a reef or wreck tour with weights and tanks is $59. They dive the outer reefs, the *Duane,* the *Bibb* and the *Eagle*. Packages drop the per-trip cost down to $45. Hotel packages with Ocean Pointe Suites. Freshwater showers and refreshments after the dive. Friendly service, night dives, Nitrox training and fills. E-6 processing. Referrals. CMAS, NAUI, PADI, PDIC, SSI, YMCA. ☎ 800-433-8946 or 305-852-4599, fax 305-852-1293. E-mail: scuba@floridakeysdivectr.com. Website: www.floridakeysdivectr.com. Write to: 90500 Overseas Hwy, MM 90.5, Plantation Key FL 33070.

Tavernier Dive Center operates two 42-ft dive boats to the ledges, reefs and wrecks. If you are staying at an affiliated hotel, the tours cost $45, $50 if not. Snorkelers join the dive boat for $30, all equipment supplied. E-mail through their website: www.tavernierdivecenter.com. ☎ 800-787-9797 or 305-852-4007, fax 305-852-0869. Write to the shop at: MM 90.7, Tavernier FL 33070.

Lady Cyana Divers offers ocean reef and wreck tours, all level PADI courses. Referrals for PADI, CMAS, NASDS, CMAS, NAUI, SSI, IANTD, YMCA, NASE. Two fast custom dive boats carry 19 and 28 passengers. Dive trips costs $52 with tanks and weights. Snorkelers pay $25 to join the trips, plus $10 for equipment use. Nitrox. E-6 processing. ☎ 800-433-8946 or 305-852-4599, fax 305-852-1293. E-mail through the website: www.ladycyana.com. Write to PO Box 1157, Mile Marker 85.9, Islamorada FL 33036.

Rainbow Reef Dive Center offers reef and wreck trips, courses and hotel packages. ☎ 800-457-4354 or 305-664-4600. Website: www.rainbowreef-divecenter.com. Write to: 84977 Overseas Hwy, Islamorada FL 33036.

Key Largo & Upper Keys Accommodations

Keys accommodations range from informal housekeeping cottages, simply furnished bayside motels and spacious condo and house rentals to luxurious resort villages, houseboats, and campgrounds, most of which are packed tight with RVs. All accommodations are air-conditioned and most have cable TV and a refrigerator in the room.

Some of the older mom-and-pop motels on the Bay have been updated and offer a certain island charm that is hard to duplicate in the large resorts. A few are badly in need of renovation and may be parking areas for RVs. Send for current brochures.

Rates listed are per room, per night, for winter and spring. Subject to change. For a complete list of home rental agencies, contact the **Key Largo Chamber of Commerce**, 106000 Overseas Hwy, Key Largo FL 33037. ☎ 305-451-1414, US 800-822-1088, fax 305-451-4726.

Amy Slate's Amoray Lodge on Florida Bay offers 16 ultra-clean, attractive, modern one- and two-bedroom apartments with full kitchens. Air-conditioning and ceiling fans. Sundeck. Scuba, snorkel and boat trips leave for Pennekamp Park from the resort dock aboard luxurious catamaran, *Amoray Dive.* Walking distance to several good restaurants. A great choice for Pennekamp divers. Winter suite rates $80 to $235. No pets. ☎ 800-426-6729 or 305-451-3595, fax 305-453-9516.

Best Western Suites, MM 100 oceanside, rents canalside apartments with kitchens and screened patios. Boat docking. Group discounts and dive packages available. No pets. Winter rates from $130. Write them at MM 100, 201 Ocean Drive, Key Largo FL 33037. ☎ 800-462-6079 or 305-451-5081.

Holiday Inn Key Largo Resort, MM 99.7 oceanside, is adjacent to a large marina with a boat ramp and docking for all size craft. The resort features 132 suites, restaurant, gift shop, freshwater pool with waterfall and fast access to diving and recreation facilities. It is also the home of the *African Queen,* used in the 1951 movie starring Humphrey Bogart and Katharine Hepburn. No pets. Winter room rates from $129 to $189. Moderate to deluxe. Write MM 100, 99701 Overseas Hwy, Key Largo FL 33037. ☎ 800-THE-KEYS or 305-451-2121.

Howard Johnson's Resort, MM102.3 Bayside, features modern rooms, swimming in the pool or Bay, sand beach, restaurant, pool, balconies, beach bar, dock, dive and other packages. Cable TV. Refrigerators and microwaves.

Some small pets are allowed. Call first. Winter rates $95 to $245. Group rates available. Write MM 102, PO Box 1024, Key Largo FL 33037. ☎ 800-654-2000 or 305-451-1400.

Manatees are often spotted behind this resort in winter.

Island Bay Resort, Bayside at MM 92.5, features eight rooms with kitchen facilities, boat dock and ramp, sandy beach and cable TV. No pets. $65 to $125. Write PO Box 573, Tavernier FL 33037. ☎ 305-852-4087 or 800-654-KEYS.

Kelly's Motel, MM 104.5, sits in a sheltered cove. Boat dock and ramp. Dive trips. Sandy beach. Cooking facilities. Some pets. Rooms $75 to $150. Write 104220 Overseas Hwy, Key Largo FL 33037. ☎ 305-451-1622 or 800-226-0415.

Kona Kai Resort, at MM 97.8, is a nine-unit motel on the Bay. Cable TV, phones, fishing pier. Boat dock and ramp. No pets. Rooms $141 to $397. Write 97802 Overseas Hwy, Key Largo FL 33037. ☎ 305-852-7200 or 800-365-STAY.

Largo Lodge, at MM 101.5, is a charming Bayside complex offering six apartments – all in a tropical garden setting. Guests must be at least 16 years old. Swimming. Small boat dock. Ramp. No pets. Rooms from $105. Write: 101740 Overseas Hwy, Key Largo FL 33037. ☎ 800-IN-THE-SUN (468-4378) or 305-451-0424.

Marriott Key Largo Bay Beach Resort, MM 103.8 Bayside, features luxury accommodations, pool, sand beach, dive shop, watersports, two fine restaurants and three bars. Packages available. Rooms from $149 to $500. ☎ 800-932-9332 or 305-453-0000, fax 305-453-0093.

Marina Del Mar Bayside, MM 99.5, has 56 comfortable rooms, freshwater pool and dock. Rooms $99 to $159. ☎ 800-242-5229, fax 305-451-9650.

Marina Del Mar, MM 100, oceanside, is a luxury dive resort on a deepwater marina in the heart of Key Largo. There are 130 rooms, suites and villas. Refrigerators in all rooms. The suites have complete kitchens. Rooms overlook the yacht basin or ocean. Dive shop on premises. Fishing charters. Meeting facilities. Waterfront restaurant. Rates $99 to $330. Write: PO Box 1050, Key Largo FL 33037. ☎ 305-451-4107, US 800-451-3483, FL 800-253-3483, Canada 800-638-3483, fax 305-451-1891.

Ocean Pointe, MM 92.5, oceanside, features one- and two-bedroom suites with Jacuzzi tubs and fully equipped kitchens, private balconies, heated swimming pool with whirlpool spa, lighted tennis courts, marina with boat ramp and rental slips, waterfront café and lounge, white sandy beach, watersports equipment. Money-saving packages. No pets. Suites $170 to $210. ☎ 800-882-9464 or 305-3000, fax 305-853-3007.

Popps Motel, on the Bay at MM 95.5, has 10 units with cooking facilities, a small beach, boat dock and ramp. No pets. Rates $79 to $89. Write PO Box 43, Key Largo FL 33037. ☎ 305-852-5201, fax 852-5200. E-mail: popps@ix.netcom.com.

Rock Reef Resort, at MM 98, offers clean, comfortable cottages and apartments on the Bay with one, two, or three bedrooms. Playground, tropical gardens. Boat dock and ramp. Sandy beach. No pets. Rates $88 to $175. Write PO Box 73, Key Largo FL. ☎ 800-477-2343 or 305-852-2401, fax 305-852-5355. E-mail: rockreefr@aol.com. Website: http://florida-keys.fl.us/rockreef.htm.

Stone Ledge Resort, MM 95.3 Bayside, offers 19 conch-style motel rooms, sandy beach, boat dock. Ten of the units have kitchens. Refrigerators in all rooms. TV. No pets. Rooms $68 to $78. Write PO Box 50, Key Largo FL 33037. ☎ 305-852-8114.

Tropic Vista Motel, at MM 90.5, sits on an oceanside canal. Dive shop on premises. Dock. Pets allowed in some rooms. Call first. Rates $53 to $90. Write PO Box 88, Tavernier FL 33070. ☎ 800-537-3253 or 305-852-8799.

Westin Beach Resort Key Largo, MM 97 Bayside, a splendid watersports resort, features 200 luxury rooms, two restaurants, lounge, nature trails, two pools with waterfall, pool bar and a large dock on the Bay. Private beach. Caribbean Watersports at the beach shack. Meeting facilities. No pets. Rooms $179 to $239. Write 97000 Overseas Hwy, Key Largo FL 33037. ☎ 305-852-5553; worldwide 800-539-5274, fax 305-852-3530.

Key Largo RV & Tent Campgrounds

America Outdoors. MM 97.5. Sandy beach, laundry, bath houses. Boat dock, ramp and marina. RV sites. Pets allowed. Write 97450 Overseas Hwy, Key Largo FL 33037. ☎ 305-852-8054, fax 305-853-0509.

Blue Lagoon Resort & Marina, MM 99.6, Bayside, rents and parks RVs. A couple of simple efficiencies for rent also. Parking is tight, but you are in the heart of Key Largo. Boat dock. Swimming. No pets. Write: 99096 US Hwy 1, Key Largo FL 33037. ☎ 305-451-2908.

Calusa Camp Resort. MM 101.5. Bayside RV park. Boat dock, ramp, marina, bait shop, camp store. Rentals. Pets allowed. Write: 325 Calusa, Key Largo FL 33037. ☎ 800-457-2267 or 305-451-0232.

Florida Keys RV Resort, MM 106, oceanside, has cable on all sites, water, electric. Good Sam Park. Pets OK. Near dive shops. ☎ 800-252-6090, fax 451-5996.

Key Largo Kampground. MM 101.5. Oceanfront RV and tent sites, boat dock, ramp, laundry and bath house. Write: PO Box 118-A, Key Largo FL 33037. ☎ 305-451-1431, US 800-KAMP-OUT.

Key Largo Dining

Key Largo is fast-food heaven, with popular chain restaurants everywhere. For all-day diving or fishing excursions there are grocery stores and even gas stations that offer packaged lunches and cold beverages to go. **Miami Subs**, MM 100, Bayside, has subs, and packaged goods to go. ☎ 305-451-3111. **Tower of Pizza**, MM 100, oceanside, delivers fabulous New York-style pizza, sit-down service too. ☎ 305-451-1461. Or try **Domino's Pizza**, Key Largo. ☎ 305-451-4951.

For a unique tropical atmosphere and superb gourmet cuisine, try the **Quay Restaurant**, MM 102.5, Bayside (☎ 305-451-0943). Indoor or garden seating. Moderate to expensive. Adjacent is the **Quay Mesquite Grill**, which serves excellent fried or broiled fish sandwiches. The complex also features a freshwater pool, boat docks, beachside bar and entertainment. Sunset cruises. Romantic, starlight seating and gourmet seafood are also found at **Snooks Bayside Club**, MM 99.9 (behind Largo Honda). ☎ 305-453-3799. Moderate to expensive. Garden patio or indoor dining.

Frank Keys Café offers romantic seating and decent Italian and seafood cuisine. MM 100.2. ☎ 305-453-0310.

The Fish House, oceanside at MM 102.4, serves excellent fresh fish, steaks and chicken for lunch or dinner. It is always packed, with a long waiting list after 6 pm. Moderate prices. Casual. ☎ 305-461-4665.

Ballyhoo's Seafood Grille is set in a 1930s conch house at MM 97.8 on the median strip. Fresh seafood specialties. Open daily. ☎ 305-852-0822.

Or try the **Cracked Conch**, MM 105, oceanside (☎ 305-451-0732) for conch fritters and fried alligator, 90 different beers and honey biscuits. Inexpensive to moderate. ☎ 305-451-0732.

Rick & Debbie's Tugboat, oceanside at Seagate Blvd and Ocean Drive off MM 100, is a locals' favorite. Specials are fried or broiled fish. Inexpensive to moderate. Opens 11 am weekdays, weekends at 7 am. ☎ 305-453-9010.

Holiday Casino Cruises, MM 100, depart the Holiday Inn docks. Features casino gambling in international waters. Complimentary hors d'oeuvres. Open bar, plus sandwiches and burgers available. Sunday brunch with fine catered food. Overnight packages. Sign up in the Holiday Inn lobby. ☎ 305-451-0000.

The Italian Fisherman offers dining on a waterfront terrace. Mile Marker 104, Bayside, Key Largo. 11 am-10 pm. ☎ 305-451-4471.

The Marlin Restaurant, MM 102.7, is the favorite après-dive, story-swapping eatery. Open daily. ☎ 305-451-9555.

Señor Frijoles, MM 103.9, Bayside, offers sizzling fajitas, seafood nachos, Mexican pizza, Cancun chili fish, enchiladas and chicken specials. ☎ 305-451-1592.

Sundowners on the Bay at MM 104 specializes in seafood, chicken, steaks and pasta. Daily 11 am-10 pm. ☎ 305-451-4502.

Early breakfasts are served at **Howard Johnson**, MM 102.5, ☎ 451-2032; **Harriets**, MM 95.7, ☎ 305-852-8689; **Holiday Inn**, MM 100; **Gilberts**, MM 107.9, ☎ 305-451-1133; and **Ganim's Kountry Kitchen**, MM 102, ☎ 305-451-3337 and MM 99.6 across from Holiday Inn. Turn off Hwy 1 northbound at MM 103.5, onto Transylvania Ave, then head toward the ocean to find the **Hideout**, a local favorite for breakfast and lunch.

Islamorada Accommodations
Plantation Key to Long Key

For a complete list of home rental agencies, contact the **Islamorada Chamber of Commerce**, PO Box 915, Islamorada FL 33036. ☎ 305-664-4503 or 1-800-FABKEYS.

Bud & Mary's Fishing Marina, MM 79.8, oceanside, consists of six motel units. Charter boats, backcountry guides, rental boats, dive boat and party fishing. No pets. Rooms $75. ☎ 800-742-7945 or 305-664-2461, fax 305-664-2461. E-mail: Budnmary@budge.net.

Breezy Palms Resort, MM 80, on the ocean, offers one- , two- and three-room villas, beach cottages or studio efficiencies. All with well-equipped kitchens and attractive furnishings. Maid service. Large swimming beach. Fresh water pool, boat harbor and ramp with a light dock for night fishing. No pets. Write PO Box 767, Islamorada FL 33036. Rates $75 to $210. ☎ 305-664-2361, fax 305-664-2572. E-mail: breezypalms@msn.com. Website: www.breezypalms.com.

Caloosa Cove Resort, MM 73.8, has 30 deluxe oceanfront condos, one- or two-bedroom, with modern kitchens. Pool, lounge, restaurant, tennis, boat rentals, free breakfast and activities. Full-service marina with dockage. No pets. Rooms $125 to $175. Write 73801 US Hwy 1, Islamorada FL 33036. ☎ 888-297-3208 or 305-664-8811, fax 305-664-8856.

Cheeca Lodge offers pampered seclusion, oceanside, at MM 82. Well described as being in "its own neighborhood," the resort offers guests a wealth of activities, including dive and snorkeling trips, a nine-hole golf course, sailing, fishing, tennis, parasailing, windsurfing – complete with a staff of expert instructors, captains or pros. Features include oversized guestrooms and villas, most with private balconies and paddle fans, a children's recreational camp, shops, gourmet dining, entertainment, palm-lined swimming/snorkeling beach, pool, 525-foot lighted fishing pier. Dockage and marina. Conference center. On-site dive shop. No pets. $240 to $1,100. Deluxe. Write: PO Box 527, Islamorada, FL 33036. ☎ 305-664-4651 or 800-327-2888, fax 305-664-2893. E-mail: Cheecalodge@aol.com.

Chesapeake of Whale Harbor, adjacent to the Whale Harbor Restaurant and Islamorada docks, sprawls across six oceanfront acres at MM 83.5. The modern resort offers motel or efficiency units, a sand beach and deep water lagoon. Walk to fishing charter boat docks. No pets. Write: PO Box 909, Islamorada FL 33036. Rates: $130-$520. ☎ 800-338-3395 or 305-664-4662, fax 305-664-8595. Website: http://florida-keys.fl.us/chesapea.html.

El Capitan Resort, MM 84, has efficiencies for two to six people in the Holiday Isle complex. Oceanside lagoon and beach. Boat dockage. No pets. Rates $120 to $240. Write MM 84, Islamorada FL 33036. ☎ 305-664-2321, US 800-327-7070, fax 305-664-2703.

Holiday Isle Resort encompasses an entire beach club community, with every imaginable watersport and activity. Guests choose from rooms, efficiencies or suites. The beach vibrates with reggae music. Vendors offer parasailing, fishing and diving charters, sailing, windsurfing, jetskiing, inflatable-island rentals, sun lounges and dancing. Fast food stands serving barbecued dishes, pizza, ice cream, drinks and more are scattered about the grounds. There is a lovely rooftop restaurant and a unique place in the parking lot where you cook it yourself on slabs of granite. Rooms are luxurious. The beach is open to everyone and is packed early during the high season. No pets. Rates $85 to $425. Write 84001 US Hwy 1, Islamorada FL 33036. ☎ 305-664-2321, US 800-327-7070, fax 305-664-2703.

Harbor Lights Motel, oceanfront, MM 85, is part of the Holiday Isle beach complex, offering efficiencies, rooms and cottages. Write 84001 US Hwy 1, Islamorada FL 33036. Rates $65 to $110. ☎ 800-327-7070 or 305-664-3611, fax 305-664-2703. Website: www.theisle.com.

Howard Johnson Resort, oceanside at MM 84.5 adjacent to Holiday Isle, features a soft sand beach. Guests wander back and forth to Holiday Isle beach. Boat dock and ramp. Restaurant. No pets. Write 84001 US Hwy 1, Islamorada FL 33036. Rooms $135 to $165. ☎ US 800-6327-7070 or 305-664-2711, fax 305-664-2703. Moderate to deluxe.

La Jolla Motel, MM 82.3, Bayside, has a quiet, tropical garden atmosphere. Kitchen units are comfortable. Boat dock and ramp. Small swimming beach, grills. Rooms $59 to $125. Write Box 51, Islamorada FL 33036. ☎ 305-664-9213. Inexpensive to moderate.

Lime Tree Bay Resort, at MM 68.5, is an older motel, but comfortable, with beautiful grounds and terrific sunset views. Kitchen units available. There is a restaurant, tennis court, boat dock and beach as well as a freshwater pool. No pets. Rates $95 to $225. Write: PO Box 839, Long Key FL 33001. ☎ 305-664-4740 or 800-723-4519. Inexpensive to moderate.

Plantation Yacht Harbor Resort, MM 87, Bayside, features tennis courts, private beach, jet skis and a huge marina with protected docking for large and small craft. A dive shop and lovely restaurant overlook the bay. No pets. Write: 87000 US Hwy 1, Plantation Key, Islamorada FL 33036. Rooms $78 to $135. ☎ 800-356-3215 or 305-852-2381, fax 853-5357. E-mail: fun@ pyh.com. Website: www.pyh.com.

Ragged Edge, MM86.5, oceanside, has one- and two-bedroom air-conditioned suites and motel rooms, color TV, laundry room, guest boat harbor, marina dockage, ramps, deep water channel, fishing pier. Nice. Rates $69 to $169. ☎ 305-852-5389.

Islamorada Campgrounds

Fiesta Key KOA, MM70, Bayside, sits on a 28-acre tropical island surrounded by warm gulf waters. 350 sites. Marina, docks and ramp. ☎ 305-664-4922.

Long Key State Recreation Area, MM66, Bayside, features two nature trails, bike and canoe rental, picnic area, observation tower, guided walks. No pets. ☎ 305-664-4815.

Islamorada Dining

Islamorada's grills sizzle with fresh seafood and the most unusual dining experiences in the Keys. You'll find the hot spot for fast food on the shores of **Holiday Isle**, MM 84, oceanside. Food stands line this sprawling beach complex with barbecued everything. Ice cream and pretzel vendors crowd in alongside the Keys' most dazzling display of string bikinis. Or take the elevator to the sixth-floor restaurant for a quieter view of the sea. Prices rise with the elevation.

Rip's Island Ribs 'N Chicken, within the same complex, features do-it-your-way meals. Diners prepare their entrées on thick granite slabs that are heated to 600° and brought to your table. Your waitress supplies hot garlic bread, fresh, ready-to-cook vegetables and a choice of sirloin, chicken, shrimp or a combination. Just toss a little salt on your rock and give your food a turn or two until it looks right. A choice of sauces adds the finishing touch. It's *easy*. Or try the ribs. They're served already cooked. Expect a long waiting line on weekends, especially in season. ☎ 305-664-5300.

Enjoy sunset views and fresh seafood at **The Lorelei Restaurant**, MM 82, Bayside. Sunday-Thursday, 5-10 pm. The outdoor Cabana Bar features burgers, fish sandwiches, breakfasts, lunches, dinners and a raw bar. 7 am-12 pm. Entertainment on weekends. Drive or boat to it. ☎ 305-664-4656.

Marker 88 offers exotic fish and steak entrées in a romantic setting. Choose from expertly prepared Scampi Mozambique, Snapper Rangoon, Lobster Marco Polo and a host of other gourmet creations. Closed Mondays. Reservations a must (☎ 305-852-9315). MM 88, Plantation Key. Moderate to expensive

Whale Harbor Restaurant features an all-you-can-eat seafood buffet nightly. Huge selection. Lovely setting in the old Islamorada lighthouse, adjacent to the Islamorada docks at MM 83.5. Moderate. ☎ 305-664-4959.

Try a hand-tossed pizza or pasta at **Woody's**, MM 82. Family dining in the early evening. Late-night food with adult entertainment every night but Monday. Inexpensive. ☎ 305-664-4335.

Cheeca Lodge offers casual dining at the **Ocean Terrace Grill**, MM 81.5. Moderate to expensive. ☎ 305-664-4651.

The Coral Grill, MM 83.5, Bayside, features a nightly buffet. Great strawberry daiquiris! Sunday, noon-9 pm; weekdays, 4:30-10 pm. ☎ 305-664-4803.

The Green Turtle Inn, MM 81.5, has an old time Keys atmosphere and excellent cuisine. Wood-paneled walls are covered with celebrity photos. Leave room for their rum pie. Gets crowded after 6 pm. Open 5 pm-10 pm. Closed Mondays. ☎ 305-664-9031.

Plantation Yacht Harbor, MM87. Live bands. Lobster, stone crab, oysters and clams. Sunday brunch with omelette and waffle bar. Daily 11am-9 pm. ☎ 305-852-2381.

Squid Row, MM 81.9, oceanside, offers excellent fish dishes and fine service. Open for lunch or dinner. ☎ 305-664-9865.

For a quick meal try a pita sandwich at the **Ice Cream Stoppe**, MM 80.5. ☎ 305-664-5026.

Best Dives of the Middle Keys

Dive sites in the Middle Keys – from Long Key Bridge Key to the Seven Mile Bridge – are similar to, but often less crowded than those in Key Largo and the Upper Keys. Besides the offshore reefs and wrecks, the Marathon area has a number of sunken vessels around the new and old bridges, which serve as artificial reefs for fishing. When currents are mild you can dive a few of these spots which abound with fish, sponges and soft corals.

☆☆ **Sombrero Reef**, Marathon's most popular ocean dive and snorkeling spot, offers good visibility and a wide depth range, from the shallows to 40 feet. Cracks and crevices shot through the coral canyons that comprise the reef overflow with lobster, arrow crabs, octopi, anemones, and resident fish. A huge light tower marks the area. Boaters must tie up to the mooring buoys on the reef.

☆ Slightly north of Sombrero lies the wreck of the *Thunderbolt*, an intentionally scuttled, 188-ft freighter lying upright in 110 feet of water with the top of its wheelhouse at 70 ft. Resident fish include big barracudas, swarms of sergeant majors, queen and grey angelfish, blue tangs and moray eels.

☆ **Coffins Patch**, just north of the *Thunderbolt,* provides good snorkeling areas with mounds of pillar, elkhorn, and brain corals at depths averaging 20 to 30 ft.

Marathon & the Middle Keys Dive Operators

Abyss Pro Dive Center, behind the Holiday Inn at MM 54, oceanside, offers reef and wreck trips to popular sites aboard their 34-ft dive boat. Snorkelers may join the trip if it is to a shallow site. Divers pay $54 for a trip, including tanks and weights. Snorkelers pay $35, equipment included. ☎ 800-457-0134 or 305-743-2126, fax 305-743-7081. E-mail: info@abyssdive.com. Website: www.abyssdive.com. Write to: 13175 Overseas Hwy, Marathon FL 33050.

Captain Hook's Dive Center operates a slick 30-ft dive boat and 26-ft catamaran. They offer all level PADI instruction and certification for all agencies. Two-tank dive trips with tanks and weights cost $49. Snorkelers pay $35 with equipment. Friendly service. ☎ 305-743-2444, fax 305-289-1374. E-mail: cpthooks@bellsouth.net. Website: www.thefloridakeys.com/captainhooks. Write to: 11833 Overseas Hwy, Marathon FL 33050.

Hall's Dive Center and Career Institute offers all level of instruction, trips and referral checkouts. ☎ 800-331-4255 or 305-743-5929, fax 305-743-8168. E-mail: hallsdive@aol.com. Website: www.hallsdiving.com. Write to 1994 Overseas Hwy, Marathon FL 33050.

Hurricane Aqua Center (dba Discount Divers) & Two Conchs Dive & Charters at MM 48. This PADI shop offers courses, referral checkouts and trips. A two-tank dive with tanks and weights costs $59. Snorkelers join for $43, equipment included. Maximum six divers aboard their 26-ft boat. ☎ 305-743-2400, fax 305-743-2221. Write to: 10800 Overseas Hwy, Marathon FL 33050.

Middle Keys Scuba Center visits all sites from Sombrero Reef to Duck Key. Divers and snorkelers mix aboard their 30-ft custom dive boat. NAUI and PADI certification courses and check-out dives for all agencies. Photo and video rental equipment and courses. Divers pay $50 for a two-tank dive, including tanks and weights. Snorkelers pay $35. ☎ 305-743-2902. Friendly service. E-mail: rdoileau.aol.com. Website: www.divingdiscovery.com. Write to: 11511 Overseas Hwy, Marathon FL 33050.

The Diving Site is the only DOT hydrostatic facility in the area. This PADI shop offers resort courses through divemaster courses, PADI referrals, dive and snorkeling trips. They operate a 40-ft custom dive boat that carries up to 24 divers and a 25 ft boat that carries four divers. Nitrox courses and fills. Morning dives are to the deeper reefs and the wreck of the *Thunderbolt*. After-noon trips are to the shallow reefs. Two-tank dives with tanks and weights cost $52.50; snorkeling trips cost $32 with equipment. Write to: 12399 Overseas Hwy, Marathon FL 33050.

Marathon Accommodations

Rates listed are for winter and spring, per night, per room or suite.

For a complete list of rental units, condos and villas, contact the **Greater Marathon Chamber of Commerce**, 12222 Overseas Hwy, Marathon FL 33050. ☎ 305-743-5417 or 800-842-9580.

Buccaneer Resort, MM 48.5, Bayside, has 76 units, beach, café, tennis, boat dock and charters. Dive shop on premises. Some kitchen units. Water-front restaurant and tiki bar, sandy beach, fishing docks, wave runners. Write 2600 Overseas Hwy, Marathon FL 33050. Rooms $59 to $249. ☎ US 800-237-3329 or 305-743-9071. E-mail: buccaneer@floridakey.com. Website: www.florida.com.

Conch Key Cottages, MM 62.3, oceanside, are situated on a secluded, private island that until recently could be reached only by boat. New owners have built a landfill roadway so you can drive the short distance from US 1. Rustic, 50s-style wooden cottages have screened-in porches and huge ceiling fans. Pool. All air-conditioned with cable TV, hammock and barbecue. Coin washers and dryers on premises. Boat dock and ramp. Rates $100 to $249. Call first. Write Box 424, Marathon FL 33050. ☎ 800-330-1877 or 305-289-1377, fax 305-743-8207.

Holiday Inn of Marathon, MM 54, oceanside, has 134 rooms, restaurant, and bar. Abyss Dives shop is on property. Boat ramp and marina. No beach. Pets OK. Write 13201 US Hwy 1, Marathon FL 33050. Rates $139 to $200. ☎ 305-289-0222. For dive/hotel packages, ☎ 800-457-0134.

Faro Blanco Marine Resort, MM 48, spreads over two shores with the most diverse selection of facilities on the Atlantic and the Gulf. Choose from houseboat suites, condos, garden cottages, or an apartment in the Faro Blanco lighthouse for a special treat. There is a full-service marina if you are arriving by yacht and wish to tie up for a stay. Dockmaster stands by on VHF Channel 16. Convenient to fine restaurants and diving. Pets allowed in the houseboats and cottages, but not the condos. Children under 18 not allowed in the condos. Good for boaters. Rates $89 to $233. Write: 1996 US Hwy 1, Marathon FL 33050. ☎ 800-759-3276.

Hawks Cay Resort and Marina offers 177 spacious rooms and suites. Heated pool, saltwater lagoon with sandy beach, 18-hole golf course nearby, marine-mammal training center featuring dolphin shows for guests. Charter fishing and diving boats leave from the marina. Protected boat slips for large and small craft. Rooms $220 to $450. No pets. Write: MM 61, Duck Key FL 33050. ☎ 305-743-7000 FL 800-432-2242, fax 305-743-5215.

Howard Johnsons Resort, MM 51, oceanside, has a private beach, dive shop, dock and marina, restaurant. Good boardsailing off the beach. Pets OK. Write: 13351 US Hwy 1, Marathon FL 33050. Rooms $125 to $375. ☎ 800-321-3496 or 305-743-8550, fax 305-743-8832.

Kingsail Resort Motel, MM 50. Bayside accommodations range from modern, attractive rooms to well-equipped efficiencies and one-bedroom apartments. There is a boat ramp, dock, grocer, pool, shaded tiki. No pets. Fishing and diving charters. Rates $75 to $125. Write: PO Box 986, Marathon FL 33050. ☎ 305-743-5246 FL 800-423-7474, fax 305-743-8896.

Ocean Beach Club MM 53.5, oceanside, features 38 guest rooms, sandy white beach, hot tub and fishing pier. No pets. Rooms $100 to $170. ☎ 305-289-0525 or 800-321-7213, fax 305-289-9703. Write: PO Box 510009 KCB, Marathon FL 33050.

Rainbow Bend Fishing Resort, oceanside at MM 58, offers free use of a motorboat or sailboat with every room plus complimentary breakfast daily. There is a wide sandy beach, pool, fishing pier, tackle shop. Dive and fishing charters. Rooms and efficiencies $135 to $225. Café. Pets OK. Write: PO Box 2447, Grassy Key FL 33050. ☎ 800-929-1505 or 305-289-1505, fax 305-743-0257. E-mail: Rainbowbend@fla-keys.com. Website: fla-keys.com/marathon/accom/rainbowbend.htm.

The **Seahorse Motel**, at MM 51, bayside, offers protected dock space, a playground, pool, barbecue patio, quiet rooms and efficiencies. Write: 7196 US Hwy 1, Marathon FL 33050. $59 to $85. ☎ 305-743-6571 or 800-874-1115, fax 305-743-0775.

Additional and varied Marathon accommodations are offered through **AA Accommodation Center, Inc.**, ☎ 800-732-2006 or 305-296-7707.

Middle Keys Dining
Long Key
Little Italy Restaurant at MM 68.5 serves early breakfasts, lunch and dinner. Italian specialties, fresh seafood and steaks in a cozy atmosphere. Open 6:30 am-2 pm, 5 pm-10 pm. Low to moderate. ☎ 305-664-4472.

Duck Key
Hawk's Cay Resort and Marina, MM61, features the **Cantina** for poolside lunch and dinners, **Porto Cayo** for elegant dining Tuesday-Sunday 6 pm-10 pm, **The Palm Terrace** for buffet style breakfast 7 am-10:30 am and **WaterEdge** for dinner 5:30-10 pm. ☎ 305-743-7000.

Marathon
Marathon is a heavily populated residential community with a wide choice of restaurants.

Key Colony Inn, MM 54 at Key Colony Beach, features well-prepared seafood specialties. ☎ 305-743-0100.

Enjoy indoor or outdoor patio dining at the **Quay** of Marathon, MM 54. Lunch and dinner. ☎ 305-289-1810.

Fast take-out food at low prices is featured at **Porky's Too** on the Marathon side of the Seven Mile Bridge. ☎ 305-289-2065.

Enjoy natural foods, vegetarian delights or grilled seafood on the porch of a charming 1935 stone house at **Mangrove Mama's**, MM 20. Open for lunch and dinner. Full take-out menu too. Moderate. ☎ 305-745-3030.

Best Dives of the Lower Keys & Key West
Dive trips from the Lower Keys – Big Pine Key, Sugar Loaf Key, Summerland Key, Ramrod Key, Cudjoe Key and Torch Key – take off to reefs surrounding **American Shoal** and **Looe Key National Marine Sanctuary**.

☆☆ The **Looe Key** reef tract, named for the *HMS Looe*, a British frigate that ran aground on the shallow reefs in 1744, offers vibrant elkhorn and staghorn coral thickets, an abundance of sponges, soft corals and fish. Constant residents include Cuban hogfish, queen parrot fish, huge barracuda, and long snout butterfly fish. A favorite dive site of the Lower Keys, Looe Key bottoms out at 35 feet. Extreme shallow patches of sea grass and coral rubble provide a calm habitat for juvenile fish and invertebrates.

☆☆ Diving off Key West includes offshore wreck dives and tours of **Cotrell Key, Sand Key** and the **Western Dry Marks**. Huge pelagic fish and graceful rays lure divers to this area.

✰✰✰ **Stargazer**, the world's largest underwater sculptured reef, sits five miles off Key West between Sand Key and Rock Key. This magnificent steel wonder, completed in 1992 by artist Ann Labriola, is 200 feet long, 70 feet wide and stands 10 feet high in 25 ft of water. Each of its 10 sections are perforated in the pattern of different star constellations, once used to navigate the seas. Divers and snorkelers become a living part of this mystical artificial reef as they locate the positions of the constellations in its surface. Corals are beginning to grow on the structure, which shelters a small community of reef fish. Good for diving and snorkeling, with depths from the surface to 25 ft.

✰✰ **Sand Key**, marked by a lighthouse, lures snorkelers and novice divers to explore its fields of staghorn coral. Depths range from the surface to 45 ft.

✰✰✰ **Cosgrove Reef**, noted for its big heads of boulder and brain coral, attracts a number of large fish and rays.

✰✰ Advanced divers may want to tour the *Cayman Salvage Master*, at 90 feet. This 180-ft vessel was purposely sunk to form an artificial reef.

✰ **Joe's Tug** sits upright in 65 ft of water, a scenic backdrop for schools of jacks, barracudas and grunts.

✰✰ Seldom visited, though pristine for diving, are the **Marquesa Islands**, 30 miles off Key West. Extreme shallows both en route and surrounding the islands make the boat trip difficult in all but the calmest seas, and docking is impossible for all but shallow draft cats and trimarans. Check with **Lost Reef Adventures** (☎ 305-296-9737) for trip availability.

Fort Jefferson National Monument

Almost 70 miles west of Key West lie the Dry Tortugas, a cluster of seven islands that make up Fort Jefferson National Monument. Visitors enjoy good fishing, snorkeling and touring the ruins of the historic fort. Famous for bird and marine life, as well as for its legends of pirates and sunken gold, the central feature is Fort Jefferson itself, largest of the 19th-century American coastal forts. High-speed ferries and seaplanes offer snorkeling excursions to the fort.

Big Pine & Lower Keys Dive Operators
The Lower Keys

Because all the reefs in the Looe Key Marine Sanctuary are shallow, dive shops group divers and snorkelers together on the same boats. Trips to the deep wrecks are reserved for scuba divers.

Looe Key Dive Center, at the Looe Key Reef Resort (MM 27.5), takes divers and snorkelers to the best reef and wreck sites in the Looe Key Marine Sanctuary, including the wreck of the *Adolphus Busch Sr.,* aboard a fast 49-ft catamaran. A two-tank dive with tanks and weights costs $60. Snorkelers pay $25 to join the trip; add $7 for equipment. Certification courses. ☎ 800-942-5397 or 305-872-2215, fax 305-872-3786. E-mail: looekeydiv@aol.com. Website: diveflakeys.com. Write to: PO Box 509, MM 27.5, Ramrod Key FL 33042.

Underseas Inc., a PADI five-star center, features reef and wreck tours for divers and snorkelers to Looe Key Marine Sanctuary aboard their 50-ft catamaran or 35-ft custom dive boat. They also offer wreck dives, night dives, Nitrox and training. Still camera rentals. A two-tank dive costs $50 with weights and tanks. Snorkelers pay $25 . Universal referrals. ☎ 800-446-5663 or 305-872-2700, fax 305-872-0080. E-mail: diveuseas@aol.com.

Key West

Dive Key West, Inc. offers a large retail shop, two fast dive boats, one 36-ft, one 26 ft, that carry six to 12 divers. Snorkelers join the dive boats for reef dives. The shop visits Western Sambo, Marker I, Joe's Tug and the *Cayman* wreck. NAUI, NASDS, PADI and YMCA referrals. Two-tank dive costs $59 with weights and tanks. C-courses. ☎ 800-426-0707 or 305-296- 3823, 305-296-0607. Website: www.divekeywest.com. Write to: 3128 North Roosevelt Blvd, Key West FL 33040.

Lost Reef Adventures, Inc. takes divers and snorkelers aboard their 40-ft custom dive boat . The shop visits the Sambos, Dry Rocks, Sand Key and the wrecks. PADI and NAUI instruction. Universal referrals. A two-tank dive costs $56. Snorkelers pay $30 for the trip and equipment. ☎ 800-952-2749 or 305-296-9737, fax 305-296-6660. E-mail: lostreefkw@aol.com. Website: www.paradise.com. Write to: 261 Margaret St., Key West FL 33040.

Subtropic Dive Center, at Garrison Bight, has PADI and SSI training, Nitrox training and service, universal referrals. They operate three boats, a 42-ft BurPee, a 28-ft dive boat, and a 48-ft catamaran used for snorkeling trips. Two-tank trips cost $55, snorkelers pay $30 with full gear included. ☎ 888-461-3483, fax 305-296-9918. E-mail: info@subtropic.com. Website: www.subtropic.com. Write to: 1605 North Roosevelt Blvd., Key West FL 33040.

Southpoint Divers offers tours and courses. ☎ 800-891-DIVE, 305-296-6888. Write to: 714 Duval St., Key West FL 33040.

Lower Keys Accommodations

Big Pine Key

Big Pine is centered between Marathon and Key West. A 20-minute drive will get you to either. For a complete list of Lower Keys accommodations call, write or visit: **Lower Keys Chamber of Commerce**, PO Box 430511, Big Pine Key, FL 33043. ☎ 800-872-3722 or 305-872-2411.

Big Pine Resort Motel, located at MM 30.5, Bayside, is close to Looe Key Marine Sanctuary. The motel has 32 rooms, efficiencies and apartments. Parking for trailers, trucks and buses. Adjacent restaurant. No pets. Rates $59 to $69. Gay-friendly. Write to: Rt 5, Box 796, Big Pine Key FL 33043. ☎ 800-801-8394 or 305-872-9090, fax 305-872-9090.

Dolphin Marina Resort, MM 28.5, oceanside, is at the closest marina to Looe Key Marine Sanctuary. Twelve simple motel rooms. No pets. Snorkel and sunset cruises daily. $99 to $149. ☎ 800-553-0308 or 305-872-2685, fax 305-872-0927. Website: http://thefloridakeys.com/dolphinmarina.

Parmer's Place Resort Motel, MM 28.5, Bayside, features 38 furnished efficiencies and one handicapped unit. Quiet. No pets. Rooms $77 to $293. E-mail: parmers@juno.com. Website: http://parmersplace.com. ☎ 305-872-2157, fax 305-872-2014.

Little Torch Key

Little Palm Island. Located on an out island, this luxurious resort offers all recreational facilities. Suites include private balcony, king-size bed, ceiling fans, air-conditioning, coffee maker, refrigerator, data-link line, wet bar and whirlpool. Dive shop on premises. Seaplane service. Launch transfers to the island are provided. No TV or phones. Two-night minimum stay on weekends. Rates: January 15 to March 31, $600 to $850; April 1 to May 31, $500 to $750; June 1 to December 16, $350 to $650. Meals add $140 per person, per day. No refunds on unused packages or meal plans. Write to Overseas Hwy 1, MM 28.5, Route 4, Box 1036, Little Torch Key FL 33042. ☎ 800-GET LOST (343-8567) or 305-872-2524, fax 305-872-4843. E-mail: getlost@littlepalmisland.com. Website: littlepalmisland.com.

Sugarloaf Key

Sugarloaf Lodge, at MM 17, Bayside, is a complete resort with miniature golf, airstrip, restaurant, boat rentals, fishing charters, tennis, pool and marina. Skydiving and airplane rides. Rooms $115 to $130 in winter, $75 to $90 in summer (May to December). Write to: PO Box 148, Sugarloaf Key FL 33044. ☎ 800-553-6097 or 305-745-3211, fax 305-745-3389.

Lower Keys Campgrounds

Sugarloaf Key KOA, MM 20, oceanside, offers 184 sites on 14 acres, full-service marina with canoe and boat rentals, game room, pool, hot tub, sandy beach, restaurant, laundry facilities and full-service store. ☎ 305-745-3549. Write to: PO Box 469, Summerland Key FL 33044.

Key West

Key West has three main resort areas – **Old Town**, the center of activity and where you'll find the island's most posh, oceanfront resort complexes, **South Roosevelt Blvd**, which runs along the south shore parallel to the Atlantic Ocean, and **North Roosevelt Blvd**, the commercial strip packed with fast food joints and strip malls that runs along the island's northern, Gulf shores. Because the island is just two miles wide and four miles long, no matter where you stay, you can travel to any point within a matter of minutes.

For a complete list of Key West accommodations, including guest houses, condominiums, apartments and vacation homes, contact the **Greater Key West Chamber of Commerce**, Mallory Square, 402 Wall St., Key West FL 33040. ☎ 800-LAST KEY or 305-294-2587.

Best Western Hibiscus Motel, 1313 Simonton St., Key West FL 33040, offers 61 rooms in a tropical park-like setting. Two queen beds and refrigerator in each room, heated pool. Gay-friendly. $99 to $139. Some kitchen units. No pets. ☎ 305-296-6711.

Best Western Key Ambassador Resort Inn, 3755 S. Roosevelt Blvd., Key West FL 33040. Airport pick-up. Pool, balconies, in-room fridge. Close to beach. 101 units. Rates $89 to $219. ☎ 305-296-3500, US 800-432-4315. Deluxe.

Comfort Inn, 3824 N. Roosevelt Blvd., Key West FL 33040. Features 100 guest rooms. Family plans, Olympic pool. Rates $120 to $360; includes continental breakfast. ☎ 800-695-5150 or 305-294-3773, fax 305-294-3773.

Curry Mansion Inn, 511 Caroline St., Key West FL 33040. Nestled alongside the original 1899 Curry Mansion, the Inn offers 15 elegant, romantic rooms, each opening onto a sparkling pool and surrounded by the lush foliage of the Curry Estate. Private baths and phones, wet bars, air-conditioning, ceiling fans and TV. Rates $160 to $275. ☎ 800-253-3466 or 305-294-5349, fax 305-294-4093. E-mail: frontdesk@currymansion.com. Website: www.currymansion.com.

Econo Lodge Resort of Key West, 3820 N Roosevelt Blvd., Key West FL 33040. This 134-room family resort features tiki bar, off-street parking, 24-hour Dennys. Rooms $115 to $355. No pets. ☎ 800-766-7584 or 305-294-5511, fax 305-296-1939.

Fairfield Inn by Marriot, 2400 N. Roosevelt Blvd., Key West FL 33040. 100 rooms, heated pool, tiki bar, cable TV, free local calls. Closest hotel to the Wharf. Some kitchen units. No pets. Handicapped-accessible. Rooms $89 to $199. ☎ US 800-228-2800 or 305-296-5700.

Holiday Inn La Concha Hotel, 430 Duval St., Key West FL 33040. This historic hotel towers over the center of Old Town and features 160 romantic

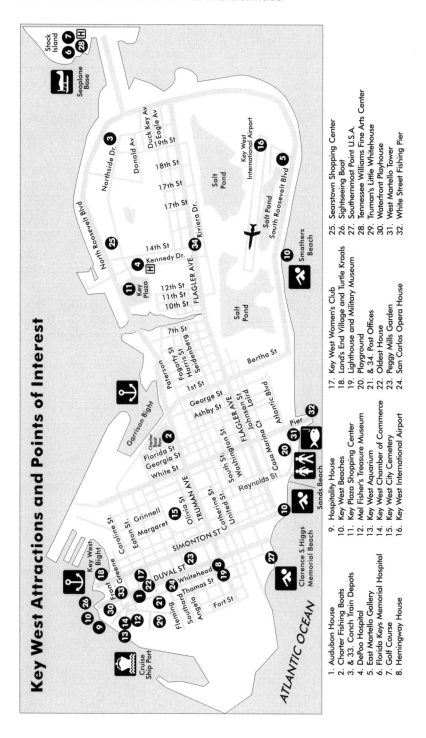

rooms, a restaurant, fitness room, whirlpool spa, shops and the best view of the city from the rooftop lounge. Walk to all attractions, fishing and sightseeing. Meetings and receptions for up to 200 people. Rates $179 to $315. ☎ 800-745-2191 or 305-296-2991, fax 305-294-3283. Handicapped-accessible. Website: www.keywest.com/laconcha/html.

Holiday Inn Beachside, 1111 N. Roosevelt Blvd., Key West FL 33040. Located directly on the Gulf of Mexico, this resort has 222 lovely rooms, 79 with water views. Amenities include large freshwater pool, whirlpool, on-site watersports and dive trips, gift ship, full service restaurant and bar, two lighted tennis courts and full catering facilities. Soft sand beach, wave runners. Oceanfront and poolside rooms. Diving and snorkeling tours. Convenient to both sides of the island and Stock Island. Rooms $119 to $160. No pets. ☎ 800-292-7706 or 305-294-2571, fax 305-292-7252. E-mail: db_wright@ msn.com.

Hampton Inn, 2801 N. Roosevelt Blvd., Key West FL 33040. Located on the Gulf, Hampton Inn features 157 units, island decor, freshwater pool, cable TV, Showtime, heated jacuzzi, tiki bar, sundeck. Handicapped-accessible. Some pets OK. Rooms from $74 (summer and winter), with much higher-priced rooms available during both seasons. ☎ 305-294-2917, US 800-HAMPTON.

Howard Johnson Resort, 3031 N. Roosevelt Blvd. Key West FL 33040. Adjacent to recreation center and Key Plaza shopping center. Pool, restaurant. Rates $159+. ☎ 800-942-0913 or 305-296-6595, fax 305-296-8351. Website: www.tarbray-hojo@travelbase.com.

Hyatt Key West Resort and Marina, 601 Front St, Key West FL 33040. Oceanfront, this stunning, 120-room landmark resort sits two short blocks from Duval and the heart of Old Town. Pool, three fine restaurants, private sandy beach and marina. Rooms $285 to $385. ☎ US 800-233-1234 or 305-296-9900.

Key Wester Resort, 3675 S. Roosevelt Blvd., Key West FL 33040. Sprawled across nine acres on the Atlantic, the 100-room resort features an Olympic pool, tiki bar and café at poolside, two tennis courts. A half-mile to beach, 2½ miles to town. No pets. Rates $128 to $355. ☎ 800-477-8888 or 305-296-5671, fax 305-294-9909.

Marriott's Casa Marina Resort, MM 00, 1500 Reynolds St., Key West FL 33040, is the island's largest oceanfront resort, featuring 314 rooms, tennis, bicycles, water sports, private beach, two pools, whirlpool and sauna. Complete health club on premises. Lovely mahogany pool bar with barbecue services. Lounge. Handicapped-accessible. Rates $309 to $795. ☎ US 800-626-0777 or FL 305-296-3535, fax 305-296-3008. E-mail: Casa@ keywest.com. Website: www.keywestparadise.com/casam.html.

Marriot Reach Resort, 1435 Simonton St., Key West FL 33040. Elegant resort located on a natural sand beach. Features 149 rooms (80 suites) each with a veranda, most with ocean view, ceiling fans, wet bar, two restaurants, oceanside dining, watersports, food store, library, five bars, entertainment. Health center, lap pool. Handicapped-accessible. No pets. Rates $309 to $419. ☎ US 800-874-4118 or 305-296-5000. E-mail: Reach@key-west.com. Website: www.keywestparadise.com/thereach.html.

Ocean Key House Suite Resort & Marina on Mallory Square at Zero Duval St., Key West FL 33040, offers deluxe suites on the Gulf of Mexico. Fully-equipped kitchens. Jacuzzi. Private balcony with water and sunset views. VCR and movie rentals. No pets. Rates $169 to $700. ☎ US 800-328-9815 or 305-296-7701. W-mail: info@oceankeyhouse.com. Website: www.keywest.com/okh.

Old Town Resorts, Inc., at 1319 Duval St., Key West FL 33040, includes the southernmost motel in the US, the **South Beach Oceanfront Motel**, and the **La Mer Hotel**. Offers three pools, jacuzzi, tiki bar, sunning pier on the Atlantic, gift shop, dive shop, concierge. Walking distance to beach, shops, nightlife and dining. No pets. Call for rates. ☎ 305-296-6577, FL 800-354-4455, fax 294-8272.

Pegasus International Motel, 501 Southard St., Key West FL 33040. Art Deco hotel with old-world service in Old Town at reasonable rates. 23 units. No pets. TV, private bath, air-conditioning. ☎ 800-397-8148 or 305-294-9323, fax 294-4741.

Pelican Landing Resort & Marina, 915 Eisenhower Drive, Key West FL 33040. Marina suites sleep two to eight people. No pets. Full kitchens, heated pool, barbecue grills, cable TV, docks, fish cleaning station, barbecue grill, HBO. Two penthouses with Jacuzzi. ☎ 800-527-8108 or 305-296-7583.

Pier House Resort & Caribbean Spa, One Duval St., Key West FL 33040. In the heart of Old Town. Offers 142 eclectic, romantic guest rooms and suites with private terraces. Private beach, full-service spa, heated pool. Five restaurants, five bars, beachside entertainment. No pets. Rates $275 to $795. ☎ 800-327-8340 (US) or 305-296-4600, fax 305-296-7568. E-mail: pierhouse@conch.net. Website: http://pierhouse.com.

Quality Inn of Key West, 3850 N Roosevelt Blvd., Key West FL 33040. Typical large chain features include pool, kitchen units, free coffee makers and coffee in each room. Free HBO. Rates $114 to $260. ☎ 800-553-5024 or 305-294-6681, fax 305-294-5618. E-mail: qualityikw@aol.com.

Ramada Inn Key West, 3420 N. Roosevelt Blvd., Key West FL 33040. On the commercial strip across highway from the Gulf of Mexico. Air-conditioned, color TV, pool, tennis. Pets welcome. Handicapped-accessible. Rates $120 to $260. ☎ 800-330-5541 or 305-294-5541, fax 305-294-7932.

Sheraton Suites Key West, 2001 S Roosevelt Blvd., Key West FL 33040. 180 suites just a quarter-mile from Key West Airport. All suites have a fridge, microwave, remote TV, complimentary breakfast. Large pool, free shuttle to and from Key West Airport and Old Town. Large meeting rooms. Rates $295 to $495. ☎ 800-425-3224 or 305-292-9800, fax 294-6009. Website: www.sheraton.com.

Southernmost Motel in the USA, 1319 Duval, Key West FL 33040. Features two pools, jacuzzi, tiki bar poolside. Walking distance to ships, nightlife, attractions, across from beach with pier on ocean. Rates $120 to $199. ☎ 800-354-4455 or 305-296-6577. E-mail: Lamer508@aol.com. Website: www.oldtownresorts.com.

Key West Campgrounds

Boyd's Campground, Maloney Ave., Stock Island FL 33040. ☎ 305-294-1465. Southernmost campground in the US. On the Atlantic Ocean at Key West city limits. Features all watersports, showers, restrooms, laundry, store, ice, city bus, telephone, dump station, bottle gas, electric, water, sewer hookups. Twenty boat slips and launching ramps. Pets OK. Pool.

Jabour's Trailer Court, 223 Elizabeth St., Key West FL 33040. Waterfront campground in Old Town. Walking distance to everything. Tent and RVs welcome. Efficiencies. ☎ 305-294-5723.

Leo's Campground & RV Park, 5236 Suncrest Rd., Key West FL 33040. Features 36 shady sites. Electric hookups, hot & cold showers, laundry, dump station. Security seven days a week. Barbecues. ☎ 305-296-5260.

Key West Dining

Key West

You'll find the locals' favorite watering hole at **The Half Shell Raw Bar** in Lands End Village. Menu features are fried or broiled fish, shrimp and conch; raw oysters and clams. Friendly service. Try for a table on the back porch, overlooking the docks, where you'll spot six or seven huge silver tarpon. Open for lunch and dinner. Moderate. ☎ 305-294-7496.

Across the wharf sits **Turtle Kraals Bar and Restaurant** serving fresh fish, hamburgers and the largest selection of imported beers in Key West. The restaurant is what remains of the days when turtles were brought in by the boatload from as far away as the Cayman Islands and Nicaragua. ☎ 305-294-2640. Website: www.turtlekraals.com.

Kraal is an Afrikans word meaning holding pen or enclosure. It refers to the concrete pilings that were driven into the ocean bottom to form a holding pen for the turtles until they could be shipped to the Northeast or slaughtered and made into soup at the cannery.

Pepe's Café, 806 Caroline St., serves the best breakfasts in the Keys. Frosted glasses of fresh orange juice and artfully prepared French toast or egg dishes are served indoors or outside under a canopy of flowering vines. Pub-style fare for lunch and dinner. Outdoor decor includes a white picket fence with peepholes for passersby at two levels – one for people and one for their pets. ☎ 305-294-7192.

The rooftop lounge at Holiday Inn's **La Concha** on Duval St. serves exotic island drinks and is the best spot in town for sunset viewing.

Mallory Market is the center of the Historic Key West waterfront and offers every imaginable fast-food outlet, plus a few you may not have imagined. One particularly good one is the conch fritter stand outside the Shipwreck Historeum, across from the Key West Aquarium.

Duval Street is lined with wonderful cafés and restaurants featuring varied, ethnic dishes. **Hooters** and the **Hard Rock Café** offer tasty fast food.

Bagatelle, 115 Duval St., features indoor or outdoor gourmet dining in a magnificent Victorian mansion. Lunch and dinner daily. Moderate to expensive. ☎ 296-6609.

The Cheese Board at 1075 Duval St. has 52 varieties of cheese, coffees and wines. ☎ 305-294-0072.

Chops, at the Holiday Inn La Concha, 430 Duval St., features venison chops, duck breast, rabbit, and seafood. 5:30-10:30 pm. ☎ 296-2991.

Kelly's Caribbean Bar, Grill & Brewery, 301 Whitehead St., serves lunch, dinner or cocktails. Decent Caribbean cuisine in a tropical garden setting. Try one of their micro-brew beers. Original home of Pan American Airways. ☎ 305-293-8484.

Exotic dishes from Southeast Asia are found at **Dim Sum**, 613 Duval St (rear). Dinner. ☎ 305-294-6230.

Yo Sake at 722 Duval (☎ 305-294-2288) and **Kyushu** (☎ 305-294-2995) at 921 Truman Avenue feature Japanese cuisine and sushi bars. Lunch and dinner.

The Banana Café, 1211 Duval St. French restaurant and crêperie. Open daily except Tuesday for breakfast and lunch from 8 am to 3 pm. Dinner from 7 to 10:30 pm. ☎ 305-294-7227.

Hog's Breath Saloon packs guests into its bustling open-air restaurant and raw bar. Nightly entertainment from sunset to 2 am. "Hog's breath is better than no breath at all!" ☎ 305-296-4222.

Louie's Back Yard, at the corner of Vernon and Waddell Streets, is one of Key West's finest waterfront restaurants. American cuisine highlights the menu for lunch, dinner and Sunday brunch. Expensive. Louie's delightful patio bar sits over the sea. ☎ 305-294-1061.

Strip malls along N. Roosevelt Blvd. feature most fast food chain restaurants.

Other Activities

Historic tours, parasailing, sailing charters, seaplane rides, and golf are available. Visit **Mel Fisher's Treasure Museum**, **Key West Aquarium**, **Ernest Hemingway's House**, the **Audubon House and Gardens**. There are also trolley tours and shopping for Haitian art, island jewelry, hand printed fabrics, handcrafted hats, masks, sandals, and hammocks.

Facts

Recompression Chamber: Paradis Hyperbarics, Marathon, ☎ 305-743-9891; Mariners Hospital, Tavernier, MM 91.5, ☎ 888-506-3638.

Handicap Facilities: Most large resorts feature full handicap-accessible facilities. State and national parks have wheelchair-accessible trails, tour boats, accommodations, restaurants.

Getting There: All major national and international airlines fly into Miami Airport. Connecting scheduled flights land in Marathon and Key West.

Driving from Miami International Airport, take LeJeune Road south to 836 West. Then take the Turnpike Extension to US 1 south, which runs the length of the Keys to Key West.

Driving from the North, take Florida Turnpike to Exit 4 (Homestead-Key West), then US 1 south. From Tampa, take 1-75 south to Naples, then east to Miami and the Turnpike Extension; or take 41 south to the Florida Turnpike, then east to the Turnpike Extension, then south to US 1.

Airlines serving Key West International Airport: American Eagle, ☎ 800-433-7300; Cape Air, ☎ 305-293-0603; Delta/Comair, ☎ 800-354-9822; Gulf Stream, ☎ 800-992-8532; USAir Express, ☎ 800-428-4322. General flight information, ☎ 305-296-5439.

Airlines serving Marathon Airport: American Eagle, ☎ 800-433-7300; Gulf Stream, ☎ 800-992-8532; USAir Express, ☎ 800-4284322.

Mile Markers: Mile Markers (MM) appear on the right shoulder of the road (US 1) as small green signs with white numbers and are posted each mile, beginning with number 126, just south of Florida City. They end with the zero marker at the corner of Fleming and Whitehead streets in Key West.

Awareness of these markers is useful, as Keys residents use them continually. When asking for directions in the Keys, your answer will likely be a reference to the nearest Mile Marker number.

Rental Cars: At Miami Airport, Avis, Budget, Hertz, National and Value. If possible, book rental cars in advance of your trip. In season you may be forced to rent a more expensive car than you planned.

Buses: Greyhound buses leave three times daily (7 am, noon and 6 pm) from the airport-vicinity bus station at 4111 NW 27th St., Miami. Travel time to Key West is 4½ hrs. ☎ (in FL) 800-410-5397, 305-876-7123 or, in Key West, 305-296-9072.

Clothing: During winter pack a light jacket, long-sleeved shirts and pants. Temperatures occasionally drop to the 50s. More usually, shorts and tee shirts cover most fashion needs, though one change of dressy attire may prove useful.

Scuba divers visiting the Keys between December and March will find a shortie or lightweight wet suit appropriate. Water temperatures drop to the 70s. Winter snorkelers will be most comfortable with a lycra wetskin or light wet suit.

Hospitals: Mariners Hospital, MM 89, ☎ 305-852-4418; Fisherman's Hospital, MM 48.5, ☎ 305-743-5533; Florida Keys Health Systems, MM 5, turn right , ☎ 305- 294-5531.

Weather: ☎ 305-296-2741.

Marine Patrol: ☎ 305-743-6542.

For Additional Information: ☎ 800-FLA-KEYS. Florida Keys & Key West Visitors Bureau, PO Box 1147, Key West FL 33041. Website: www.fla-keys.com.

The Shipwreck Trail

Courtesy of the Florida Keys National Marine Sanctuary

Nine shipwreck sites in the Florida Keys National Marine Sanctuary have been designated for historic preservation as The Shipwreck Trail. Each site is identified with a spar buoy and is accessible by private boat or dive shop charters. A brief history and description of each wreck follows.

The City of Washington

This two-masted sailing vessel, built in 1887 at Roach's Shipyard in Chester, Pennsylvania, served as a combination passenger and cargo transport between New York, Cuba, and Mexico. During 1889 she was refitted with a 2,750 hp steam engine, which dramatically increased her range and speed.

On February 15, 1898 a blast that rocked Cuba's Havana harbor and destroyed the USS Maine also damaged the neighboring *City of Washington* with flying debris that smashed awnings and tore up her deckhouse. Despite the imminent danger and chaos, crew members from the City of Washington rushed to rescue the *Maine*'s survivors.

Current research supports possible spontaneous combustion aboard the *Maine*, though bad relations between the US and Spain at that time made sabotage the only possibility considered. The explosion sank the *Maine* and started the Spanish-American War.

During the war, the *City of Washington* sailed as a transport ship carrying troops. She returned to her passenger and cargo runs following the war until retirement in 1908. Three years later she was converted into a coal-transporting barge.

On July 10, 1917, *The City of Washington* sank while being towed by the tugboat *Luchenbach #4*, after it ran aground on Elbow Reef. The *Luchenbach #4* was refloated, but *The City of Washington* broke apart and could not be salvaged.

Dive site

The City of Washington sits off northern Key Largo in 25 ft of water on Elbow Reef. The wreck is 325 ft long, with most of the hull's lower, bilge section intact. The bow section is badly damaged with pieces scattered over a 140-ft radius.

Wreck features include half of a cargo hoisting gear, a segment of the forward mast, a chock from the port side of the vessel, a deck ladder, the bilge pump assembly, the propeller shaft log running through the hull, several hull plate sections with port holes, the top rail with deck egging holes, and the stern rail assembly.

Resident marine life includes yellowtail snappers, schools of sergeant majors, moray eels, midnight parrot fish, and blue tangs.

Sea fans, plumes, branching fire coral, brain coral and star corals border the wreck.

The *Benwood*

Built in England during 1910 for a Norwegian company, the *Benwood* operated as a merchant marine freighter carrying precious ores. She spanned 360 ft in length with a 51-ft beam and was armed with 12 rifles, one four-inch gun, six depth charges and 36 bombs.

On April 9, 1942 the *Benwood* was on a routine voyage from Tampa, Florida, to Norfolk, Virginia, carrying a cargo of phosphate rock. Rumors of German U-boats in the area required her to travel completely blacked out with the Keys coastal lights three miles abeam. The *Robert C. Tuttle*, also blacked out, was traveling in the same area, bound for Atreco, Texas. The two ships were on a collision course. The bow of the *Benwood* collided with the port side of the *Tuttle*. The *Tuttle* was not in immediate danger, but the *Benwood's* bow was crushed and taking on water.

The captain turned her toward land and a half-hour later gave orders to abandon ship. The next day the keel was found to be broken and the ship declared a total loss. Local rumors were that the ship was hit by a German submarine.

Salvage began soon after the sinking and continued into the 1950s. She was later dynamited by the Coast Guard as a navigational hazard and continued to serve the US Army for aerial target practice after World War II.

Dive Site

The *Benwood* wreck sits between French Reef and Dixie Shoals in 25 to 45 ft of water. Usually low seas, good visibility and a close proximity to John Pennekamp Park make this one of the most popular wreck dives in the Keys.

The remains of the wreck scatter across a wide area. The 25-ft-high bow of the ship is the most intact feature. The hull structure is partially intact up to the first deck. Large steel knees join the deck plate to the outer hull and sides of the vessel. These knees are massive reinforced triangles of steel that outline the ship's hull shape despite the loss of the hull plates.

The first deck has been punctured in many places, forming a network of "nooks and crannies" perfect for fish habitat. Divers can peer through these holes into the cargo hold and see the space where ore was once carried.

Swarms of yellowtail rove the Benwood *wreck*

During summer, swirls of glass minnows hover over the wreck. Schools of grunts, snappers and sergeant majors are year-round inhabitants. Stingrays, angels, eels, and snappers are usually nearby.

Coral rubble, brain coral, fire coral and encrusting sponges cover the wreck.

The *Duane*

The *Duane* was built in 1936 at the US Naval Yard in Philadelphia. She was a 327-ft Treasury Class Cutter, one of seven such vessels, and was named for William J. Duane, Secretary of the Treasury under Andrew Jackson. She had various assignments before being sent to the Atlantic in 1941, where she eventually served with the US Atlantic Fleet. Her service included an impressive wartime and peacetime record. On April 17, 1943, she and her sister ship, the *Spencer*, sank the German U-Boat U-77. She participated in four rescues at sea, picking up a total of 346 survivors. In 1980 she was an escort vessel for thousands of Cuban refugees coming to the United States. Her last assignments included Search and Rescue work and Drug Enforcement.

Dive Site

The Coast Guard Cutter *Duane* lies upright on a sandy bottom in 120 ft of water, one mile south of Molasses Reef off Key Largo. After being decommissioned on August 1, 1985 as the oldest active US military vessel, the *Duane* was donated to the Keys Association of Dive Operators for use as an artificial reef. On November 27, 1987 she was towed to Molasses Reef, her hatches opened, her holds pumped full of water, and down she went to begin her final assignment.

On a clear day, the outline of the *Duane's* intact hull can be seen from above. The mast and crow's nest, protruding high above the hull, lie at 60 ft, the navigating bridge at 70 ft, just forward of amidships. The superstructure deck is at 90 ft and the main deck at 100 ft. The hull structure, completely intact, with the original rudders, screws, railings, ladders and ports, makes an impressive display.

Barracuda, yellowtail snappers, angelfish, wrasse, damselfish, spotted blennies, butterflyfish, trumpetfish, grunts, winged mollusks, and an occasional sea turtle inhabit the wreck. Finger corals, watercress algae, cup coral, star coral, sea fans, and sea plumes abound.

The *Eagle*

The *Eagle*, first known as the *Raila Dan*, was launched at Werf-Gorinchem, Holland, in December 1962 as a conventional hull freighter. She had several owners and seven name changes after her launching. On October 6, 1985, she caught fire. Two US Coast Guard cutters responded to her distress call, but the ship's superstructure was destroyed. After being declared a total loss, the Florida Keys Artificial Reef Association purchased her for $30,000 and Joe Teitelbaum, a private citizen, donated another $20,000 to help create an artificial reef. The ship was renamed the *Eagle Tire Company*, and was cleaned and gutted of all wooden parts. Oil and fuel was removed to protect the marine life in the area.

Dive Site

The *Eagle* lies on her starboard side in 110 ft of water three miles northeast of Alligator Reef Light. On the night of December 19, 1985, while waiting to be sunk as an artificial reef next to the *Alexander* barge, the *Eagle* broke from her moorings. Her port anchor was dropped to prevent further drifting in the current and she was sunk at that spot.

The *Eagle* offers several interesting structural features that make it a notable dive attraction. A large anchor chain exits the hawse pipe on the port bow, and continues a considerable distance before disappearing in the sand. Two large mast assemblies rest on the bottom. One is set on the forecastle; the other, amidships between cargo bays. Each has its own ladder and observation platform in place. Toward the stern there is a tandem set of cargo booms. Heat damage from the fire can be observed in the stern quarter. The deck railings at 70 ft, and her propeller and rudder at 110 ft, are still intact. In 1998, the *Eagle* was broken in two by Hurricane Georges.

Watch for groupers, snappers, cobia, amberjacks, silversides, and grunts.

The *San Pedro*

The *San Pedro*, a member of the 1733 Spanish treasure fleet caught by a hurricane in the Straits of Florida, sank in 18 ft of water 1¼ miles south of Indian Key. She is the oldest shipwreck on the Shipwreck Trail, with the mystique of a Spanish treasure ship.

The 287-ton Dutch-built vessel *San Pedro* and 21 other Spanish ships under the command of Rodrigo de Torres left Havana, Cuba, on Friday, July 13, 1733, bound for Spain. The *San Pedro* carried 16,000 pesos in Mexican silver and numerous crates of Chinese porcelain. Upon entering the Straits of Florida, an oncoming hurricane was signaled by an abrupt wind change. The Spanish treasure fleet, caught off the Florida Keys, was ordered back to Havana by their captain. But it was too late. The storm intensified and scattered, sank or swamped most of the fleet.

The wreck of the *San Pedro* was found in the 1960s in Hawk Channel. The site was heavily salvaged by treasure hunters. Silver coins dating between 1731 and 1733 were recovered from the pile of ballast and cannons that marked the place of her demise. Elements of the ship's rigging and hardware as well as remnants of her cargo were unearthed and removed.

Dive Site

The large pile of ballast, dense stones from European river beds, typically stacked in lower holds of sailing ships to increase their stability, marks the spot where the San Pedro went down. Mixed in with the ballast are red ladrillo bricks from the ship's galley. In 1989 this site became a State of Florida Underwater Archaeological Preserve. Replica cannons, an anchor from another 1733 shipwreck site and a bronze plaque were placed on the site to enhance its interpretation.

Red snappers, grunts, spadefish, stingrays, parrot fish, angelfish and an occasional barracuda roam the wreck, which sits in turtle grass and hard corals.

Adelaide Baker

The *Adelaide Baker*, originally called the *F.W. Carver*, was built in 1863 in Bangor, Maine. She measured 153 ft between perpendiculars, had a beam of 35 ft and a hold depth of 21 ft. Her double-decked hull was constructed of oak and hackmatack (like snowshoe wood). Two years after being built she was sheathed with copper. After being sold to the British she was renamed the *Adelaide Baker*.

On January 28, 1889, while en route to Savannah with a load of sawn timber, the ship floundered and sank on Coffins Patch Reef. Wreckers assisted the captain and crew to safety. The irregularly shaped granite ballast concentrated along the edge of the reef marks where she was first holed, spilling ballast and lower cargo.

Dive Site

The remains of this three-masted, iron-rigged ship, locally known as the *Conrad*, and believed to be the *Adelaide Baker* scatter over a square quarter-mile area in 20 ft of water, four miles south-southeast of Duck Key.

The *Adelaide Baker's* remains litter a north-northwest path 1,400 ft long. Most of the eroded material clusters over two areas. Cluster A is thought to be about where the ship went down. Large iron hold-beam-knee-riders and deck-beam-hanging-knees dominate this cluster. Nearby lie the lower portion of the mizzen mast and a metal water tank. Cluster B appears to have been segregated and placed there by early salvors. The iron main mast, 77 ft long, is the dominant feature here. The remains of a bilge pump, knee-riders, iron deck bit, hawse-hole frames, and miscellaneous rigging and tackle are also parts of Cluster B.

Other features, separate from these clusters, are two additional mast sections, a pile of rigging, and a second water box. The widely dispersed nature of the wreck site and identifiable ship components makes it fun to try and identify shipwreck materials.

Expect to see snappers, nurse sharks, lobsters, moray eels, parrot fish, goatfish, angelfish, and groupers. Sea fans, brain coral and branching corals adorn the bottom.

The *Thunderbolt*

The *Thunderbolt* was built, along with 15 sister ships, by Marietta Manufacturing Company at Point Pleasant, West Virginia, under contract to the US Army during World War II. First named *Randolph*, the *Thunderbolt* was launched on June 2, 1942.

Initially, these ships were built to plant and tend defensive coastal minefields for the Army's Coast Artillery Corps. However, in 1949 this function and the *Randolph* were transferred to the Navy. While in the Navy, this vessel was never commissioned. It remained in the Naval Reserve Fleet, first in South Carolina, then in Florida. In 1961, Caribbean Enterprises of Miami purchased the vessel. Later on, Florida Power and Light bought and used her for researching electrical energy in lightning strikes – hence her new name, *Thunderbolt*. Eventually, Florida Power and Light donated the vessel to the Florida Keys Artificial Reef Association.

Dive Site

The *Thunderbolt* was intentionally sunk on March 6, 1986, as part of the Florida Keys Artificial Reef Association project. Intact and upright, she rests on a sand bottom in 120 ft of water, four miles south of Marathon and Key Colony Beach.

The ship's hull is 189 ft long with a forecastle, which served as the cable handling area, and with a cruiser stem. Prior to being sunk, the ship was stripped of all but a few major pieces of equipment. The most prominent remaining features are a horizontal cable-handling reel at 80 ft , centered on the after-end of the forecastle deck, and the remains of the ship's superstructure including the observation deck located at 75 ft. The aft end of the superstructure has been cut away, exposing the interior of the hull at the engineering space. The rudder and propellers, which lie at 120 ft, also remain to complement the stern section of the hull.

Jack crevalle, amberjacks, groupers, barracudas, cobia, sharks, tarpon, jewfish, and spiny sea urchins are usual residents. Hydroids, flaming scallops, sea whips and sponges grow among the hard corals.

The *North America*

James B. Hall of New York and George S. Hall of Bath, Maine were part owners of the *North America,* based in New York. The 130-ft ship-rigged vessel had two decks, three masts and a 29-ft beam.

During the 19th century, three ships sank near Sombrero Light on Delta Shoals, a shallow reef. The wreckage lying immediately north of the shoal on a sand and grass flat at 14 ft is thought to be the *North America.*

Admiralty Court Records show that a three-masted, square-rigged vessel named *North America*, carrying dry goods and furniture, sank November 25, 1842 on Delta Shoals while en route from New York to Mobile, Alabama. Documents credit local wreckers with saving Captain Hall and his crew.

Four ships were registered by the name of *North America* in 1842, but the size of the remains on Delta Shoals and Captain Hall's name in the court records match those associated with the *North America* built in Bath, Maine in 1833.

Dive Site

Vessel remains include a large section of wood hull filled with ballast. The wreckage measures approximately 112 ft long and 35 ft wide. Only small sections of the lower hull protrude above the sandy bottom. Ballast covers most of the structural remains.

The southwest extremity of the site consists of the keel and several iron drift bolts that attached the keel and keelson to the floor timbers. The majority of the remaining hull is covered by sand and only small sections of the keel can be found exposed. The ballast pile is oval-shaped and appears to be largely contained within the surviving hull structure. The longitudinal axis of the ballast pile is southwest to northeast and extends for 85 ft. Beyond the ballast, the remainder of the hull structure is covered by sand and turtle grass. The ceiling and planking are primarily attached by wooden trunnels (treenails). A few ¾-inch square copper spikes can be seen where they held the planks in position during construction before the trunnels were installed. Cement can be found between several of the frames where it was probably used as a temporary patch material.

The remains of two barrels containing cement can be found within the confines of the ballast scatter, one near the north end and one at mid-section.

Marine life includes groupers, lobsters, crabs, snappers, blue tangs, wrasse, damselfish, hogfish, scorpionfish, moray eels, barracudas and angelfish. The bottom is a mix of turtle-grass, manatee-grass, anemones, sponges, fire coral, brain coral, sea whips, and sea plumes.

The *Amesbury*

The *Amesbury* (DE 66) was launched and commissioned in 1943 as a destroyer escort. She was named for Lt. Stanton Amesbury, who was killed in enemy action over Casablanca on November 9, 1942 while attached to an aviation squadron in the Atlantic Area.

The *Amesbury's* first assignment was duty with the Atlantic Convoy 7, followed by participation in the Normandy invasion. Returning to the United States in August, 1944, she was assigned temporary duty with the Fleet Sonar School in Key West. In 1945, she was one of the 104 destroyer escorts converted to high speed transports at the Philadelphia Navy Yard. *Amesbury* was then assigned hull number APD-46 and equipped with a five-inch turret gun and three twin-mount 40-millimeter antiaircraft guns. Proceeding to the Pacific she supported landings in Korea and China during 1945, carrying Underwater Demolition Team Twelve. The *Arnesbury* returned to Florida in 1946, was decommissioned and never performed active service again. Chet Alexander Marine Salvage of Key West purchased her in 1962 for scrap.

Dive Site

The remains of the steel-hulled *Amesbury* lie in 25 ft of water five miles west of Key West. This vessel was being towed by Chet Alexander Marine Salvage of Key West to a deep water location to be sunk as an artificial reef. While en route she grounded and before she could be refloated a storm broke up her hull. The site is locally known as Alexander's Wreck.

The remains of the *Arnesbury* consist of two sections of hull and superstructure lying 200 yards apart. The southern section contains the remains of the bow and port side. The northern section of the wreck consists of the stern and starboard side. Fifty feet back from the stem of the bow is the five-inch gun mount behind a semicircular shield. Behind that is the twin 40-millimeter Bofors-style anti-aircraft gun mount on an elevated pedestal. A debris field on the east side of the hull contains pieces of the collapsed upper hull, bridge, and superstructure. The northern section of wreckage includes the stern, another Bofors gun and mount, miscellaneous debris, and heavy Welin davits used to transport and launch four Landing Craft Vehicle Personnel boats.

Watch for lobsters, crabs, scorpionfish, moray eels, barracudas, angelfish, parrot fish, yellowtail snappers, damselfish, sergeant majors, southern stingrays, jewfish, black and Nassau groupers, spadefish, red snappers, cobia, and pompano. Surrounding star and brain corals mix with sea rods and sponges.

For additional information about The Shipwreck Trail or the Florida Keys National Marine Sanctuary, write to PO Box 500368, Marathon FL 33050. ☎ 305-743-2437, fax 305-743-2357. Website: fknms@ocean.nos.noaa.gov.

Eco-Tips

Help our finned and web-footed friends stay healthy by practicing good diving, snorkeling and boating habits. The following tips developed by leading ocean environmentalists provide a good start.

Dispose of Trash Properly

Each year more than 100,000 marine animals die from eating or becoming entangled in plastic debris. Sea turtles, whales, dolphins, manatees, fish and sea birds mistake plastic bags and balloons for jellyfish. Swallowing a plastic bag or balloon has caused many of these animals a slow and painful death by blocking their digestive tracts, thus starving them to death. Sea birds' bills and heads have gotten twisted up in the plastic rings from six-packs of beer and soda cans.

You can help prevent these mishaps by disposing of all your trash properly and discouraging others from throwing trash overboard.

Never release a helium-filled balloon into the air. Pick up any discarded fishing line you see around docks and marinas. Plastic six-pack rings should be cut up before placement in the recycling bin.

Hit the Beach

Fourteen billion pounds of garbage are dumped in the world's oceans each year, most of it in the Northern Hemisphere. Volunteers with the Center for Marine Conservation have collected nearly 900 tons of beach trash. In one clean-up, 8,000 plastic bags were found along the shores of North Carolina.

If you wish to find out about beach clean-ups, contact the **Center for Marine Conservation**, 1725 De Sales St., NW, Suite 600, Washington, DC 20036, ☎ 202-429-5609. Website: www.cmc-ocean.org.

Practice Good Buoyancy Control

Learn to adjust weights and vest or jacket inflation to maintain neutral buoyancy. This enables you to hang where you want without kicking up the bottom or surrounding corals, critters and fellow divers.

Avoid Dangle Damage

Dangling consoles, gauges, cameras, and other assorted dive gear and instruments wreak havoc when they bang into delicate corals and tiny invertebrates, often crushing or battering tiny critters to death. Avoid slamming gear into your subsea surroundings. *Courtesy Paul Sieswerda, Collection Manager, New York Aquarium*

Keep Your Hands to Yourself

Mother Nature protects fish bodies from bacterial invasion with a layer of invisible slime. Even gently touching fish disturbs the slime layer and produces an area similar to a sunburn on human skin. The fish may seem fine when they swim away, but two days later will suffer skin infections where touched. If you are in a marine sanctuary that allows hand-feeding fish, avoid the temptation to pet or handle them. *Courtesy of Paul Sieswerda, Collection Manager of the New York Aquarium*

Watch Your Bubbles

Long stays under ledges or any area where your exhaust bubbles can't rise to the surface can create air pockets that may engulf overhead sea anemones and stationary invertebrates. Being trapped in your air will cause them to dry out and die. Use discretion. *Courtesy Paul Sieswerda, Collection Manager, New York Aquarium*

Keep Sea Snacks All Natural

Feeding fish is frowned upon in all but a few marine sanctuaries. Hand-feeding lessens the animals' instinctive reaction to flee, and certain foods eaten by humans can be unhealthy and often fatal to fish. In areas such as Honduras and Mexico where spear fishing is a way of life for the natives, the grouper or turtle that learns to trust snack-carrying, vacationing divers will also stay put long enough to be speared.

In areas where fish feeding is acceptable, be sure to feed only foods that a fish or turtle would naturally eat. Frozen squid or freeze-dried shrimp or flakes are acceptable choices. Fishin' Chips makes waterproof, cardboard dispensers that hold pop-out pills. The pills are an all-natural fish food that stay dry until use. They don't cloud the water. Available at many dive shops or call ☎ 800-522-4269 for sales locations. Be sure to recycle the packaging!

De-silt Sponges and Corals

To breathe and eat, sponges must be able to suck in water for oxygen and nu-

trients. Wave action cleanses them of most natural silting, but they have no mechanism to rid themselves of silt kicked up by divers and snorkelers.

If you see a silt-covered sponge or coral, give it a hand by fanning the surrounding water to "blow" off the residue. *Courtesy of Dee Scarr, Touch the Sea, Bonaire*

Bail Out a Crab

Plastic materials are often smoother than some ocean animals' feet were meant to walk on. Plastic buckets lying mouth up on the sea floor trap hermit crabs, who crawl in, then can't get out. They eat the bottom ring of algae, then slowly starve to death.

When you see a new bucket or container on the sea floor, simply bring it back up to the surface and dispose of it properly. If the bucket is coral-encrusted on the outside, leave it, but put a pile of debris or coral rubble inside to form an exit ramp for wandering crabs. If no rubble is at hand, cut an escape hole in the bottom or side with your dive knife or shears. Take care not to handle any coral directly or you may get a nasty infection. *Courtesy of Dee Scarr, Touch the Sea, Bonaire*

BOATERS

Obey Restricted Access Signs

Boaters should stay a minimum distance of 100 yards from bird roosting, nesting and feeding areas. If your presence appears to be flushing birds from their activities, you are too close and should move farther away.

Approach Seagrass Beds Gently

Seagrass beds provide nursery areas, feeding habitat and shelter for a wide variety of marine animals. Alert and knowledgeable boaters can help protect this precious resource.

Accidental groundings and turbidity from boat wakes destroy seagrass beds. Recovery may take as long as 10 years.

Use navigation charts and make sure you have adequate water depth to avoid scraping the flats. Color changes in the water indicate differences in depth and bottom types. Shallow sea grass beds, hard-bottom, patch reefs and sand shoals in near-shore areas will appear beige, brown or light green. Deeper adjacent waters are darker green. Wearing polarized sunglasses greatly enhances subtle differences in water color.

First Aid

SEA STINGS, CORAL CUTS, AND SUNBURN

Painful swelling and redness may occur if you brush into stinging corals, fire sponges or jellyfish. Allergic reactions are also common. Most injuries are not serious, but can become infected if not cared for immediately.

Sea sting kits, sold by dive shops, offer immediate relief, but if you don't have one on hand, some common household products may help, including meat tenderizer, ammonia water, rubbing alcohol, antibiotic salve and vinegar.

CORAL CUTS

Coral animals have a hard external skeleton that is frequently razor-sharp and capable of inflicting deep, painful wounds. Some have stinging cells that produce a tiny puncture, which rapidly disappears but may leave itchy welts and reddening.

Fire corals, though delicate in appearance are often the most dangerous. All coral cuts, while usually superficial, can take a long time to heal.

Avoid exploring reefs or wrecks subject to heavy surge and wave action or surface current. It is easy for the unprepared diver to be swept or tumbled across a reef. Coral should not be handled. Many marine parks have outlawed wearing gloves so as to protect the coral.

First Aid

Live coral is covered with bacteria. Wash the bruise with a baking soda or weak ammonia solution, followed by soap and fresh water. A tetanus shot is recommended. When available, apply cortisone ointment or antihistamine cream.

An application of meat tenderizer may speed up the healing process since the venom from stinging sea creatures is a protein, which the tenderizer destroys. Mix the tenderizer with water to make a paste and apply. The wound should be covered with a sterile dressing to prevent infection.

JELLYFISH STINGS

When you come in contact with a jellyfish, you are exposed to literally thousands of minute stinging organs in the tentacles, yet the stinging results only in painful local skin irritation. The Portuguese Man-of-War is an exception and its sting has, in rare cases, resulted in death.

Man-of-War jellyfish

Do not handle jellyfish. Even beached or apparently dead specimens may sting. Tentacles of some species may dangle as much as 165 ft. Stay away to prevent contact.

First Aid

If you're stung, remove any tentacles and attempt to prevent untriggered nematocysts from discharging additional toxins by applying vinegar (acetic acid), 10% formalin solution, sodium bicarbonate, boric acid, or xylocaine spray.

Vinegar appears to be the most effective in reducing additional nematocyst discharge. DO NOT USE FRESH WATER OR RUB SAND ON THE AREA – you may cause additional nematocyst discharge.

Antihistamines or analgesics have been useful in relieving itching and redness. Meat tenderizer may also be useful in relieving the pain.

SEA URCHIN PUNCTURES

Sea urchins are radial in shape with long spines . They are widespread in the Western Hemisphere. Penetration by the spines can cause intense pain.

First Aid

Large spine fragments may be gently removed but be careful not to break them into smaller fragments that might remain in the wound. Alternately soaking the injured extremity in hot, then cold water may help dissolve small fragments. Get immediate medical attention for severe or deep punctures.

Treatment

Clean wound removing as much of the spine with tweezers. Spines which have broken off flush with the skin are nearly impossible to remove and probing around with a needle will only break the spines into little pieces.

Most of the spines will be dissolved by the body within a week. Others may fester and can then be removed with tweezers. Some have small venomous pincers that should be removed, and the wound should then be treated as a poisonous sting. Small fragments may reabsorb. Some divers have found the use of a drawing salve helpful. In severe cases, surgical removal may be required when spines are near nerves and joints. X-rays may be required.

Spines can form granulomas months later or may migrate to other sites.

STONEFISH & SCORPIONFISH STINGS

Stings by these fish have been known to cause fatalities. Divers and snorkelers should avoid handling them or any venomous fish.

Venoomus fish are often found in holes or crevices or lying well-camouflaged on rocky bottoms. Divers should be alert for their presence and should take care to avoid them at all times.

First Aid

Get victim out of the water. Lay patient down, Observe for shock. Wash wound with saltwater (cold) or sterile saline solution. Soak wound in hot water for 30 to 90 minutes (not hotter than 50°C or 120° F). Use hot compresses if wound is on the face. Get immediate medical assistance

SUNBURN

Some of the most severe sunburns can occur on cloudy days when the sun is not visible. Snorkelers spending a great deal of time floating face down on top of the water often end up with badly sunburned backs and legs. Long-sleeved shirts and long pants are recommended. At the very least a tee shirt should be worn.

Treatment

A variety of sunburn ointments and sprays are commercially available and should be carried in every dive bag. If no special ointment is available, bandages soaked in tannic acid, boric acid, or vinegar will provide some relief. The victim should avoid further exposure until the condition has passed.

First Aid

What About Sharks?

Two opposing attitudes predominate when you mention sharks to ocean explorers – irrational fear or total fascination. Most of us share a little of each. Statistically, sharks have generated more sensational publicity as a threat to divers than any other animals, even though their bites are among the least frequent of any injuries divers sustain.

Paul Sieswerda, shark expert at the New York Aquarium, warns divers about taking either approach to this honored and feared species. Common sense and a realistic understanding of the animals should be combined, he says, adding that "anything with teeth and the capability of biting should be treated with the same respect we give to any large animal having potential to inflict injury." The vast majority of sharks are inoffensive animals that threaten only small creatures; but some will bite divers that molest them. Nurse sharks, commonly seen sleeping under reef ledges, appear docile largely because they are so sluggish, but large ones can seriously injure a diver when provoked.

Most sharks are timid. Fewer than 100 serious assaults by sharks are reported worldwide each year, with the average being closer to 50. Less than 35% of these are fatal. Statistics isolating attacks on divers alone are not available, but they would be far fewer than 50. A majority of those few fatal attacks are not cases of the infamous great white shark biting the diver in two; they involve four- or five-foot sharks causing a major laceration in an arm or leg. Loss of blood due to lack of immediate medical attention is usually the cause of death.

Overplaying the danger is equally unrealistic. Encounters with dangerous sharks by divers on shallow reefs or shipwrecks are rare. Except in the case of special shark dives offered in the Bahamas, when a shark encounters man, it tends to leave the area as suddenly as it appeared.

So use common sense. Avoid diving in areas known as shark breeding grounds. Avoid spearfishing and carrying the bloody catch around on the end of the pole. If you do see a shark and are uncomfortable about its presence, leave the water. Above all do not corner or provoke the shark in any manner.

Snorkelers should not attempt to join shark dives meant for scuba-equipped explorers. The relationship is different. When sharks feed, they often trap fish against the surface. Sharks have poor eyesight. In cloudy water the dangling hand of a snorkeler may resemble a small fish.

Our favorite shark danger story comes from former Florida divemaster Bill Crawford. A young diver begged to see a shark in the water. Finding one presented quite a problem. The area was largely shallow reefs, so shark sightings were rare indeed. Thinking hard, the divemaster remembered a big old nurse shark who could be found sleeping under a ledge on one of the outer reefs. The shark had been there for years, totally ignoring the daily stampede of divers and snorkelers. So the divemaster took the young man to that spot and, as luck would have it, there was the shark. Upon seeing it sleeping under the ledge, the young diver became frozen with fear. In a wild panic he backed into a wall of coral, putting his hand deep into a hole where a big green moray eel lived. The nurse shark, true to its calm reputation, just kept sleeping. But the moray, incensed at the intrusion, defended its home by sinking its sharp teeth deep into the diver's hand.

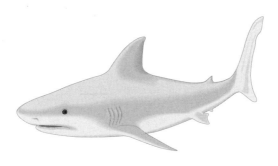

Index

Abaco Islands (Bahamas), 11, 29-30; accommodations, 32-35; best dives, 29-31; dive operators, 31-32

Accommodations: Abaco Islands, 32-35; Bermuda, 99-101; Big Pine Key, 131-132; Bimini, 43; Cat Island, 44-45; Crooked Island, 45; Elbow Cay, 32; Eleuthera, 48; Exumas, 51; Grand Bahama, 27-29; Grand Turk, 71, 73; Great Abaco, 33; Great Guano Cay, 33-34; Green Turtle Cay, 34; Harbour Island, 48-49; Islamorada, 122-124; Key Largo, 118-121; Key West, 105, 106; Little Torch Key, 132; Long Island, 55-56; Marathon, 127-128; New Providence Island, 14, 20-22; Providenciales, 77-79; Salt Cay, 74; San Salvador Island, 59-60; South Caicos, 80; Spanish Cay, 34; Sugarloaf Key, 132; Treasure Cay, 34-35; Walker's Cay, 35

Andros (Bahamas), 11, 35-39; best dives, 36, 38; dive operators, 38-39; getting there, 35-36; history, 36; map, 37; snorkeling, 38

Artificial reefs, 112-114; Alligator Reef, 114; Bibb, 112-113, 117; Conch Reef, 113; Duane, 112-113, 117; Eagle, 113, 117; Pickle Reef, 113; Speigel Grove, 113

Bermuda, 83-103; accommodations, 99-101; best dives, 86-94; climate, 103; currency, 103; dining, 101-102; dive operators, 94-95; documentation, 103; dolphin encounters, 99; dress code, 103; getting there, 102; glass bottom boats, 96; golf, 97; helmet diving, 97; history, 83; horseback riding, 97; laws and regulations, 84; map, 85; parasailing, 98; recompression chamber, 102; shipwrecks, 84, 86; shopping, 99; sightseeing, 98-99; snorkeling, 91, 93-94; snorkeling tours and rentals, 95-96; taxes, 99, 103; time zone, 103, transportation; 102; when to go, 83-84

Berry Islands (Bahamas), 39-40, 62-63; best dives, 39; dive operators, 40; snorkeling, 39-40

Big Pine Key (Florida Keys), 105; accommodations, 131-132; best dives, dive operators, 130-131; Looe Key National Marine Sanctuary, 105, 108, 109, 130; climate, 106, 108, 140; diving, 106; dress code, 140

Bimini (Bahamas), 11, 40-43; accommodations, 43; Alice Town, 40; best dives, 40-42; dive operators, 42-43; getting there, 42; snorkeling, 42

Blue Lagoon Island (Bahamas), 22

C-Cards on Board for Divers Down, 9

Cat Island (Bahamas), 11, 43-45; accommodations, 44-45; Arthur's Town, 43; history, 44; sightseeing, 44; climate, 64

Columbus, Christopher, 12, 52, 56, 57

Crooked Island (Bahamas), 11, 45; accommodations, 45; dive operator, 45; getting there, 45

Cruise ships' private island retreats, 62-63

Cruises, 2-4

De Leon, Ponce, 67

Dining: Bahamas, 14; Bermuda, 101-102; Florida Keys, 121-122, 124-125, 129, 137-139,

Dive operators: Abaco Islands, 31-32; Andros, 38-39; Bermuda, 94-95; Berry Islands, 40; Big Pine Key, 130-131; Bimini, 42-43; Caicos, 76-77; Crooked Island, 45; Eleuthera, 48; Exumas, 50-51; Grand Bahama, 25-27; Grand Turk, 70-71; Harbour Island, 48-49; Islamorada, 117-118; Key Largo, 114-117; Key West, 131; Long Island, 55-56; Marathon, 126-127; New Providence Island, 19-20; Salt Cay, 74; San Salvador Island, 59-60

Dive sites: American Shoal (Florida Keys), 129; Amos' Wall (Turks & Caicos), 79; The Anchor (Turks & Caicos), 69-70; Anchor Alley (Turks & Caicos), 79; Angel's Camp (Bahamas), 23; Angelfish Reef (Bahamas), 39; The Arches Reef (Turks & Caicos), 79; the Barge (Bahamas), 36; Ben's Cavern (Bahamas), 23, 24-25; Bimini Road (Bahamas), 41; Bimini Wall (Bahamas), 40; the Blue Hole (Bahamas), 36; Blue Holes (Bermuda), 92; Blue Lagoon Reef (Bahamas), 19; Brad's Mountain (Bahamas), 36; Cathedral (Bahamas), 31; The Caves (Bermuda), 92; Carysfort Reef

(Florida Keys), 111-112; Christ of the Abyss (Florida Keys), 108-109; Coffins Patch (Florida Keys), 126; Conception Island Wall (Bahamas), 53; Conch Cay (Bahamas), 50; Coral Reef (Bahamas), 50; Cosgrove Reef (Florida Keys), 130; Cotrell Key (Florida Keys), 129; Crab Cay Blue Hole (Bahamas), 50; Current Cut (Bahamas), 46; Dolittle's Grottos (Bahamas), 57; dolphin dives (Bahamas), 24; Double Caves (Bahamas), 57-58; The Dungeons (Bahamas), 38; Eden Banks (Bahamas), 23; Edge of the Ledge (Bahamas), 24; Egg Island Lighthouse Reef (Bahamas), 46; The Elbow (Florida Keys), 112; Fish Farm (Bahamas), 23; the Fishbowl (Bahamas), 39; Flamingo Tongue Reef (Bahamas), 53; Fowl Cays National Park (Bahamas), 31; French Reef (Florida Keys), 111; The Gardens (Bahamas), 46; The Gardens (Turks & Caicos), 69; Giant's Staircase (Bahamas), 36; Gold Rock Blue Hole (Bahamas), 23; Gouldings Cay (Bahamas), 18; Grouper Alley (Bahamas),30; Grouper Hole (Turks & Caicos), 75; Healing Hole (Bahamas), 41-42; Hole in the Wall (Bahamas), 56-57; The Hump (Bahamas), 58; Lobster Reef (Bahamas), 50; Long Reef (Bahamas), 50; Looe Key National Marine Sanctuary (Florida Keys), 129; Lost Blue Hole (Bahamas), 18; Marquesa Islands (Florida Keys), 130; Miller's Reef (Bahamas), 46; Molasses Reef (Florida Keys), 109, 111; The Nodules (Bahamas), 42; Pelican Cay National Park (Bahamas), 30; The Pinnacles (Turks & Caicos), 75; The Plane (Turks & Caicos), 79; The Point (Turks & Caicos), 79; Point Pleasant (Turks & Caicos), 73-74; Rainbow Reef (Bahamas), 23, 40; Sand Key (Florida Keys), 129, 130; Sand Mounds of Bimini (Bahamas), 41; Schoolhouse Reef (Bahamas), 18; Shark Alley (Bahamas), 31; Shark Rodeo (Bahamas), 30; Shark Wall (Bahamas), 18; Sombrero Reef (Florida Keys), 126; Southwest Breaker (Bermuda), 88; Southwest Reef (Bahamas), 18; Spiral Cavern (Bahamas), 30; Stargazer (Florida Keys), 130; Stella Maris Shark Reef (Bahamas), 52; Sting Ray Reef (Bahamas), 50; Telephone Pole (Bahamas), 57; Thunderball Reef, (Bahamas),16; The Tower (Bahamas), 30; Tuna Alley (Bahamas), 42; The Tunnels (Turks & Caicos), 69; Turnbull's Gut (Bahamas), 36, 38; Tutts Reef (Bahamas), 31; West Wall (Turks & Caicos), 74-75; Western Dry Marks (Florida Keys), 129

Diving etiquette, 151-153
Dolphin Assistant Trainer Program, 24
Duck Key (Florida Keys), 146; dining, 129

East Caicos (Turks & Caicos), 67
Elbow Cay (Bahamas), 11, 32; getting there, 30
Eleuthera (Bahamas), 11, 14, 43, 46-48, 66; accommodations, 48; best dives, 46-48; dive operators, 48; snorkeling, 47-48
Exumas (Bahamas), 11, 14, 49-51; accommodations, 51; best dives, 50; dive operators, 50-51; Exuma Cays Land and Sea Park, 49; getting there, 50; history, 49-50; Little Exuma (Bahamas), 50; snorkeling, 49; getting there, 11, 63-64

Fisher, Mel, 106
Florida Keys Artificial Reef Association, 146, 147;
Florida Keys National Marine Sanctuary, 108, 149; map, 110, 111
Florida Keys National Marine Sanctuary Shipwreck Trail, 141-149; *Adelaide Baker*, 145-146; *Amesbury*, 148-149; *Benwood*, 142-143; *The City of Washington*, 141-142; *Duane*, 143-144; *Eagle*, 144; *North America*,147-148; *San Pedro*, 145; *Thunderbolt*, 146-147; *USS Maine*, 141
Fort Jefferson National Monument, 130

Getting there: Andros, 35-36; the Bahamas, 11, 63-64; Bimini, 42; Crooked Island, 45; Elbow Cay, 30; Exumas, 11, 63-64; Grand Bahama, 22; Bermuda, 102; Florida Keys, 139; Great Abaco, 33; Great Guano Cay, 33; Green Turtle Cay, 34; Long Island, 52; Out Islands, 29; San Salvador Island, 56; Spanish Cay, 34; Treasure Cay, 34
Grand Bahama (Bahamas), 11, 14, 15, 22-29; accommodations, 27-29, best dives, 23-27; Blue Holes, 22-23; dive operators, 25-27; dolphin encounters, 24; getting there, 22; map, 23; snorkeling, 25; West End, 22

Grand Caicos (Turks & Caicos), 67; history, 67-68; live-aboards, 80; North Caicos (Turks & Caicos), 67; photo service, 77

Grand Turk (Turks & Caicos), 67, 68-73; accommodations, 71, 73; best dives, 68-70; Cockburn Town, 68, 70; dive operators, 70-71; map, 72; Nitrox, 71; sightseeing, 68; snorkeling, 70;

Great Abaco (Bahamas), 11

Great Guano Cay (Bahamas), 4, 33-34

Green Turtle Cay (Bahamas), 30, 31

Gulf Stream, 24, 40

Handicap facilities: Florida Keys, 139

Handicapped Scuba Association (HSA), 4

Harbour Island (Bahamas), 11, 14, 48-49, 66; accommodations, 48-49; dive operators, 48-49; getting there, 48

Hemingway, Ernest, 1, 40, 41

History: Andros, 36; the Bahamas, 12-13, 13-14; Bermuda, 83; Turks & Caicos, 67-68; Cat Island, 44; Exumas, 49-50; Florida Keys, 106; Long Island, 51-52; Salt Cay, 73; San Salvador Island, 56

Insurance, 4-5

Islamorada (Florida Keys), 105, accommodations, 122-124; campgrounds, 124; dining, 124-125; dive operators, 117-118; Dolphin Research Center, 105; snorkeling, 117

Island Passage, 67, 68

Junkanoo, 13-14

Key Largo (Florida Keys), 105; accommodations, 118-121; best dives, 108-114; campgrounds, 120-121; dining, 121-122; dive operators, 114-117; John Pennekamp Coral Reef State Park, 105; Key Largo National Marine Sanctuary, 105, 108; snorkeling, 116

Key West (Florida Keys), 105, 106; accommodations, 133, 135-137; best dives, 129-130; campgrounds, 137; dining, 137-139; dive operators, 131; map, 134; laws and regulations, 109

Little Abaco (Bahamas), 11; Nitrox, 31; sightseeing, 29; snorkeling, 31

Little Torch Key (Florida Keys), 132; accommodations, 132;

Live-aboards; Bahamas, 60-62; Turks & Caicos, 80

Long Island (Bahamas), 11, 51-56; accommodations, 55-56; best dives, 52-53, 55; dive operators, 55-56; getting there, 52; history, 51-52; map, 54; snorkeling,53, 55

Long Key (Florida Keys), 129; map, 107

Lost Ocean Hole, 16

Lucayans, 12, 52, 56

Maps; Andros, 37; the Bahamas, 12; Bermuda, 85; Florida Keys, 107; Florida Keys National Marine Sanctuary, 110, 111; Grand Bahama, 23; Grand Turk, 72; Key West, 134; Long Island, 54; New Providence Island, 17; San Salvador Island, 59

Marathon (Florida Keys), 105, 108; accommodations, 127-128; best dives, 125-126; dining, 129; dive operators, 126-127; snorkeling, 126

New Providence Island (Bahamas), 11, 15-22; accommodations, 14, 20-22; best dives, 16, 18-19; dive operators, 19-20; dolphin encounters, 19; gambling, 15; map, 17; Nassau, 11, 14; snorkeling, 19

Out Islands (Bahamas), 11; getting there, 29; snorkeling, 27

Overseas Highway (Florida Keys), 106

Package tours, 2-4

Packing checklist, 6

Paradise Island (Bahamas), 11

Providenciales (Turks & Caicos), 67; accommodations, 77-79; best dives, 74-76; gambling, 67; recompression chamber, 81; snorkeling, 75-76; transportation, 81

Safety tips, 7-8, 9, 155-160

Salt Cay(Turks & Caicos) 67, 73-74; accommodations, 74; best dives, 73-74; dive operators, 74; history, 73; snorkeling, 73-74; taxes, 81; when to go, 68

San Salvador Island (Bahamas), 11, 12, 56-60; accommodations, 59-60; best dives, 56-59; dive operators, 59-60; getting there, 56; history, 56; map, 59; snorkeling, 58-59;

Security, 7

Index

Shipwrecks, 11; *Adolphus Busch Senior* (Florida Keys), 105; *Adelaide Baker* (Florida Keys), 145-146; *Amesbury* (Florida Keys), 148-149; *Aristo* (Bermuda), 87; *Bahama Mama* (Bahamas), 18; *Bahama Shell* (Bahamas), 16; *Benwood* (Florida Keys), 111, 142-143; *Bibb* (Florida Keys), 112-113, 117; *Caraquet* (Bermuda), 92; *Cayman Salvage Master* (Florida Keys), 130; *City of Washington* (Florida Keys), 112, 141-142; *The Constellation/Montana* (Bermuda), 86-87; *Cristobal Colon* (Bermuda), 87; *Darlington* (Bermuda), 91; *David Tucker II* (Bahamas), 18; *De La Salle* (Bahamas), 16; *Deborah K* (Bahamas), 30; *Duane* (Florida Keys), 143-144; *Eagle* (Florida Keys), 144; *Etheridge* (Bahamas), 24; *Duane* (Florida Keys), 112-113, 117; *Eagle* (Florida Keys), 113, 117; *Helena C* (Bahamas),16; *Hermes* (Bermuda), 90; *HMS Endymion* (Turks & Caicos), 70, 73; *HMS Looe* (Florida Keys), 129; *Joe's Tug* (Florida Keys), 130; *The José* (Bahamas), 24; *Kevin's Wreck* (Bermuda), 92; *L'Herminie* (Bermuda), 90-91; *Larington* (Bermuda), 88; *Madiana* (Bermuda), 92; *The Mahoney* (Bahamas), 16; *Marion* (Bahamas), 38; *Mary Celestia* (Bermuda), 88-89; *Minnie Breslaur* (Bermuda), 89-90; *MS Comberback* (Bahamas), 53; *North America* (Florida Keys), 147-148; *Poppa Doc* (Bahamas), 24; *Rita Zovetta* (Bermuda), 92; *San Pedro* (Florida Keys), 145; *Sapona* (Bahamas), 40; *Southwind* (Turks & Caicos), 75; *Speigel Grove* (Florida Keys), 113; *Taunton* (Bermuda), 92; *Theo's Wreck* (Bahamas), 24; *Thunderbolt* (Florida Keys), 126, 146-147; *Tonawanda* (Florida Keys), 112; *USS Adirondack* (Bahamas), 30; *USS Maine* (Florida Keys), 141; *Willaurie* (Bahamas), 18; *Xing Da* (Bermuda), 90
Shopping: Bahamas, 14-15; Bermuda, 99
Sightseeing: Abaco Islands, 29; Bermuda, 98-99; Cat Island, 44; Florida Keys, 139; San Salvador Island, 13
Snorkeling sites: the Bight Reef (Turks & Caicos), 75-76; Church Bay (Bermuda), 93; *Cienfuegos* (Bahamas), 47; Coral Gardens (Bahamas), 55; Devil's Back-

bone (Bahamas), 47-48; Devonshire Bay (Bermuda), 93; Eagle Ray Run (Turks & Caicos), 76; Elbow Beach (Bermuda), 93; Fort George's Cut (Turks & Caicos), 76; Freighter Wreck (Bahamas), 47; *The Frescate* (Bahamas), 58-59; Gibbs Cay (Turks & Caicos), 70; Islamorada (Florida Keys), 117; John Smith's Bay (Bermuda), 93; Key Largo (Florida Keys), 116; Little Abaco, 31; Little Exuma (Bahamas), 49; Love Hill (Bahamas), 38; Marathon (Florida Keys), 126; Memory Rock (Bahamas), 25; Moma Rhoda's Reef (Bahamas), 39; Mystery Reef (Bahamas), 47; Out Islands (Bahamas), 27; Paradise Cove (Bahamas), 25; Pollockshields (Bermuda), 93; Poseidon's Pint (Bahamas), 55; Rainbow Reef (Bahamas), 55; The Reef at Chub Cay (Bahamas), 39-40; the Road to Atlantis (Bahamas), 42; Round Cay (Turks & Caicos), 70; Salt Cay, 73-74; Shelly Bay (Bermuda), 94; Smith's Reef (Turks & Caicos), 75; Snapshot Reef (Bahamas), 58; Snorkel Park (Bermuda), 94; Somerset Long Bay (Bermuda), 93; South Dock (Turks & Caicos), 70; Southampton Reef (Bahamas), 53; Sunshine Reef (Bahamas), 42; Tobacco Bay (Bermuda), 93; Treasure Reef (Bahamas), 25; Train Wreck (Bahamas), 47; Trumpet Reef (Bahamas), 38; Vanaheim (Bahamas), 47-48; West Bar Reef (Bahamas), 53; Wheeland Cut (Turks & Caicos), 76
South Caicos (Turks & Caicos), 67, 79-80; accommodations, 80; best dives, 79
Spanish Cay (Bahamas), 31, 34
Sugarloaf Key (Florida Keys), 132; accommodations, 132; campgrounds, 132; transportation, 140

Tongue of the Ocean (TOTO), 11, 16, 18
Tropic of Cancer, 51
Treasure Cay (Bahamas), 11, 34-35
Tucker, Teddy, 84, 86

Underwater Explorers Society (UNEXSO), 22, 24, 25-26

West Caicos (Turks & Caicos), 67
Walker's Cay (Bahamas), 35

ADVENTURE GUIDES
from Hunter Publishing

BAHAMAS

2nd Edition, Blair Howard

Fully updated reports for Grand Bahama, Freeport, Eleuthera, Bimini, Andros, the Exumas, Nassau, New Providence Island, plus new sections on San Salvador, Long Island, Cat Island, the Acklins, the Inaguas and the Berry Islands. Mailboat schedules, package vacations and snorkeling trips by Jean-Michel Cousteau. 280 pp, $14.95, 1-55650-852-2

EXPLORE BELIZE

4th Edition, Harry S. Pariser

"Down-to-earth advice.... An excellent travel guide."
– *Library Journal*

Extensive coverage of the country's political, social and economic history, along with the plant and animal life. Encouraging you to mingle with the locals, Pariser entices you with descriptions of local dishes and festivals. Maps, color photos. 400 pp, $16.95, 1-55650-785-2

BERMUDA

2nd Ed. Blair Howard

"Promises everything but boredom."
– *San Antonio Express*

Bermuda retains much of its legendary charm, despite being a major tourist destination. Botanical gardens, historic houses, 17th-century forts, pink sand beaches. Abundant golf courses and tennis clubs.
224 pp, $14.95, 1-55650-906-5

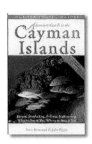

CAYMAN ISLANDS

Paris Permenter & John Bigley

The only comprehensive guidebook to Grand Cayman, Cayman Brac and Little Cayman. Encyclopedic listings of dive/snorkel operators, along with the best sites. Enjoy nighttime pony rides on a glorious beach, visit the turtle farms, prepare to get wet at staggering blowholes or just laze on a white sand beach. Color photos. 224 pp, $17.95, 1-55650-915-4

COSTA RICA

3rd Edition, Harry S. Pariser

"... most comprehensive... Excellent sections on national parks, flora, fauna & history."
– *CompuServe Travel Forum*

Incredible detail on culture, plants, animals, where to stay & eat, as well as practicalities of travel. E-mail and Web site directory. 560 pp, $16.95, 1-55650-722-4

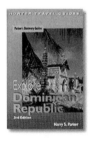

EXPLORE THE DOMINICAN REPUBLIC

3rd Edition, Harry S. Pariser

Virgin beaches, 16th-century Spanish ruins, the Caribbean's highest mountain, exotic wildlife, vast forests. Visit Santa Domingo, revel in Sosúa's European sophistication or explore the Samaná Peninsula's jungle. Color. 340 pp, $15.95, 1-55650-814-X

FLORIDA KEYS & EVERGLADES

2nd Edition, Joyce & Jon Huber

"... vastly informative, absolutely user-friendly, chock full of information..." – Dr. Susan Cropper

"... practical & easy to use." – *Wilderness Southeast*

Canoe trails, airboat rides, nature hikes, Key West, diving, sailing, fishing. Color. 224 pp, $14.95, 1-55650-745-3

TAMPA BAY & FLORIDA'S WEST COAST

2nd Edition, Chelle Koster Walton

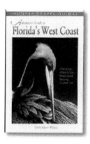

A guide to all the cities, towns, nature preserves, wilderness areas and sandy beaches that grace the Sunshine State's western shore. From Tampa Bay to Naples and Everglades National Park to Sanibel Island. 288 pp, $16.95, 1-55650-888-3

ANTIGUA, BARBUDA, NEVIS, ST. BARTS, ST. KITTS, ST. MARTIN

2nd Edition, Paris Permenter & John Bigley

Far outdistances other guides. Recommended operators for day sails, island-hopping excursions, scuba dives, unique rainforest treks on verdant mountain slopes, and rugged four-wheel-drive trails. 360 pp, $16.95, 1-55650-909-X

NORTHERN FLORIDA & THE PANHANDLE

Jim & Cynthia Tunstall

From the Georgia border south to Ocala National Forest and through the Panhandle. Swimming with dolphins and spelunking, plus Rails to Trails, a 47-mile hiking/biking path made of recycled rubber. 320 pp, $15.95, 1-55650-769-0

ORLANDO & CENTRAL FLORIDA

Disney World, the Space Coast, Tampa & Daytona

Jim & Cynthia Tunstall

Takes you to parts of Central Florida you never knew existed. Tips about becoming an astronaut (the real way and the smart way) and the hazards of taking a nude vacation. Photos. 300 pp, $15.95, 1-55650-825-5

PUERTO RICO

3rd Edition, Harry S. Pariser

"A quality book that covers all aspects... it's all here & well done." – *The San Diego Tribune*

"... well researched. They include helpful facts... filled with insightful tips." – *The Shoestring Traveler.*

Crumbling watchtowers and fascinating folklore enchant visitors. Color photos. 344 pp, $15.95, 1-55650-749-6

SOUTHEAST FLORIDA

Sharon Spence

Get soaked by crashing waves at twilight; canoe through mangroves; reel in a six-foot sailfish; or watch as a yellow-bellied turtle snuggles up to a gator. Interviews with the experts – scuba divers, sky divers, pilots, fishermen, bikers, balloonists, and park rangers. Color photos. 256 pp, $15.95, 1-55650-811-5

VIRGIN ISLANDS

5th Edition, Lynne Sullivan

"Plenty of outdoor options.... All budgets are considered in a fine coverage that appeals to readers."
– *Reviewer's Bookwatch*

Every island in the Virgins. Valuable, candid opinions. St. Croix, St. John, St. Thomas, Tortola, Virgin Gorda, Anegada. Color. 400 pp, $17.95, 1-55650-907-3

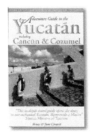

THE YUCATAN
Including Cancún & Cozumel

2nd Edition, Bruce & June Conord

"... Honest evaluations. This book is the one not to leave home without." – *Time Off Magazine*

"... opens the doors to our enchanted Yucatán."
– Mexico Ministry of Tourism

Maya ruins, Spanish splendor. Deserted beaches, festivals, culinary delights. 400 pp, $16.95, 1-55650-908-1

LANDMARK VISITORS GUIDES

A terrific new look from the producers of the highly respected Visitors Guides, acknowledged as among the most reliable and useful guides for sightseers. With full color maps and photos throughout, the new Landmark Visitors Guides are highly detailed, giving you the information you need to get the most from your trip. They serve as a useful reference tool before you leave home, and are the perfect travel companion while on the road.

Area-by-area tours highlight in-town sights and attractions, including art galleries, museums, historic buildings and churches. They also lead you out into the countryside, with recommended stops en route. Colorful call-out boxes reveal tidbits of the area's local culture, interesting sidelights on how the landscape has been shaped and other details lacking in competing guidebooks. The comprehensive Fact File in back provides opening times, fees and contact information for all places mentioned in the text. Index.

ANTIGUA & BARBUDA
96 pp, $9.95, 1-901522-02-4

BERMUDA
160 pp, $13.95, 1-901522-07-5

DOMINICAN REPUBLIC
160 pp, $13.95, 1-901522-08-3

FLORIDA'S GULF COAST
160 pp, $12.95, 1-901522-01-6

FLORIDA KEYS
160 pp, $12.95, 1-901522-21-0

ST. LUCIA
160 pp, $13.95, 1-901522-28-8

THE VIRGIN ISLANDS
286 pp, $17.95, 1-901522-03-2

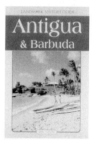

TASTE OF... GUIDES

These unique combination cookbook/travel guides make the perfect gift for the gourmet traveler, or just about anyone who enjoys mouth-watering island dishes! Merging the cuisine and culture of each destination, they start with a look at what has influenced the food and the local ingredients that make it unique. The main section of each book is dedicated to restaurants, from five-star resorts to plush hotel restaurants to independently owned establishments island-wide. Each book has a section that details annual food festivals and culinary contests on each island, so you can plan your visit to taste the creations of the islands' most respected chefs. Written by Paris Permenter & John Bigley. Photos throughout. 5 x 8 pbks

THE BAHAMAS

A Taste Of The Islands
276 pp, $15.95,
1-55650-832-8

JAMAICA

A Taste Of The Island
276 pp, $15.95,
1-55650-833-6

ONE-OF-A-KIND GUIDES

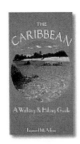

THE CARIBBEAN
A Walking & Hiking Guide

3rd Edition, Leonard M. Adkins

"... anyone who likes to experience the Caribbean with their feet: this book is for you." *Caribbean Travel & Life*

A wealth of information about enjoying the Caribbean on foot. Easy walks and rugged hikes are profiled. Anguilla, Antigua, Dominica, Guadeloupe, Martinique, Nevis, Saba, Statia, the Virgin Islands. All hikes rated. Maps and photos. 380 pp, $15.95, 1-55650-848-4

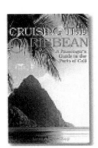

CRUISING THE CARIBBEAN
A Guide to the Ports of Call

2nd Edition, Laura & Diane Rapp

Tailored to the needs of cruise ship travelers. How to make the most of time ashore: walks, shopping, excursions, historical sights, beaches. Recommended places to eat at each port. Written by pursers of a major cruise line. Maps. 288 pp, $15.95, 1-55650-799-2

THE SECRET CARIBBEAN
Hideaways of the Rich & Famous
Brooke Comer

Celebrity-style vacations for a real-person price. How about Mick Jagger's Mustique, known for its wildlife (and wild life)? Or quiet Nevis, a royal favorite? This unique book offers an impressive selection of places to stay – all frequented by stars – at affordable rates.

400 pp, $16.95, 1-55650-851-4

BEST DIVES OF THE CARIBBEAN
2nd Edition

Joyce & Jon Huber

"A trustworthy publication." *Undercurrent Magazine*

"The bible of Caribbean dive-travel." *The Travel Show*

Covers 24 islands in the Caribbean.

384 pp, $18.95, 1-55650-798-4

BEST DIVES OF THE
WESTERN HEMISPHERE
2nd Edition

Joyce & Jon Huber

Florida Keys, California, Hawaii, Galapagos, The Caribbean, Brazil, Belize

400 pp, $18.95, 1-55650-858-1

ALIVE GUIDES

Alive Guides give you the option to live, love and breathe your destination. Just ask the authors. They have been visiting these places for years – and still keep going back for more! Up-to-the-minute and packed with valuable advice, Alive Guides cover every aspect of travel in each exciting destination. Shopping, nightlife, area-by-area sightseeing, transportation, culture. Restaurants and accommodations are described in detail, based on repeat visits

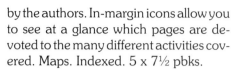

by the authors. In-margin icons allow you to see at a glance which pages are devoted to the many different activities covered. Maps. Indexed. 5 x 7½ pbks.

ANTIGUA, BARBUDA, ST. KITTS & NEVIS ALIVE!
Paris Permenter & John Bigley
400 pp, $16.95, 1-55650-880-8

ARUBA, BONAIRE & CURAÇAO ALIVE!
S. Brushaber & A. Greenberg
304 pp, $15.95, 1 55650 756 9

CAYMAN ISLANDS ALIVE!
Paris Permenter & John Bigley
360 pp, $16.95, 1-55650-862-X

JAMAICA ALIVE!
Paris Permenter & John Bigley
400 pp, $14.95, 1-55650-882-4

MARTINIQUE, GUADELOUPE, DOMINICA & ST. LUCIA ALIVE!
Lynne M. Sullivan
656 pp, $19.95, 1-55650-857-3

NASSAU & The Best of The Bahamas ALIVE!
Paris Permenter & John Bigley
400 pp, $14.95, 1-55650-883-2

ST. MARTIN & ST. BARTS ALIVE!
Harriet Greenberg
320 pp, $15.95, 1-55650-831-X

ORDER FORM

Yes! Send the following guides:

TITLE	ISBN #	PRICE	QUANTITY	TOTAL
SUBTOTAL				
SHIPPING & HANDLING (United States only) (1-2 books, $3; 3-5 books, $5; 6-10 books, $8)				
ENCLOSED IS MY CHECK FOR				

NAME:

ADDRESS:

CITY/STATE/ZIP:

VISIT US ON THE WORLD WIDE WEB
http://www.hunterpublishing.com

Secure credit card orders may be made at the Hunter Web site, where you will also find in-depth descriptions of the hundreds of travel guides we offer. All Hunter titles are also available at bookstores nationwide. Or order direct by sending a check for the total of the book(s) ordered plus the shipping and handling charge shown above to Hunter Publishing, 130 Campus Drive, Edison NJ 08818.